THE THREE OF US

Also by Julia Blackburn

FICTION

The Book of Colour
The Leper's Companions

NON-FICTION

Charles Waterton
The Emperor's Last Island
Daisy Bates in the Desert
Old Man Goya
With Billie
My Animals & Other Family

JULIA BLACKBURN

THE THREE OF US

A Family Story

PANTHEON BOOKS

NEW YORK

Grateful acknowledgment is made to Alfred Publishing Co., Inc. for permission to reprint an excerpt from "Mama Look a Boo Boo," words and music by Lord Melody, copyright © 1956 (Renewed) by Ice Music International Ltd. All rights administered by Artemis Muzikuitgeverij B.V.; and "Travelin' All Alone," words and music by J.C. Johnson, copyright © 1930 (Renewed) by WB Music Corp. All rights reserved. Reprinted by permission of Alfred Publishing Co., Inc.

Library of Congress Cataloging-in-Publication Data
Blackburn, Julia.
The three of us : a family story / Julia Blackburn.
p. cm.
ISBN 978-0-375-42474-8
1. Blackburn, Julia—Family. 2. Authors, English—20th century—Family relationships. 3. Children of authors—England—Biography. 4. Children of alcoholics—England—Biography. 5. Mothers and daughters—England—Biography. 6. Blackburn, Thomas, 1916–1977. I. Title.
PR6052.L3413Z46 2008   823'.914—dc22   2007050147

www.pantheonbooks.com
Printed in the United States of America
First American Edition
2 4 6 8 9 7 5 3 1

⋇ CONTENTS ⋇

CONTENTS

For Herman

⟨ I ⟩

This Is the Story

This is the story of three people. It is the story of my two parents and the three of us together, but it is also the story of the tangled fairy-tale triangle, which took shape between me and my mother and the succession of solitary men who entered our lives after my father had left.

⊙ ⊙ ◉ ⊙ ⊙

My father Thomas Blackburn was a poet and an alcoholic who for many years was addicted to a powerful barbiturate called sodium amytal, which was first prescribed for him in 1943. When the cumulative effect of the drug combined with the alcohol made him increasingly violent and so mad he began to growl and bark like a dog, he was tried out on all sorts of substitute pills, including one which he proudly said was used to tranquillize rhinoceroses.

He had two divorces and several breakdowns, but then at the age of sixty he had a vision of the afterlife, which made him happy because he realized he was no longer afraid of dying. A year later, in the early morning of 13 August 1977, he finished writing a long letter to his brother with the words 'I am now going to lie down in a horizontal position and breathe long and deep.' He then went upstairs and died from a cerebral haemorrhage, just as he was getting into bed.

He was disastrous in so many ways, yet I never felt threatened by him. I could be frightened of the madness and the drunken rages, but I never doubted the honesty of his relationship with me and that was what really mattered.

My mother, Rosalie de Meric, was very different. She was a painter by profession and she rarely got drunk and didn't use prescription drugs, and she was sociable and sane and flirtatious, and I was always afraid of her. Right from the start I was her sister and her confidante and, eventually, her sexual rival, as the boundaries between us became increasingly dangerous and unclear. The battle we fought reached a crisis in 1966 when I was eighteen, and that crisis never really passed, the scent of rage and adrenaline hanging in the air as sharp as gunpowder.

On the first day of March 1999, when she was eighty-two years old, my mother was told she had only a short time to live and she came to stay with me for what proved to be the last month of her life. Something crucial happened and the spell that had held us for so long in its grip like an icy winter was finally broken, and we were able to laugh and talk together with an ease we had never known before. 'I have never been so happy in all my life,' she said. 'How curious to be dying at the same time.'

And when she was near the end and her voice had become so slow and deep it seemed to be emerging from the bottom of a well, my mother said, 'Now you will be able to write about me, won't you!'

'Yes, I will,' I replied, because in that moment I felt she was giving me her blessing, making it possible for me to tell a story that otherwise I could never have told.

During her final month I kept a journal, which recorded this brief and joyful time. I also exchanged faxes with my old friend Herman, who was living in Holland. He had come to visit me just a couple of days before my mother learnt that she was ill. Herman and I had first been lovers in 1966 and we finally parted in 1973. He was the one person who knew all about the past and how important it was to sort things out before it was too late.

I have used excerpts from my journal and from the faxes throughout the telling of this story; they are the thread that connects the beginning to the end.

Herman and I were married in December 1999.

A Supper Party

Friday, 2 April 1965 and I know the date because I still have the diary I kept for that year.

The supper party was at my father's house: the house where he now lived with my stepmother and her daughter and a black-and-white Parson Jack Russell terrier called Henry, whom I liked very much.

Here I am at the front door of the house. I ring the bell and it makes an optimistic bing-bong, bing-bong noise, as if it were an ice-cream van telling the children to come and buy, quick, quick. There are thick panes of red and

blue glass in the door and when I press my face to them I can just see a blue and red Henry dancing a welcome. My father is looming into view and I can hear his sharp cough.

He opens the door. He is pasty-faced from all the pills and hangovers. His spectacles are low on his nose and he is gazing over the top of them with a lop-sided smile, which was made lopsided ages ago when he climbed over a high spiked fence and fell and was caught by his upper lip on one of the spikes. He is wearing a beige cardigan that has cigarette burns in it and when he kisses me on the cheek I can smell Fisherman's Friend extra strong cough sweets, as well as beer and wine and Capstan Full Strength cigarettes, untipped.

'There you are, darling,' he says, which is true, I am.

'Come in, come in. How nice! You look well. Looked ghastly the last time I saw you. I'm just finishing something. Won't be long. Peggy's in the kitchen.' And he's gone, back to his study.

I know that just last week, my father threw my stepmother into an empty bathtub. Naked, or at least I presume she was naked, although she might have been in her pyjamas. They were having a fight and the neighbours came because of all the shouting and screaming, but they didn't call the police, not this time.

'Imagine that,' said my mother, who laughed when she told me the story. My mother had always been too heavy to be lifted or thrown, but she was punched and slapped instead.

My father never hit me; except once when the three of us were sitting down to Sunday lunch at the big round table and he had lunged sideways at my mother with his fist, but got me instead by mistake. 'So sorry darling,' he said, genuinely apologetic. 'No blood I hope?'

◦ ◦ ◉ ◦ ◦

But now here's Peggy and I can't see any bruises. She also smells of cigarettes and wine, and she has her own sharp and foxy smell, which mixes with the sweetness of her perfume. She wears a lot of perfume and carries a lipstick with her wherever she goes. She has put some on now and her lips are dark red and shiny. She has a big wide mouth with very regular teeth, a sharp nose and almost lidless eyes like little almonds, that will flicker and close later, when the wine kicks in. Her black hair is cut in a bob with a fringe. She is shorter than me and delicately built, with thin wrists and narrow shoulders. Even I could pick her up if I chose to. She is wearing a green silk shirt.

I've told the two of them that I'm going to stay the night. I have never stayed the night here before, but I'm having a lot of trouble at home with my mother, so I thought I'd give it a try and then, if it worked, I could move in and stay for a while.

My father had been very pleased when I told him the first part of my plan.

'Good, good, good!' he said and he rubbed his hands together with a papery sound, which was one of his ways of expressing pleasure.

There is a spare room and my stepmother leads me to it and opens the door. There are boxes of remaindered books of my father's poetry on the floor and a bedcover that I remember from long ago. The sheet has been turned down in readiness for my arrival.

I go to the bathroom and open the medicine cupboard. I take out a pot of Elizabeth Arden rich moisturizing night cream and rub some on my face. I look at the bright colours of the lipsticks that stand higgledy piggledy in a corner of the cupboard and marvel at how they are all worn down to such a round blunt stub. I sniff at a bottle of my father's Jochem's Hair Oil. He used the same stuff when he lived with me and my mother. It's got bay rum in it and a sweet smell that I like.

I go down to the kitchen, which is very small, with just enough room for a sink and a cooker. Last week, maybe it was after the business with the bathtub, my father phoned to tell me he had thought of killing himself. He said he was going to gas himself in the cooker because he felt so depressed.

At that moment Peggy had snatched the phone from him and I heard him grunting with surprise. 'He turned on the gas,' she said, 'but when he saw the cold roast chicken in the oven, he ate it, all of it, at two o'clock in the morning. We had nothing for lunch the next day!'

My father reclaimed the phone. 'I have been very depressed, darling. Black despair. The poems won't come like they used to.'

⊙ ⊙ ◉ ⊙ ⊙

7

Peggy is preparing things in the kitchen. She has bought half a dozen little pots of lumpfish caviar and ham and cheese and salami and smoked salmon and lots of Jacobs Cream Crackers. Tonight's supper is to be a long stream of hors d'oeuvres, with coffee and brandy to round it all off.

My father has finished whatever he was doing in his study and he comes to join us, a full glass in his hand. 'Drink?' he says. 'I've got sherry and Martini and lots of sweet German hock, which nobody likes except me.'

The table has been laid and the little bits and pieces of cold this and that are displayed on plates. David Wright, the deaf poet who wrote a poem about an Emperor Penguin, arrives with his wife Pippa. She is an actress and she has white skin and red hair, and she holds his hand all the time; later she even manages to keep hold of his hand while she is eating.

David Wright talks in a booming monotone. His big face is solemn but curiously without expression and he keeps his eyes fixed on his wife and doesn't try to understand what people are saying, but turns to her instead, so she can translate with her lips. According to my diary another couple is here as well, along with one of my father's students from the college where he teaches, but they have all disappeared from my memory without trace.

We sit on hard chairs round the table and we put things on our crackers, which splutter their jagged crumbs over the tablecloth and down on to our laps. David Wright booms and Peggy's eyelids are fluttering and I am trying to impress everyone with my cleverness.

I tell David Wright that I enjoyed his poem about the unhappy penguin in the London Zoo who didn't appreciate how comfortable his life had become and missed the icy storms of the Antarctic.

David Wright stares at me with blank incomprehension, then turns to his wife to translate my words for him. 'Thank you,' he says solemnly.

I notice that my father's bottom lip is getting looser. He has stopped eating and he is finding it increasingly difficult to locate his mouth with the end of a cigarette and impossible to light the cigarette once it is in position. He holds the flaring match head down, the flame burning the skin and nails of his thumb and forefinger and filling the room with a brief acrid smell.

'Let me do it for you, Tom,' says Pippa with the red hair, and he grins and holds his face close to hers, greedily sucking in anticipation of success. By now he is mixing red wine with the sweet German hock and adding a slosh of sherry as an afterthought. Peggy has also stopped eating. She stands behind him with her hands gripping his shoulders.

'Darling!' he says and pats her hand.

'Darling!' she says and moves her hand away.

My father has read us a new poem and we have talked about William Blake and how he felt that death was nothing more than walking into the next room. We have also talked about the friability of Cream Crackers and whether salami is made out of donkeys, but the conversation is faltering.

Henry has been watching things very closely and he senses that trouble is on its way. He turns on his heels and, with a short bark, demands to be let out of the room.

'Stay here, damn you!' says my father, a note of pleading in his voice. 'That dog disapproves of me. He acts like a moral policeman.'

But Henry is insistent and when the door is opened for him he goes to find one of his hiding places. He won't reappear until the morning.

'The head of the English Department is a cunt!' says my father and he smiles benevolently at his own reflection in the dark night of the window.

'Shut up, darling!' says Peggy. Her eyes are tightly closed and the inside edges of her lips are stained with wine.

'I said he is a cunt because he is a cunt. A fascist cunt! I told him so and he didn't like it!'

Pippa with the red hair laughs and says she didn't know that cunts had political allegiances, but she doesn't translate the conversation to her waiting husband. Everyone else stays silent.

'My wife is a lesbian!' says my father and he begins to cry.

Peggy makes tut-tut noises and asks me to help her clear the table.

'I don't love him, I love you!' she says once we are in the kitchen dealing with a heap of plates. She grabs hold of my arm and squeezes it and her eyelids flicker. 'I didn't marry him for this!' she says.

Next door, my father is making loud clock noises, to show that he is bored. 'Tick-tock, tick-tock, tick-tock.' Then he yawns very loudly. 'You're all hypocritical shits!' he says to his guests.

9

I return to the table with Peggy. We are both smoking. My father snatches the cigarette from my mouth and stubs it in the ashtray.

Peggy picks it up and lights it and pushes it back between my lips.

'Let her smoke, damn you!' she says and she smiles at the guests.

◎ ◎ ◉ ◎ ◎

Everyone is suddenly ready to leave. There is an urgent fumbling of coats and bags as they make their way towards the safety of the front door. They hardly say goodbye, but as they step out into the night they look back at me and my father and stepmother with pitying glances.

I go to bed without washing or brushing my teeth. I climb between the cold sheets. My nightie is very flimsy and I wish I'd brought the red flannel one, which would have felt safer.

Peggy arrives first. She looks down at me and tells me how lucky I am. 'You have no idea how lucky you are. You are luckier than anyone I have ever met . . . Your father loves you,' she adds, to prove the point. 'But you are always blaming people. That is why I hate you.'

My father comes in. He groans and throws himself on to his knees beside the bed, great sobs heaving out of him.

'Darling, I really miss reading you bedtime stories,' he says. 'I love you. Do you know how much I love you? Peggy, do you know how much I love this girl?'

'Yes,' says Peggy, 'that's what I was telling her just now.'

I start to scream. It seems like the only thing to do.

'She is very unstable,' says Peggy, staring at me, her eyes wide open for the first time this evening.

'She needs to go back to that psychiatrist,' says my father. 'What's his name? Can you remember his name?'

'Kollestrom!' says Peggy, suddenly very efficient.

'Kollestrom. Remind me to phone him in the morning. First thing!' says my father.

They leave the room and after a while dawn breaks through the window and I fall asleep.

When we meet for breakfast my father says, 'Good morning, darling! Hope you slept well. It was fun last night, wasn't it, although that David can be a bit of a bore. His wife's very handsome. Peggy thinks she's frigid. Peggy is very intuitive you know.'

'Toast?' says Peggy from out of a white cloud of cigarette smoke. She has put five jars of Cooper's Oxford Marmalade on the table, a little flock of them, all with their lids off.

And then we go into the pocket handkerchief of a garden and Henry appears out of nowhere and offers each of us a very dignified and friendly greeting.

It seems that every time someone is about to speak, at that exact moment a big jet aeroplane cruises low above our heads like a great white shark, wiping out all the words and any thoughts that went with them.

My father shows me the stone lion's head he has just bought for his rockery and I admire it. Peggy goes to make more coffee, then appears with a camera. She takes several photographs of me and my father, standing side by side, holding our striped mugs in the morning air and smiling contentedly, as if we have just been told a good joke.

⊙ ⊙ ◉ ⊙ ⊙

I walk back to the house where I live with my mother and the lodger. It is not very far away, about ten minutes if you are quite fast. I go inside. It is very silent and cold in the hall and no one answers or appears out of a door-way when I call out.

I go upstairs to my room; it used to be my father's study, in the days when the three of us lived together. I have recently painted the walls of this room a dark purple and I have hung red striped curtains in the window.

I close the curtains and put on a record of American Negro work songs. I take off all my clothes and lie on the double bed, listening to Josh White singing about old Jack O'Diamonds who can't rob his pocket of silver or gold.

⊙ ⊙ ◉ ⊙ ⊙

1 March 1999

How wonderful to see you again after so long, although from the moment you arrived, I hardly noticed the so-longness of the gap of time. I've been doing the mathematics. It's thirty-four years since we first met and twenty-nine since we parted. What an odd thought!

This morning I took Rosalie to the hospital for a routine check-up. When they did the blood tests they discovered she had no red platelets, or hardly any, and very few white whatever-they-ares either. The white cell count is six instead of six hundred I think they said, or was it six thousand? They are keeping her in for observation.

It hasn't stopped raining since you left. A great emptying of celestial bathtubs. The meadows behind the house are turning into lakes.

Goodnight, or if you are already asleep when this fax gets through, good morrow when you wake,
Julia

(Fax to Herman)

12

Back Home

The year is 1964 and this is my first diary. I have stuck a painting of a naked couple on the front cover, but the painting is very abstract and you only see that it's a naked couple if you look carefully. On the back cover there's a magazine photograph of three little black boys and a girl playing in a street, and the girl and one of the boys have been tied to the trunk of a tree with a thick length of rope. She looks towards the camera, while the others look away. I have written the word PRIVATE three times on the front cover and on the back I have written 'diary – please don't read it'.

I write about how I go to school every day, except when I am sick, or tired, or hung-over, in which case I stay in bed and write about that instead. On school days the alarm clock rings at seven. I get up and pull back the red curtains. I am naked. I have been sleeping naked ever since I lost my virginity a short while after my sixteenth birthday. I like the fact of naked-ness. In my diary I make little drawings of naked men and women lying together and drawings of breasts and bottoms.

I wash in the sink in the corner of the room. My father used to piss in the sink when this was his study and the white enamel is stained with a pale yellow tidemark, which I have tried to scrub out with Vim, but it won't go. And I have his table, covered with black circles that show where the glasses of beer once stood.

I look at myself in the mirror above the sink. I don't see a face, just the details of a face. I see a fringe that has curled sideways in spite of having been taped down to my forehead with Sellotape all through the night. I see a nose that is big and broad like my mother's and eyes that are dark brown like my father's.

I smile at the mouth and it smiles back, but not in a very trusting way. I draw a line of black kohl round my eyes and put some pale make-up on my face. I also put on some lipstick, but then I change my mind and kiss it off on to a sheet of paper. The creased and parted lips seem to be trying to say something. I think I might send them as a love letter, but maybe that's silly. I backcomb my hair and brush a thin layer of smoothness on top of the self-made tangle.

I put on a white padded bra, a white poplin shirt, white knickers, a grey pleated skirt, a grey cardigan, long grey socks and brown sandals just like the ones in the Start-Rite advertisement, 'children's shoes have far to go', in which a little girl and a little boy walk with such confidence, hand in hand into the future.

I put on a purple blazer. It has the school emblem stitched to the breast pocket: an embroidered oak tree growing below the motto *fortiter et recte*, 'strong and straight', as we all must surely try to be. I pick up my navy-blue felt hat with its badge and ribbon, and stuff it into the blazer pocket where it nestles against a packet of Woodbines and a metal cigarette lighter.

I go down one flight of stairs to the hall. Here is a zinc-lined mahogany chest, made to withstand the heat and damp of the tropics. There are no labels on it and I don't know which side of the family it comes from. The Burmese gong stands on top of it and that belongs to my mother's childhood. She says it represents the only time she was happy as a child; during the years when she and her family lived in Burma: the scent of flowers in the air and a dark-skinned ayah who was kind to her and sang her songs. Two wooden elephants hold a bronze disc suspended from their ivory tusks and you must beat the disc with a stick that has its round head muffled in chamois leather. We use this gong to announce mealtimes, when we can remember.

One of my mother's oil paintings hangs above the gong. It shows a woman with a horned headdress sitting with her hands in her lap, and she has very odd breasts, attached to her chest like limpets. A wooden crate is there next to her and a rat is emerging from it, just his front paws and his head, the eyes bright and the whiskers twitching. The woman in the painting does not notice the rat. She has never noticed it.

Down another flight of stairs and into the dark basement where you find the kitchen and the narrow bathroom and a little room that has no particular use, its walls erupting into powdery blisters as if they had caught some horrible disease.

⊙ ⊙ ◉ ⊙ ⊙

Paul, our Swiss lodger, is in the kitchen. We have had a number of lodgers living with us since I moved into my father's study, leaving my old bedroom empty. There was Bob the architect, he was the first and my mother was sure he wanted to marry her; then Richard, the American painter with a withered leg; Ian, David, another Richard, Ken the Conman and of course Great-Uncle Guy for a while, but he never seemed like a lodger because he was surrounded by a wonderful aura of family and there was no danger there. Anyway, Great-Uncle Guy was a homosexual, as my mother kept telling me, her eyes lighting up as she asked if I could imagine what sort of things two men could do with each other.

Paul is sitting at the round table that was given to us by Great-Aunt Molly. He is smoking Gauloises, drinking a little glass of French brandy and reading the *Economist*, which is on top of *Playboy*, which is on top of *Der Spiegel*. He is wearing a scrupulously white towelling dressing gown – he has all his clothes dry-cleaned at a shop on Putney High Street and that's why it's so much whiter than my school shirt. The dressing gown is slightly open at his bare chest and it just reaches his bare knees. Elegant Moroccan leather slippers encase his bare feet. I always assumed he was naked under the dressing gown, but I suppose he might have been wearing a pair of boxer shorts.

Paul certainly looks like a boxer. He would have liked to be a boxer, but he trained as an economist instead, hence the magazine on top of the pile.

That was because it was the wish of his father who was a wealthy business-man, but not a very nice man as far as I can gather.

Paul has a round bullet head and very short-cropped, soft blond hair. He wears wire-framed spectacles that hide his eyes. He has a little button nose, which I know he hates, and big cheeks, which he also hates, and a wide, straight mouth, which opens and shuts rather mechanically, as if it were on hinges like the mouth of a ventriloquist's doll. When he looks in the mirror – and he looks in the mirror quite often – he always seems to get a terrible shock. He must expect someone quite different to be there. He scowls at the person who scowls back at him and he clenches his jaw and gets ready for a fight, if a fight is necessary.

'Good morning, my beauty,' he says. He always calls me his beauty and I hope it's a compliment, although it might be a way of teasing me, I'm never sure. I'm never sure of anything with Paul.

'I have been waiting for you,' he says and he lets out an elaborate and noisy yawn, stretching his hairy arms above his shoulders, so that the dress-ing gown falls a bit more open at his chest and tumbles sideways at his knees.

'Brandy?' he says and gives me a twinkly smile that reveals a gold tooth.

'No thank you, Paul,' and I concentrate on making my breakfast. I have two Weetabix with milk and a cup of instant coffee. Looking back now I realize I was very bound by certain rituals. Always the same breakfast and the same packed lunch as the one I am packing now while Paul watches my every movement. A fruit pie in a little cardboard packet – *'Ring the bell, ring the bell, for Lyons individual fruit pies!'* And a pork pie or a cheese sandwich and an apple if there is an apple to be found. All carefully placed in a tin lunch-box with a blue lid. I put this feast into my satchel and drink my coffee.

Paul is yawning again, even more noisily than last time. He asks if I would mind rubbing his back because it aches. So I stand behind him and rub his back, feeling the tightness of his muscles. I still have the habit of obedience to grown-ups. There are all sorts of things I will do, simply because I am told to do them.

◦ ◦ ◉ ◦ ◦

I set off for school. Left on to the street, over the zebra crossing, past the Polish delicatessen shop owned by Mr Novac who my mother says fancies her, up the hill, over the pedestrian railway bridge as fast as possible because of that middle bit which is so narrow and closed in, and it's hard to know which way to run if you need to run. Then to the right and down another hill and up a bit and there we are. School.

At Assembly we sing 'The Church's One Foundation Is Jesus Christ Our Lord' and Miss Jonson the singing mistress goes red in the face with effort, or is it anger? The two seem very closely bound. Miss Smith the headmistress asks God to bless us and our parents and the Queen and the Prime Minister, then she makes a special plea that there might be 'no more Wars, or Hunger, or Unhappiness, anywhere in the World'. We all say 'Amen' to that.

We set off down corridors to our classrooms. We do History with Miss Lloyd-Jones, who doesn't agree with Evolution, but is sure that God did it all with great flashes of His long arm, emerging from a robe even more brightly white than the one worn by our Swiss lodger. Then it's Maths with Miss Buss, who does have the most amazing bust, a solid plinth-like structure that seems to have been carved in stone. On 3 June a man from the Red Cross comes to give us a lecture on Artificial Respiration and some of us can't stop laughing when he says you mustn't give the Kiss of Life to a deformed or damaged mouth.

During lunch, I go with my best friend Peggy to the lavatories and we smoke a couple of cigarettes and talk about sex and make plans for the weekend. My mother has said she is going to be away from Friday until Monday.

◦ ◦ ◉ ◦ ◦

School ends and I walk home.

Paul is still sitting in the kitchen, drinking brandy and smoking.

'Ah!' he says. 'Time to get dressed!'

I ask him if he has seen my mother and at that same moment her feet are pounding on the stairs and she bursts in. She must have heard us talking. She is wearing an overall spattered with layers of oil paint and she is looking very pleased with herself, beaming with health and energy. 'I wondered where you

both were,' she says and she has that special hungry look on her face, which comes whenever a man is close by, so that I sometimes expect her to open her mouth and make a groaning, yowling noise, like a cat on heat. She offers Paul her broad smile, which brings dimples into both her cheeks and reveals a row of white and even teeth.

'I'm going out tonight!' she says. 'I have an admirer and he's taking me to the opera and I might not be back until the morning!'

'Then I will have the pleasure of looking after your little girl,' replies Paul, and he lights another Gauloise and winks at me.

I go upstairs to my red and purple room to do my homework. I have found a new quotation, which I write in careful letters on the cupboard by my bed: *The sickness of the oyster is the pearl.* It's there next to *baking in sensuality like an apple in its jacket* and *I am nobody, who are you?* I begin an essay about the Reformation and the death of Archbishop Cranmer, who I think looks very mean in the portrait in my textbook.

I can hear Paul talking in German on the telephone in my mother's studio. He must have left the door open. He is talking to the woman called Merrit, who doesn't love him any more. She is the reason why he had to leave Switzerland and come here, to mend his broken heart.

Paul finishes his conversation and the house is silent. It's getting late and I'm tired and hungry. Suddenly there is the sound of the gong being beaten and when I come down to the kitchen Paul has made a huge dish of kidneys and onions. He has laid the table for two and he pours me a glass of red wine with a flourish, the bottle wrapped in one of his own white handkerchiefs.

He is wearing a very smart suit and a tie. It's like being in a restaurant. I sit down cautiously and he sits opposite me and grins with his mouth slightly open. The kidneys are delicious.

We don't talk, but every time I look up Paul is still staring at me and his mouth is still slightly open. He makes me think of a fish.

Suddenly the front door bangs shut with a crash and my mother comes clattering down the stairs and bursts into the kitchen. She is wearing her leopard-skin jacket, the one she exchanged for a painting, and she looks every bit as fierce as the leopard must have once looked.

'Oh!' she says sarcastically, 'am I interrupting a little party?'

'Damn! I was just about to seduce your daughter, but now my plans are ruined!' says Paul, laughing at his own joke.

He gets up from the table, wipes his mouth with the white handkerchief and steps towards my mother with his head down, shoulders hunched, making punching movements in the air and grunting.

'What happened to your date?' he asks.

'The bastard went home on his own,' says my mother, removing her leopard skin and letting it drop to the floor. She pours herself a glass of wine. She walks over to the stove, takes the lid off the saucepan and starts eating what's left of the kidneys and onions with her fingers.

'Yum yum!' she says, wiping some of the gravy from her chin with the back of her hand.

I go to have a bath and she tells me to leave it in for her.

⊙ ⊙ ◉ ⊙ ⊙

When I am lying in the water, my mother comes in and stares abstractedly at my naked body. She takes off her own clothes, throwing them down in a heap and trampling on her salmon-pink knickers and grey-white petticoat. She sits on the lavatory and does a noisy pee and looks at her own belly. 'See what you did to me,' she says, scooping up a roll of soft white flesh covered with the little criss-crossing scars of striation marks. 'You were a very heavy baby. I've even got scars on my thighs from carrying you.'

I keep silent because there is nothing to say. I get out of the bath and wrap myself in a towel.

My mother climbs in and turns on the hot tap. She rubs her face with a big sponge, then she farts and laughs when the bubbles burst on the surface of the water.

As I walk out she tells me to leave the door open.

'Paul won't come near me,' she says, 'but at least this way I can watch the cowardly little sod running up the stairs.'

After I have gone to bed I can hear the two of them shouting at each other.

'But we have no relationship!' Paul says.

'Oh yes we do!' says my mother and I think she begins to cry.

⊙ ⊙ ◉ ⊙ ⊙

March 1999

. . . Just back from the hospital. Rosalie has been given a private room with a view of the car park. When I arrived she was sitting on the edge of the bed, wearing a bright-red caftan, which she brought back from a guru hunt in India just a few years ago. I remember her telling me how they had all danced naked together and what fun it was.

She looked wonderfully well: pink-cheeked and beaming, fluffing up her feathers like a broody hen.

'I've lost my entire immune system,' she announced rather proudly, and she showed me the dark bruises that are gathering like storm clouds on her arms and shoulders. We decided this must be something to do with the absence of platelets.

They are doing a marrow biopsy this afternoon and tomorrow we'll be introduced to the oncologist in charge of the ward.

Rosalie has asked me to go to her house to collect a few things and defrost the fridge. And she also wants me to talk to her cats, although to be honest I have never known what language her cats speak, they are very blank and distant creatures. I dread going. I always feel like a ghost or a robber when I'm in that house on my own.

(Fax to Herman)

4

Visiting Doctor Kollestrom

I was sent to Doctor Kollestrom because I had developed the habit of scream-ing. The first time I screamed was not long after my father had left. He came to our house and I hadn't seen him for several weeks and I didn't know what to say and he and my mother were talking about me without noticing that I was there. All three of us were standing in the hall at the bottom of the stairs and I screamed so loud that I passed out, just for a moment. I enjoyed the sliding sensation when the energy of my voice took over and drowned me in it, and there was nothing else in all the world but that one sound.

After that I often screamed if my mother and I were getting stuck in an argument, then I screamed on the night when I stayed with my father and his wife, but the real turning point came when I screamed at school, during a history exam. I was quickly bundled off to see Miss Smith, the head-mistress. I began to explain about the problems I was having at home with my mother and the lodgers, and that my father wasn't that easy either, but Miss Smith interrupted me. 'Do you believe in God?' she asked.

'No, I'm very sorry, but I don't.'

She looked rather pained, as if I was treading on her toe, but then she brightened up and said she thought I should go to boarding school.

I said, 'No thanks, thank you very much,' and with that our conver-sation ran out of steam.

Miss Smith promised she would have a word with my parents and she was sure everything would be all right. She sounded really confident, but then as I was leaving her room she said, 'The school has your best interests at heart, so don't hesitate to come and see me again if you need to. Goodbye, Jane dear!'

After that I never screamed again while I was at school, but I went on screaming at home, which was why Doctor Kollestrom was asked to sort me out.

Doctor Kollestrom looked exactly like my idea of what Freud must have looked like. He wore a brown suit over a carefully buttoned brown waistcoat and I don't remember the colour of his shirts, but they can't have been white or I am sure I would still see their brightness. He had big pale hands and long fingers that folded themselves together. He had a goatee beard, which twitched when he spoke, while his eyes were lost behind the gleam of heavy-rimmed spectacles. His voice was soft and whispery, and seemed to float on the wind.

He sat in a high-backed green velvet armchair, a notebook on his lap and a pencil poised in his hand. I was placed on a red velvet couch like a patient awaiting an operation, and I kept my legs crossed at the ankles because that somehow made me feel safer and less like someone in bed. It was very odd to be talking to a stranger while lying down and even odder because I was facing a wall, so that when I spoke I was addressing a painting of a river with a bridge crossing over it.

If Doctor Kollestrom had something to say to me, his disembodied voice crept up at me from behind my head. If he had nothing to say I couldn't bear the echoing silence, so I would fill it up with lots of words. This was partly because I was paying for these sessions myself with some money I had inherited from my grandfather and it seemed like a waste to pay for silence. The paying was my father's idea. He said it was a crucial Freudian principle, although I often thought about the sexy dress, or the haircut, or even the camera I could have had, instead of fifty minutes in an almost dark room with an old man who wanted to know all my secrets and told me none of his in return.

I went on seeing Doctor Kollestrom for about eighteen months, but not on a regular basis; an appointment was usually made shortly after I had screamed. At first I wrote quite a detailed account of everything we had talked about, but after a while there is often nothing more in my diary than just his name, alongside the date and the time of the appointment.

◦ ◦ ◉ ◦ ◦

Doctor Kollestrom was very keen on dreams, so I showered him with mine and they flourished under so much attention, and became wilder and wilder. He jotted them all down in his notebook.

He was much less at ease with family matters, but he did his best. I told him I was in a crisis and needed his help. He would ask questions and he'd listen to my answers, and make a few notes. Every so often he'd let out a little sigh.

'Tell me more about your father,' said Doctor Kollestrom's voice. 'When he lived with you at home he was often drunk and violent, so you must have been frightened of him?'

It was difficult for me to know how to answer this one. It was true that I had sometimes been very frightened of my father. I'd hear the sharp ringing sound of his cough as he approached the house and I knew that meant trouble. I'd wait in my room, listening as the voices began to rise and fall: my mother plaintive and pleading and always on the edge of tears, my father growling and snapping like a wolf. And then, when it sounded as if things were turning really dangerous, I'd get out of bed and go closer to the fight, standing just outside a closed door and waiting until I couldn't wait any longer, before bursting in to protect my mother from danger.

Sometimes, if she noticed that I didn't seem to be arriving in time, she'd come and fetch me. 'Quick, quick! Your father's going mad!' And she would take me by the hand and return to face him with new courage, holding me like a shield in front of her.

'I wasn't really frightened of my father,' I said after a long pause during which this scene had been playing before my eyes. 'But I didn't like being made into a shield.'

'A shield?' I could hear the pencil making a note of the term. 'How exactly, a shield?'

'My mother would hold me by the shoulders, so that my father couldn't hit her. He would get a funny look in his eyes, because he knew he didn't want to hit me, it was her he was after.'

I didn't go on to explain to the doctor, how my father would sometimes stare at me with bloodshot eyes, as if he was sure he had seen me somewhere before but couldn't quite remember where. That seemed like a shameful admission, as if it showed he had forgotten I was his daughter. Then, when he had recognized me again, he'd make a low growling noise of disappointment in the back of his throat, because the fight couldn't go ahead, at least for the time being.

'So you were very powerful! What did that make you feel?'

'Like a knight in shining armour, slaying the dragon and saving the princess,' I said, the image so vivid in my mind it helped to drive out all other thoughts.

'Your father the dragon? Your mother the princess?'

'I suppose so, but I liked him and he was nice to me in a way, even when he was being horrible to my mother. And he always said sorry in the morning. My mother never said sorry. She said it was all *his* fault. But I wanted her to apologize, to me, for what she did.'

◦ ◦ ◉ ◦ ◦

Now, of course, all such troubles were a thing of the past. There were no more acts of bravery to be accomplished, no more dragons to be slain. I lived on my own with my mother and the lodgers.

'Tell me about your mother,' says Doctor Kollestrom and his armchair lets out a reassuring creak.

Where to begin?

'She's thirty-one years older than me, so she's forty-six, she'll be forty-seven on November the fifth, Guy Fawkes Day. She says everyone has a big bonfire party to celebrate her birth. That's her joke.'

I pause and take a deep breath. 'People say we look like each other but I don't think we do. I have got her nose and a bit of her mouth, but she has dimples when she smiles. And I have my father's brown eyes, while she has green eyes with flecks of yellow in them. And we've got different shaped bodies. I am much thinner than she ever was, and taller.'

'Do you get on well?' asks Doctor Kollestrom hopefully.

'No,' I say, not sure where to go from there. Still, I give it a try. 'My mother is only interested in sex. It happened after the divorce, I mean that's when she changed so much. And now she dresses as if she were still young, but she's not young any more and she looks ridiculous. She's always making dirty jokes, which I find embarrassing, and she only wants male friends and that's why she has male lodgers in the house. She says she can't have any women friends, because solitary women are in competition with each other and not to be trusted.'

'Not to be trusted,' says Doctor Kollestrom, as if he wants to discuss this idea, but I can't wait, there is so much more to say before the hour is up.

'She wanted to have sex with Bob and she wanted to marry him. He was our first lodger but he wouldn't even kiss her and she said it was my fault and I was trying to be her rival by flirting with him. It's true I liked him, he was very nice to me, but I don't think I flirted and anyway I was only thirteen. Since then we've had Richard and Ian and Swiss Paul and some others, and there's been trouble with all of them. Because I am a rival. Now there's someone called Geoffrey.'

○ ○ ◉ ○ ○

I want Doctor Kollestrom, safe in his green armchair, to try to understand what it means to have lodgers in the house: these solitary men who arrive out of nowhere with a little suitcase and a friendly shifty smile, and a private collection of habits and smells and likes and dislikes. They eat at our table and wash in our bathtub and shit in our lavatory and behave like friends, but they are not real friends because they pay rent.

'Tell me about Geoffrey,' says Doctor Kollestrom and I try.

'Geoffrey arrived after Swiss Paul. His wife came to our house first, to arrange a room for him because she wanted to get rid of him. She is very pretty with long red hair and she's not much older than me, although she has two young children. She sat on the lawn with my mother and I heard her say, "I've had enough! You can have him!" and they both started to giggle.'

'What does Geoffrey look like?'

'He's very tall, my mother says he's six foot four, and his legs are sort of bendy in the middle. He has a lot of teeth and gentle eyes and he teaches at an art school and he wears nice shirts. I think he's very clever, but he looks like a poof!'

'Do you like him?'

'Of course not! I hate him! He's pompous and artificial and I told you he's a poof. Anyway I'm not allowed to like him. My mother started an affair with him about six months ago and after that she said I must keep away from him.'

I shift a bit on the couch. It's not nice to be told to keep away from someone, it makes me feel as if I've got a contagious disease.

'You see, Geoffrey has always been attracted to young girls and he has had affairs with several of his students. He even told my mother that he fancies his own daughter, which I think is disgusting. She's from an earlier marriage and she's just a year younger than me but I haven't met her.'

'But how can your mother be sure you don't see Geoffrey? After all, aren't the three of you living in the same house?'

'I can't help *seeing* him of course, but I am forbidden to talk to him and sometimes my mother tells me I must leave the room when he comes in.'

'Leave the room?' says Doctor Kollestrom and I imagine his eyebrows rising above the frames of his spectacles.

'He's not with us all the time,' I add, as if that helps. 'He has a cottage in the country and a flat in London somewhere, which he's doing up and my mother goes and stays with him whenever she can. But if I'm left on my own, I don't like it. It's such a big house when it's empty. I can't go to my father's; I tried that once and it didn't work. I always ask my best friend Peggy to be with me for the weekends and she does come quite often. Sometimes she comes with her boyfriend.'

I'm on a gallop now, the words stumbling over each other.

'A little while ago my mother wanted to go to Geoffrey's cottage and when she saw me looking sad, she invited a boy I hardly knew to stay with me. He'd only dropped by to collect something after a party and she put on her baby voice and said to him, "My poor *likkel girl* is going to be all by herself. I bet you'd like to *look after* her this weekend!" He blushed bright red and that made her laugh. But he agreed to do it, as if it were a favour to her. When my mother was leaving she winked at him and said, "Have fun, won't you!" I slept in the same bed with him, but I didn't let him do it.'

Had a dream — I was Cathy
Earle being killed by a man who
was herself but I couldn't
explain — chased by a tribe
of Indians — one followed to
a huge forest made of dense
string standing upright & shivering
at the top. The Indian
would always catch up. he
advised me to give up as the
wood would soon die as it
wouldn't grow — one had to run
through it — at the other side
we met Pat's family — we had
to go across the ice from
island to boulder — down
a cliff face with instead in
routing which kept crumbling
& splitting — couldn't climb was left
don't wouldn't come & he kept
saying that he would show
us the way — the ice we
saw Joan on the other
side we saw a girl with
let her bob — the
water — & enjoying herself
when she came out she was very
fat — she was held — the
by a long rope. We were
— a huge field — yellow

'And what about last weekend?' asks Doctor Kollestrom. His voice sounds nice and gentle.

'It was just me. I felt like a ghost walking from room to room and when the phone rang I didn't dare to pick it up. And then there was someone at the front door and I thought it was a murderer who knew I was inside.'

⊙ ⊙ ◉ ⊙ ⊙

Doctor Kollestrom listens as well as he can, but I have the sense that he is out of his depth. He keeps steering me back to my dreams, as if they might be able to help. I have written them all down in my diary for him and I tell him the ones I think he'll enjoy the most. Like the one about a big black bull in a field full of thistles.

'It had spreading branches growing out of its head instead of horns and ripe plums were hanging from the horns,' I say and I hear Doctor Kollestrom's pencil going scribble, scribble in the notebook.

'I knew that if I touched the plums the bull would kill me,' I say. I wait for more scribbling, but instead I hear a gentle whizzing of breath.

I raise myself up on the couch and turn my head to look at the man who is supposed to be getting me out of my muddle. The pencil has fallen from his hand and he is fast asleep, the tip of his goatee nestling against the lapels of his brown suit.

He wakes up with a little snort of surprise. He gazes at me through the velvety gloom of his consulting room and a Buddha sitting crossed-legged on a shelf behind his head gazes at me as well.

A look of deep sadness passes across his face. He puts the tips of his fingers together as if he is about to pray and says, 'As far as I can tell, you are sane and intelligent, but really your situation is impossible.'

He pauses for a moment and then with a mournful sigh he adds, 'Ah, my poor child. Whatever are you going to do?'

I don't know the answer to that, but I write his words in my diary and hope for the best.

⊙ ⊙ ◉ ⊙ ⊙

March 1999

I've been to Rosalie's house and now I'm back.

The curtains were half drawn. The cats had left offerings of headless mice on the carpet in the bedroom and the fridge in the kitchen was grinding its teeth, as fridges do. I removed the mice and turned off the fridge and got the hairbrush and knickers that Rosalie had asked me to collect for her and then I found the notebook she wanted.

It's a little sketchbook which I gave her a year ago. I opened it up. On the first page she had made a pencil drawing of a plant called a Bleeding Heart, quite a nice drawing, and for some mysterious Darwinian reason each heart-shaped flower has a tiny extra petal hanging from its pointed end, like a drop of blood. On the next page my mother had written in blue biro, 'I will never, never, never forgive Julia for what happened in 1966,' and all the nevers were heavily underlined.

I felt as though I had been slapped in the face. I told you when we were talking about it the other day, that I knew the battle between her and me was not really over, but it was horrible to be confronted with it like this, in all its rawness.

I've got the notebook here on the table in front of me. The past is buzzing around my head like a cloud of mosquitoes. One part of me longs for my mother's forgiveness, the other part is hungry for retribution. What happened, happened. But Herman, you know that, you were there!

Are you there now? Are you reading this fax as it grumbles its way through the machine on your table? Can you tell me what I should do?

(Fax to Herman)

5

Marriage

It began as a love affair. Towards the end of 1943 my father was looking for someone to go rock climbing with him in north Wales and a friend recommended Rosalie de Meric, saying she farted in bed but was very brave, with lovely green eyes.

My mother had never been mountaineering before, but on that first weekend she followed my father up some of the most difficult climbs in the area without a moment's hesitation. She managed a very exposed route on the steep face of Triffan and then learnt what was called 'backing and footing', which was the only way to get up a tight chimney on a climb called the Devil's Kitchen. Her green eyes were shining with a new-found joy and when her gym shoes were too slippery to get a grip on the wet granite she took them off and continued in her socks.

My father was delighted, and after a couple more climbing weekends he said he wanted to marry her just as soon as the divorce from his first wife came through. In the letters he wrote to her from those early days – which she kept in her black briefcase – he told her she *made all the old climbs new again.*

Throughout the sixteen years they were together they were more or less happy on the rocks, even when they were miserable everywhere else. The last holiday that we spent as a family was in Corsica and in the photographs you see all three of us smiling contentedly on one hot and exposed summit after another. But then, only a month after our return, my mother was suing for divorce on the grounds of adultery and mental cruelty, and she and I were hiding in an attic room belonging to a friend, while my father was steaming through the streets and banging on the door of anyone he suspected of harbouring us.

'One thing a marriage can't stand is divorce,' he said later, pleased with the depth of such wisdom.

⊙ ⊙ ◉ ⊙ ⊙

They were both based in London during most of the war and in 1944 they started to live together. I always wanted to know about their experience of the Blitz and what they thought of Hitler and Churchill and the death camps, and I asked them lots of questions, but neither of them had much to say. Maybe they had been too busy with their own lives to notice what was going on around them.

My father was a Conscientious Objector. For a while he was in the London Fire Brigade and he told me he had picked up a helmet after a bombing raid and the metal was still hot and contained the shattered fragments of a human head. Before that he had been stoking coal in a merchant ship going round the coast of Scotland and he had found enough time to read all twelve volumes of Proust's *Remembrance of Things Past.* He showed me the books, the pages stained with his blackened fingerprints.

In one of his early letters to my mother he admitted to a *slight breath of jealousy* for his younger brother John, who *looked fine in his uniform* and went to Suez. John even managed to get badly wounded on a battleship in the Mediterranean and had the evidence of a deep scar cut across his belly to prove it. After the war was over my father pretended that this was *his* story and he even wrote a poem about how much pain he had suffered, lying bleeding in his bunk on that naval vessel. It led to one of numerous quarrels with his brother.

⊙ ⊙ ◉ ⊙ ⊙

My mother worked as a secretary at the Admiralty, then for a couple of years she was a nurse in a hospital in London's East End, but all she was willing to remember were her lovers.

There had been lots of them, as many as three different ones in a single week, and in her diaries she'd write a first name and draw a little star to mark each sexual act, but she made no further mention of the men involved or what became of them later. She loved to show me the slippery black velvet party dress, edged with white rabbit fur, that had clung so suggestively to the contours of her body, leaving her shoulders bare. She kept it like a religious relic, wrapped in tissue paper and stuffed into a plastic bag, and it was still there in her wardrobe when she died.

She also showed me two little photographs taken just before she and my father were introduced to each other. In one she is naked, but holding a strip of cloth draped round her middle, and in the other she wears nothing but a silver necklace. She looks plump and beautiful and curiously preoccupied, as if she was all by herself and not aware of being watched. At some point she had cut round the soft contours of her own body with a pair of nail scissors and when one foot had dropped off at the ankle, she put it back with Sellotape.

'Do you want to see Mummy with nothing on?' she'd say, laughing and yet serious as well, as she carefully extricated these delicate treasures from one of the tight pockets in that leather briefcase filled with its many strange secrets.

⊙ ⊙ ◉ ⊙ ⊙

Before my parents could get married, my father had to get his divorce. He always said he had married his first wife Joan because she was so wild and mad and such a liability in public places. He boasted that she had once pulled down her knickers and pissed on the pavement in Oxford Street in the middle of the day, while people passed by and pretended not to notice. And whenever she was riding on a double-decker bus, she couldn't resist fondling the balls of the bus conductor who came to sell her a ticket. 'You should have seen the look on their faces!' said my father proudly.

35

I met Joan's sister quite recently. She asked me if I was easily shocked and when I reassured her that I wasn't, she told me Joan and my father came to see her and her husband in Surrey in 1942. The two of them stayed in the smart local hotel and they signed their names in the guest book as Mr and Mrs Orgasm.

'It created quite a stir in the village!' said this friendly octogenarian and she gave me a series of photographs commemorating the visit. Both my father and Joan look terribly pleased with themselves.

◦ ◦ ◉ ◦ ◦

Anyway, early in 1945 the divorce had come through and my parents were ready to get married. I don't know whom they had as witnesses or if there was some sort of party afterwards, but in another of the tight pockets in her black leather briefcase my mother kept a little appointment card from the Register Office in Kensington where the ceremony had taken place. On the back of it someone had written, *Decree Absolute. Brit. Nat. of Miss de Meric?* and on the front, just above the address of the office they were to attend, my father had written *Friday 2nd Feb 2.15*, underlining the time with two heavy strokes of his pencil, as if it were a dentist appointment that he shouldn't forget.

My mother told me that on their way there they stopped at a jeweller's and my father asked for the cheapest wedding ring in the shop. She said the jeweller gave her a pitying look because it was obvious the ring was only needed to legitimize a dirty weekend. Still, in spite of her own divorce some sixteen years later and her fury with my father, she went on wearing that same ring for the rest of her life and it was still on her cold hand when I saw her for the last time.

⊙ ⊙ ◉ ⊙ ⊙

They moved to Chatham. My father was teaching at a school for boys and my mother was employed as a secretary, but they saw these jobs as a front, a means of making enough money to support their real vocations as artists. They took themselves extremely seriously and had a notice fixed on the front door of their little flat on which was written: Thomas Blackburn, Poet. Rosalie de Meric, Painter.

When they escaped to the mountains, my mother made wonderful paintings of boulders and lowering skies and crowded trees. But at home she produced terrifying portraits of men and women, their faces merging together, tears like stones running down their cheeks and their mouths wide open in a scream that reveals rows of sharp teeth.

My father's early poems were equally violent. I have just been reading one of his notebooks from 1944. His handwriting is quite careful and precise, nothing like the wild hieroglyphs it became later, but his thoughts are filled with darkness, blood and chaos. One poem begins,

> Come carrion birds of an appalling menace,
> Violence in coils of claws, thick ropes and knives,
> Sinews of strangled grief and nets of scream,
> Stormy cold filling him who is all beast . . .

It was in Chatham that my father took a carving knife and chased my mother round a table saying, 'You are the Angel of Death and I must kill you!'

After a while he grew calm and apologized, and put the knife back in the kitchen drawer where it belonged.

I asked my mother how she had defended herself from him.

'I kept telling him I loved him,' she said. 'Over and over again I told him and in the end he heard me.'

And that was the pattern for all the years that followed: the more my father drank and swallowed the powerful barbiturates prescribed by his psychiatrist, the more he betrayed my mother by sleeping with other women, the more he hit her and insulted her and chased her round tables and through dark streets, the more she responded with tears and protestations of love.

Even when she hated him with a cold and angry hatred, she went on telling him how much she loved him. He'd go out on his own and come back in the early hours of the morning, and when he blundered into the conjugal bedroom I would hear her plaintive cry, 'Do you love me? Do you love her? How can you do this to me? Why don't you love me? Did you make love to her? Kiss me! Please kiss me, my darling!'

A year or so before my mother's death I asked her if she had any gentle memories of my father. It was as if I had sprung the jaws of a trap that had been lying in wait for exactly this moment.

'Gentle memories? Well, let me think. I remember he came back early one morning – this was not long after your birth – and he leant over the bed where I was lying and he put his hand close to my face and he said, "Smell my fingers!" and that was the smell of the woman he had been with!'

◦ ◦ ◉ ◦ ◦

But never mind the drinking and the pills and the bursts of violence and the infidelities that were there right from the beginning, my mother was eager to complete the magic circle of marriage by having a baby as soon as possible. My father was less keen. He said he wanted to wait until he had finished his analysis; a process he was sure would finally free him from the trauma of his own childhood. Until that had been achieved he felt he wasn't ready for the parental role and was afraid his wife would become his mother and he would be overwhelmed by jealousy of the new child who was ousting his place in her bed. I think he was particularly terrified of having a son and repeating the pattern of hatred into the next generation.

hal haysom   chelsea

In spite of all this earnest reasoning, my mother was not to be put off in her purpose; a child was what she needed above all else and after a while my father relented and she was able to throw away her Dutch Cap. When she still hadn't conceived after almost three years of trying, the two of them went and had fertility tests and were told that my father had a very low sperm count. He was advised to dip his balls in a basin of cold water before sexual intercourse took place. This apparently worked, because by the spring of 1948 my mother was pregnant.

○ ○ ◉ ○ ○

March 1999

In spite of everything that's going on, or maybe because of it, I have booked a flight to Italy. So if I can, I'll come and stay for a few days in your mountain house, one month from now. And then I can see the eagles floating above the valley, the wall containing the family of hibernating dormice and I'll hear the owls at night. It's nice to be looking forward, it gives a different dimension to this present time.

(Fax to Herman)

~⊶ 6 ⊷~

And Then a Baby

Just before the birth of my own first child, in August 1978, my mother presented me with a fat little hard-backed blue notebook. 'I feel you should have this now darling,' she said. 'It's all about my experience of giving birth and what it was like having a baby to look after. I'm sure you'll find it interesting, now that you are about to become a mother too.'

I thanked her with the usual formality that we had got used to maintaining by then, but although I kept the notebook, I didn't read it. At that time I didn't want to know what my mother thought or felt when I emerged into the world, and I also had a strong sense that I might be upset or even frightened by whatever it was she had written and I wanted to protect myself from that.

I wonder if she sat down and studied the contents of this strange and sad account of what motherhood meant to her before passing the notebook on to me. I think not, but perhaps what I really mean is – I hope not.

⊙ ⊙ ◉ ⊙ ⊙

The notebook begins quite straightforwardly with lists of the things my mother had been given by friends and lists of the things she still needed to buy: *a brush for scrubbing nappies, four flannelette cot sheets, safety pins and a rubber apron.*

A couple of rather obscure dreams follow, along with a few hurried notes made during an antenatal class, explaining how to bath a baby: *face, cotton wool (avoid eyes) no soap. Dry. Nappy off. Soap baby all over with hands.*

And then she began a new page with the title, *The Birth of 'Julia' 12.8.48.*

The Birth of "Julia" 12. 8. 48.
1.10. p.m.

Perhaps partly because of
the uncertainty of starting labour, but
as well the feeling of the
climax of the 9 months
since conception, each new
stage & even the knowledge
that the next would be
more painful, was a
greedily welcomed.

At 4.30 am. I rejoiced
at the return of the 1st stage
pains, & rushed to the ward
with excitement to
announce a show of blood.
I wanted to be congratulated.
I'd felt a fraud before
though I wasn't really going
to have a baby at all.

She started writing this account while she was still in hospital and I was just two days old. She described how excited she was when her waters broke at 4.30 a.m. and she was taken into the labour ward. The contractions began in earnest a couple of hours later and she found huge pleasure in the *orgasmic relief at the height of pain*, and the *life-or-death challenge* of the struggle she was going through. She said it reminded her of climbing mountains with my father.

And then, amid cries and shouts and excrement and the exhortation of two midwives, *the head was out . . . Dark hair . . . wet warmth and the body of a baby girl.*

⊙ ⊙ ◉ ⊙ ⊙

So far so good, but as soon as my mother looked at the little creature lying beside her, something from her own troubled past kicked into action. She felt that she hadn't given birth to a new life, but instead had given birth to herself. *I was her and she was me . . . me as a helpless newborn thing in the greatest need.* And when it was time to feed the baby, any feelings of love and protectiveness were swept to one side by what she called *a wave of ambivalence* and she was overcome by resentment at the demands that were being made of her.

⊙ ⊙ ◉ ⊙ ⊙

By 15 August she was still in hospital and suffering from the *exasperating boredom of motherhood.* She was stuck in a ward in the company of four *silly women* and a *bitter sarcasm kept rising to my lips* whenever they tried to engage her in their talk on such *meaningless trivialities as knitting, food and babies.* They even distracted her from her reading with their silly chatter.

My mother ended the account of her days in hospital with the words *All babies crying – infernal din – stupid women – wretched brats – probably stupid too anyway.*

⊙ ⊙ ◉ ⊙ ⊙

She continued to use the notebook once she was back at home, following the confused meanderings of her own thoughts and fears, and keeping a record of her dreams. During the first month after the birth she dreamt she had brought the wrong baby home with her: a blond boy and not the dark-haired girl she had given birth to. She hated this changeling child and was very rough with it. My father didn't realize it was the wrong child and this made her furious with him. When she wrote the dream down, she interpreted it to mean that her husband wasn't appreciating her creativity, he wasn't recognizing what she called her 'thing'.

In another dream she drowned the baby in the bathtub and then went to a party where she had a lot of fun.

⊙ ⊙ ◉ ⊙ ⊙

On 29 August she wrote that she was finding it hard to start painting again and as a result of this creative block, her own *internal child* was suffering and she kept bursting into tears. She knew the baby was responsible for her feelings of inadequacy, which were making it very difficult for her to fulfil herself as a painter.

She said she realized that the baby was young, but still she couldn't help blaming it for her unhappiness and that was why she didn't want to feed it, or pick it up when it cried. But when she rejected it with a denial of food and comfort, it punished her by looking at her critically and becoming what she called *a mirror to my conscience*.

By now my poor mother was quite frightened of the seventeen-day-old moral authority that lay in its cot and judged her so harshly with its staring eyes and its tendency to make a fuss. She desperately wanted the baby's approval, but she had the distinct impression that it was able to see through her *pretence of love* and knew it was being rejected. As she explained in a wonderfully circular sentence, *Didn't I know she knew, even though she couldn't express or comprehend it.*

After each of these battles of will, she was forced to relent and pick up the baby and feed it. But even that led to further confusions because as she offered her breast, she was left with the disconcerting feeling that she was *forcing the baby to swallow the refused self of myself.*

By 31 August I was almost three weeks old and my mother was determined to get a firmer grip on things.

Must quickly learn to master the problems of motherhood in the minimum of time, because I am not one of those silly women who make babies a full-time job. I am an Artist first and a mother second – only to fulfil myself as an Artist.

In contrast to my mother, my father was pleased to realize that he enjoyed parenthood enormously and didn't feel that his personality or his poetry was in any way threatened by his new role. This was partly due to the fact that even though he occasionally changed nappies and pushed the pram through the streets on a Sunday afternoon, he left home promptly at eight o'clock every morning to go to work and didn't come back until five in the afternoon at the very earliest. And because he mustn't be disturbed by a crying baby during the night, he often slept in the spare room. And because he said there was not enough money to pay for a babysitter, he often went out drinking on his own and sometimes didn't come back until the early hours of the morning. Such abandonment filled my mother with despair, but the more she wept and protested and said she felt betrayed, the more indignant and unfaithful my father became.

⊙ ⊙ ◉ ⊙ ⊙

There is a long and rather ominous silence in the blue notebook, starting from when I was a few weeks old and lasting until October 1949. By then I had passed my first birthday, my father had enjoyed several brief love affairs and my mother was clearly suffering from a deep depression.

She had been going every week to talk about her problems with Joseph Jacobs, her Freudian analyst. With the encouragement of Jacobs, she composed sad poems in which she waited for her heartless lover *in the rain cursed air.* She also began a series of paintings showing three figures.

In one of them, which she called *Mother and Child,* a bald and naked

woman sits on a chair and offers her breast to a terrifying naked baby who is perched on her lap and has the face of an old man. The woman is not looking down at the baby, but sideways at a very aggressive clown who is standing next to her. The clown is shouting at her and his hand is raised as if he is about to strike her. Another rather sad-looking clown is approaching from the far distance.

In the pages of her little notebook my mother struggled to understand what was happening to her marriage and how her unhappy state of mind was

46

reflected in the savagery of her dreams and her paintings. But the Freudian interpretations she was being offered only seemed to make her more muddled than ever. After she had completed the *Mother and Child* painting, she reached the confident if somewhat confusing conclusion that *this must be the finding of the final penis within myself. This must be the small, frail, dark child, locked in a room in another house.*

○ ○ ◉ ○ ○

March 1999

I have kept the notebook with its drawing of a Bleeding Heart plant, but as you suggested I have torn out the page in which my mother swore she would never, never forgive me for what happened all those years ago.

And yes, I have burnt it, watching the harsh words curl and blacken and turn into fragments of ash. And when I go to see her at the hospital later today, I'll take the notebook with me and I'll tell her that the fight is over, we can't go on like this, not any more.

It was so odd being in her house just now. I was surrounded by all the old unease; the sense of threat and blame as the tidal wave of the past swept over me. It was like that tumbling moment when one falls over some edge while going to sleep, only to be woken by the shock of it.

It's still raining and the dip in the fields has become a perfect circular pool.

(Fax to Herman)

Bright Eyes

Just before my birth, my parents had moved back to London and they rented a top-floor flat in a big noisy street quite close to where my father was teaching at a boys' grammar school.

Our address for the next seven years was 55B Warwick Road, the number fifty-five and the letter B painted in black on one of the round stone pillars that stood guard by the front door of our house. That door was also painted black and it opened into a dark hall smelling of disinfectant. The stairs leading to our flat were as steep as a ladder, so it seemed to me, and covered with shiny red linoleum that had little squares printed into its surface to make it less slippery. I did once slip on those stairs and as I tumbled down them I was sure I was going to be dead when I reached the bottom and was surprised to find myself alive, the blood sticky on my forehead.

Up one flight and up another and you were in our flat. The first room on your right was a cold lavatory, then came my father's study. Sometimes I'd stand outside and give a tentative knock and, if he didn't answer, I'd post letters to him under the door. He kept one of these letters for years. It was written in a laboured six-year-old's script and it read, *Dear Daddy I hate you. Lots of love Julia.*

○ ○ ◉ ○ ○

Entering that room was like stepping into another world. The air was thick with the smell of cigarette smoke and stale beer, old wine and sweat. There were armies of empty bottles standing in a corner and a gathering of half-empty glasses on the table, often with cigarette stubs floating in what was left

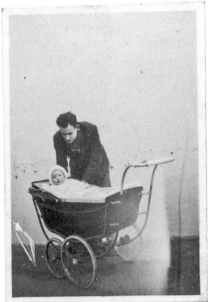

of the red or brown liquid. My father's Olympia typewriter was surrounded by drifts of paper, which fell to the floor like autumn leaves, and all these pages were covered with words written in red and blue biro, in pencil and coloured crayon and in the hammered typeface of the Olympia.

On the wall my father had a framed photograph of William Blake's death mask, the eyes closed and the jaw firmly set. Next to that was a framed postcard of a wooden mask from the Congo, with narrow slits instead of eyes. There must have been other pictures as well, but I can't remember them.

Up more stairs and into the kitchen, and I can see a white metal-topped table and a flat medicine bottle of Welfare State cod liver oil, and a packet of Stork margarine with the picture of a bird standing on one leg. A muslin cloth containing cottage cheese in the making hangs from a hook and drips into a white basin. And there is my plate, which has an orange dragonfly hovering at its centre.

Our bath is in the kitchen and when none of us is using it, it's covered with a sheet of plywood, but right now my father is in the bath and he's talking about something with the steam rising around his thin shoulders. Or maybe he's reciting a poem. He always liked to recite poetry in the bath, slapping out the rhythms with the flat of his hand on the white enamel. I learnt poetry very easily, so we could recite it together:

> Death is an elephant! *Slap!*
> Torch-eyed and terrible! *Slap!*
> Foam-flanked and horrible! *Slap!*
> Boom, steal the Pigmies!
> Boom, steal the Arabs!
> Boom, kill the Whitemen! Hoo! Hoo! Hoo!

Our sitting room was also my mother's studio. She had an easel by the window and a table piled with tubes of oil paints and jam jars filled with brushes and little mountains of rags smelling of turpentine. The first of her paintings that I became aware of showed two naked women with no hair, sitting with their arms round each other and howling in a yellow wilderness of rock and stone. And there was another from those early days in which a snarling dog was emerging out of a barrel, a spiked collar round his neck. A chain leading back into the barrel was attached to the collar and I very much hoped the chain would stop him from attacking anyone. 'That dog represents your father,' said my mother, looking at the painting. I wasn't sure what she meant, but her words frightened me as much as the painting did.

I had a tiny bedroom next to the sitting room. There were bars across the window, which I was told were to stop me from jumping out, although I thought jumping out seemed like a bad idea since the street was very far below. My mother had pinned a big glossy black-and-white photograph of herself on the wall next to my bed, 'So you can see me if I am not with you,' she said. In the photograph her illuminated face emerged out of a thick darkness and even though there were no colours I could see that she was wearing lipstick. She was smiling a lush and intimate smile, which wasn't the kind of smile that mothers made when they looked at their children, and her hair was tousled as if she had just got out of bed.

My parents slept in the room next to mine, except when they quarrelled, in which case my father slept in his study. I had mumps quite badly when I

was about four years old and I slept between them, their bodies hot and sweaty, their faces close to mine on the pillow. Then my father had mumps too and his face swelled up so that he seemed like a different person and his voice changed as well and became all hollow and quavering. I wondered if he was going to die.

My mother said I had given him my mumps and that meant that my father couldn't make any more babies, so I would never have a baby brother to play with. It was as if this eager sibling had been waiting for the moment to step into the world, but now the waiting was all in vain and he had to withdraw to some other place. He was my second baby brother. The first one had been lost while we were on holiday in Wales and although I can't remember the event, my mother told me that she had been two months pregnant and when she stopped to do a pee, he fell out on to the rough grass and that was the end of him. In my thoughts I missed the companionship of both my brothers and often imagined how nice it would have been to not feel there was something odd about being a child with two grown-ups. We could have sung songs and talked and shared things.

◦ ◦ ◉ ◦ ◦

I had very bad eyesight, but nobody knew that yet. I inhabited a world with blurred edges in which a box could turn into a dog when you got closer to it and a tree could become a person just as a person could become a tree. Sometimes I'd go and stand on the flat metal roof that served us as a garden and I would look at the round chimney-pot covers on all the chimneys and see them as row upon row of grey pigeons. I'd clap my hands, but the pigeons were not afraid of me and they didn't fly away, not even when clouds of smoke billowed around them.

I had a pigeon of my own for a while. My mother found him lying bedraggled on the side of the street and he couldn't fly, even though there seemed to be nothing wrong with his wings. I called him Bright Eyes and his home was a wooden crate on the roof. He'd sit on my lap while I talked to him and I liked to feel his beak stabbing gently into the palm of my hand when I fed him with corn. I'd let him drink the bubbled saliva from my lips while he stared at me, his eyes round with surprise.

My father had often told me that all of us had been animals of one sort or another in our previous lives. He said he had been a bee and he buzzed to prove it. He had also been a wolf once, long ago, and I remembered that suddenly years later, when he crawled under the kitchen table and growled and barked and showed his teeth.

According to my father, all birds and animals and fishes could speak our human language if they wanted to, or if you really wanted to listen to them and understand what they were saying. He'd read to me from the unabridged

Grimm's Fairy Tales, his voice rolling on until late into the night, while I moved in and out of sleep and the stories merged with each other, more vivid than dreams:

> Jorindel went to the tree where the birds were gathered and they sang to her, 'Hist, hist, there's a man in the kist! He is your brother and the child of another!' And the wolf said, 'You must cut off my head' and so the boy took the sword. And the raven said, 'I am the king of the ravens! Take this feather and if ever you are in need, throw it into the air and call for me and I will come back to help you!'

I kept waiting for Bright Eyes to speak to me in a language that I would understand. One day he stood on my hand, his head cocked, his eyes staring into mine and I knew this was the moment, but just as he was about to say something, he flapped his wings and launched himself into the sky and disappeared. I was shocked that he had left me so abruptly without a word and had even forgotten to give me a feather. I told my father what had happened and he promised me that Bright Eyes would come back, if ever I really needed his help.

⊙ ⊙ ◉ ⊙ ⊙

March 1999

I went to the hospital, taking the notebook with me.

I had planned a slow and dignified entrance, but instead I burst into tears when I walked in and saw Rosalie sitting in bed, looking so lonely and solemn.

I showed her the place where I had torn out the page and I said that if she was going to be seriously ill then I wanted to help her, but how could I help her if she still hated me and blamed me for what happened.

I thought she would fight back at once, angry and dismissive, but instead she started to weep. And then she started talking, very quietly, as if she was talking to herself.

She said how odd it was, she had always hated me, as well as loving me of course. 'Just like I hated and loved my sister,' she said. 'I hated you because your father stopped sleeping with me when you were born, and then I hated you because he had his mistresses and would stay out all night and I was stuck at home. I hated you because he was kind to you, even when he was being horrible to me. And then there was the divorce and I hated you because you went on seeing him and because you were growing up with your life ahead of you and I was growing old and so much had gone wrong and I hadn't realized until then how much I'd lost. And then there was Geoffrey and after that I could hate you with all my heart and blame you for everything.'

She stopped and looked at me very shyly and said, 'I suppose it can't have been easy for you either. I've never thought of that before. What a dreadful muddle. Something must have got stuck. I hope it's not too late, to unstick it, I mean.'

(Fax to Herman)

⤝ 8 ⤞

Dancing with Francis Bacon

Freud played a big part in the lives of my parents in those days. My mother had her Freudian analyst Joseph Jacobs, who busied her with thoughts of her *inner penis,* while my father had his Freudian analyst with whom he discussed the Oedipal and what he referred to as 'Mother's septic tit', which he saw as the direct cause of his alcoholism. His analyst was called Rosalind Vasher and although I can't remember hearing Jacobs being mentioned, Vasher's name was always in the air: 'Vasher says I need . . . Vasher doesn't want . . . I must tell Vasher.'

My father started going to her in 1943; he was having a lot of trouble with his first wife Joan and seemed to be on the edge of a second breakdown – he had already spent a year or so in a mental institution when he was in his early twenties. His mother and his wealthy Aunt Molly agreed to pay for the treatment, and they went on paying for as long as they were alive and then left him legacies when they died that were also swallowed up on the analyst's couch. My father saw Vasher twice or even three times a week for the next twenty-seven years and could never manage more than a fortnight's holiday away from her.

I met Vasher once in 1955, when we had just moved from London to Leeds. She was small and solidly built with grey hair and she asked me a fast stream of questions in a cold, dry voice. Then she turned to my father and said, 'Your daughter lacks confidence!' as if she was giving her prognosis on a disease.

It was Vasher who first prescribed the barbiturate called sodium amytal. My father had agreed to give a series of lectures on Biology to the men in his division of the London Fire Brigade and the prospect of standing up in front of so many strangers made him nervous, so he tried out this brand-new medicine and it did the trick, all fear was wiped away. Vasher continued to write out prescriptions for sodium amytal in ever-increasing amounts. Of course, no one at that time was aware of the addictive power of the drug and it apparently didn't occur to either doctor or patient that it might be partly responsible for my father's increased confusion and despair.

Although there was never any talk about the pills, Vasher and my father were happy to talk about alcohol in their sessions. They agreed that my father's dependence was not his fault; it was because he associated nourishment with causing pain and on top of that he never got enough milk. Now, of course, he wanted to drink himself into oblivion to forget his guilt and make up for the early loss.

Vasher was also very busy with my father's poetry. During their sessions he read each new poem to her and together they worked out the layers of meaning it contained. He dedicated several poems to her, along with a volume called *The Outer Darkness*.

The two of them had a very odd relationship. They were never lovers, but she encouraged him in his infidelities, telling him that as a poet he must have an anima figure in order that the male and female principles could be united into the energy of creation. This meant that it was important to explore new sexual encounters whenever he could and there was no need to feel guilty about such unnecessary concepts as marital fidelity. If my mother fussed, it showed she was not properly integrated with her own psyche and she should discuss the problem with her analyst as soon as possible.

My father had a number of brief encounters with other women, but as far as I know, the first serious love affair that he embarked on in the years soon after he had married my mother was with the painter Francis Bacon.

My mother had met Francis a couple of times during her childhood, because her bourgeois parents knew his bourgeois parents, so when she heard that he was in London she went to visit him with my father. The two men recognized something in each other straight away – 'a shared blackness' was how my father put it – and there was an immediate rapport. At their first meeting Francis decided to call my father Tony, 'because you don't look like a Thomas, you look like a Tony'. In one of his notebooks my father remembered being very impressed by the 'red curtained studio' where Francis was living with a *middle-aged and important official in the London County Council who had left his wife and two children for love.*

Not long afterwards the important official died and Francis was on his own. My parents went on seeing him, but my mother felt increasingly excluded and rightly so. As my father said in his notebook:

When his friend died, I visited him alone. He had moved to a flat in Victoria and his flat, full of newspaper photographs of the mysterious and terrible, tubes of paint, paint-stained plates – he scorned palettes – was creative and chaotic. He was, he said, trying to get to the nerve, the sudden moment of truth when the mask disintegrates and the raw animal appears.

We had long hours of conversation and although I am a heterosexual, I fell in love with him and there were kisses in taxis; my love trying in vain to ignore the repulsion of bristles on his face.

My mother was filled with jealousy. She said Francis was her childhood friend and on top of that he was a painter like she was and my father had no right to steal him away. She took her revenge by falling in love with an Indian called Kuldeep, who rented the spare room in our flat for a while.

Kuldeep was a Sikh and I can remember his beard and his turban and his serious face. I can also remember my mother telling me that my father didn't love her any more and so she wanted to run away with Kuldeep and be happy. She said he had let her watch the unwinding of his long hair and when it was down around his shoulders he looked like a god. She showed me the little wooden comb inlaid with a silver dagger that he had given her as a sign of his affection and she showed me where she kept it, in another of those tight pockets in her black leather briefcase. She made me promise never to mention the comb to my father or tell him where it was hidden.

I kept quiet, but still there were some terrible scenes, during which Kuldeep was punched in the face and told to leave, and after that his name was sometimes mentioned like a curse. But my father did agree to stop excluding my mother so totally from his relationship with Francis and for a while, when my mother discovered she could communicate with the dead by

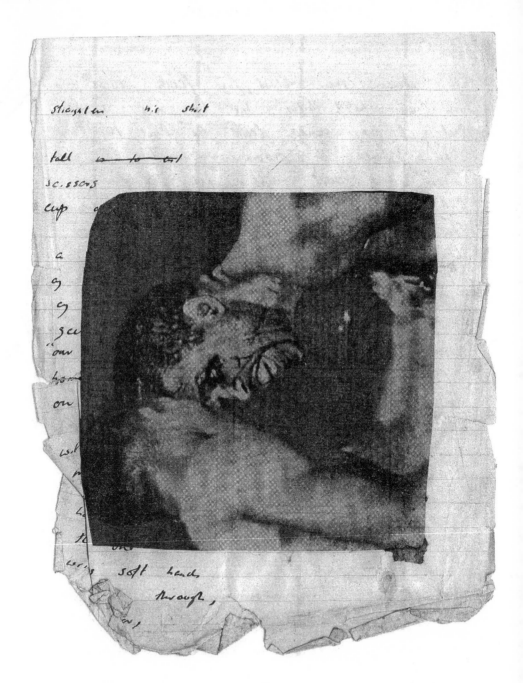

means of automatic writing, the three of them were united in a strange union. They would sit round the heavy rosewood table in my mother's studio and the two men asked the questions to the ghosts of the departed, while my mother's hand wrote faster and faster in a wild script that was nothing like her own. They got in touch with a very unhappy creature who began to tell them how his life had gone all wrong and how it was no fun being dead either. But then the novelty faded and either the ghost went away or the two painters and the poet ceased to be concerned with him.

I was told that I saw Francis quite often during those years that we lived in Warwick Road and although I can't pinpoint any of these meetings, I can remember my father showing me the scrapbook they had made together, which he said showed how much they had in common. There was a photograph of a child in Bergen-Belsen, walking past a line of emaciated corpses, laid out very regularly along the side of a wooded lane. Then came Sugar Ray Robinson, punching Joe Louis on the jaw, and you could see the long tentacle of spit floating in the air and the punched jaw had gone all soft and Sugar Ray had a swollen eye. And there were hippos in a drought and they were all stuck in the mud. After my father's death his wife Peggy threw away the scrapbook and only the one loose page has survived.

⊙ ⊙ ⦿ ⊙ ⊙

The relationship between my father and Francis reached a crisis when it was finally consummated:

> One night, drunk and disintegrated, I briskly sodomised him. He divined there was no love in the act, only infinite revulsion, and our relationship terminated.

I had thought they stopped seeing each other after that, but from my mother's diaries I realize that they went on meeting quite regularly until we moved from London to Leeds in 1955, although there were clearly fights and tensions. On 20 March of that last year my mother wrote: *T sees F Bacon* and on 19 April, *Soho p.m. Francis Bacon attacks T. Champagne. Sick.*

My father kept a single letter that Francis had sent him from Monte

Carlo. It was hidden between the pages of a book of poems and it was written in a soft pencil scrawl. It is without a date:

My dear Tony,

I wonder if you would like it here. It seems by the daylight not so totally different to London . . . the heat and the light give the really torrid quality and the whole place is fairly deserted. I head to the Casinos and throw away a lot of money. Perhaps it's what I wanted, I don't know, but I believe I can work now. Do you manage to defeat the terrible boredom? Love, or whatever you like to call it and work, seem to be the only things that do at all for me – even the gambling has lost its potency and the love thing seems to start off with so many complications, especially the homosexual side now that everyone knows as much and are afraid of everything. How wonderful if we could live the gay and magic idea, all as one. Do write when you have time. All my love, Francis.

Years later, when I saw Francis again, his flat wide face and his thin voice were suddenly deeply familiar from long ago. I was in my early twenties and living in London, and my father phoned to say they had arranged to have a drink at the Colony Room in Soho and would I come too.

During the previous few weeks I had been working for the Ceylonese poet and editor Tambimuttu. I told him of the planned meeting and he was keen to come too, so at the end of the day we set off together. Tambimuttu was wearing one of his exquisite Ceylonese silk jackets and in those days he had a big tight belly on him like an eighth-month pregnancy. We met my father on the corner of Frith Street and went through the open door and up the narrow stairs that led to the Colony Room. Muriel Belcher, who ran the place and called everyone Cunty, was not there and the room was almost empty. A man played soft jazz tunes on the piano.

My father went to the bar and ordered a bottle of rum. He kept rubbing his hands together in the glee of anticipation. He told me that the first time he came here with Francis, Muriel Belcher had pointed a pudgy finger at his reefer jacket and said, 'Take that thing off, Cunty! It looks so *vulgar!*'

Then Francis entered the room, four or five young men dancing attendance, like a flurry of courtiers around their king. He stared at my father and wavered a moment in uncertainty before lunging towards him. He grasped him by the shoulders, almost bringing their two faces into contact. 'My God, Tony!' he said, 'you look awful! You used to be so beautiful!'

'You look pretty horrible yourself,' said my father hopefully, bobbing up and down like a courting bird, his head bent slightly forward and his mouth pulled into a tight grin.

Francis was dressed in a black leather biker's jacket and black leather trousers, while my father had put on his best white linen suit, which was by now far too tight for him so that his arms, his chest and his legs seemed to be trying to burst out from the confines of the cloth.

'Champagne!' said Francis. 'Champagne to celebrate the death of love!'

'You know Tambi, of course you do, and this is my daughter, Julia,' said my father, still bobbing. 'You must remember her from Warwick Road.'

'I'm not interested in your daughter or in anyone else. It's you I am interested in, Tony. Only you! Drink up your champagne, there's a dear, and let's dance!'

They curled into each other's arms, the man in white and the man in black, and they began a slow waltz, each holding an almost empty glass of champagne over the other's shoulder. They were ironic in their manner, yet they were also tender.

Tambi was sitting next to me on a sofa. Watching the two dancers was rather like being at the cinema. 'You must write this down as soon as you get home,' he said. 'You are here witnessing the meeting of three very important people. It is an event you must remember for the rest of your life.'

○ ○ ◉ ○ ○

March 1999

Rosalie and I hugged each other, which was something we'd never done before, at least not like that with so much warmth, and then we grinned rather sheepishly.

At that moment there was a knock on the door and the doctor and two nurses appeared like an angelic apparition, all dressed in white.

Rosalie and I sat there on the side of the bed, hand in hand, waiting for the verdict.

The doctor pulled up a chair and looked at my mother with steady blue eyes. I think he was trying to assess the type of person she was and how she would respond to what he had to say.

He said he was sorry, but she had acute leukaemia, the sort normally associated with a much younger person.

'So what do you suggest?' asked my mother, very matter-of-fact.

'We could try Vitamin K treatment,' he replied, but without much conviction. 'And of course there's always chemotherapy.'

'Will it make me better?'

'Oh no,' said the doctor hurriedly, 'we can't make you better. It might give you more time, but there would be side effects . . . breathing problems. We'd keep you here, of course. You see, I have no . . .' and he trailed off.

'How much time if we do nothing?'

'It's impossible to know. A couple of weeks, a month, perhaps a few months if your body accepts the blood transfusions.'

'Thank you, doctor,' said my mother, still with this wonderful calm and poise. 'I'll talk it over with my daughter. Don't you worry, I'm sure everything will be fine.'

(Fax to Herman)

9

The Old Bs

For as long as my mother and father were together the three of us would spend every Christmas with my father's parents. They lived in Hove in the south of England and their house must have been quite close to the sea, although I don't remember ever seeing the sea when we were there.

A few days before we were ready to leave, my father became increasingly tense. I'd hear him muttering to himself, 'Oh no, no, no! I hate the bastard! God, I hate him!'

He'd begin to do his chiming-clock cough even when he was sober and he'd grind his back teeth together, so you could see the muscles of his jaw rippling. When he was in that sort of mood he had a special way of folding over his bottom lip and pulling it tight, making his face look like a mask.

We'd set off on the morning of Christmas Eve in our black Ford Prefect, my father at the wheel, sucking at a chain of cigarettes, my mother beside him in her shaggy fur coat if it was very cold, otherwise she wore the leopard skin.

I was in the back, next to a suitcase, looking at the silhouette of their heads. I was sitting on a penny that had been placed under a brown paper bag, because I had once been told by a man from the Automobile Association that this was the best way to stop car sickness and I believed him, so it worked.

The moment we arrived at our destination and my father stepped out of the car, something happened to him. A special grin appeared on his face and it remained there, locked in position for as long as our visit lasted. His body changed as well. His head went down and one shoulder rose up, giving him a crooked shape and an odd lurching bounce to his walk. If he stood still, he held his knees pressed together, like a child who needs to do a pee.

⊙ ⊙ ◉ ⊙ ⊙

The vicar and his wife appeared at the vicarage door to welcome us.

'Hello, Mummy! Hello, Daddy!' said my crooked father in a strange sugary voice and he offered them his cheek to be kissed.

'Hello, Eliel! Hello, Adelaide dear,' said my mother hopefully, standing beside my father, but no one seemed to notice her and they certainly didn't notice me, next to my parents.

My grandmother Adelaide was from Northumberland farming stock, but I hardly know anything about her family, except that her uncle Featherstone Fenwick had *breath that could slay a man.* And am I right in thinking that Adelaide's mother died from giving birth to her and that was why as a child she was never allowed to sit on her father's knee, because it would remind him of his grief and her part in it?

In the photographs of her as a young woman she looks remarkably similar to my father's first wife Joan, but without the laughter. Adelaide had auburn hair and a pale skin and hooded pale eyes, which she left to science when she died. My father said this was a noble gesture and never mind that science rejected the gift.

When she was still young, Adelaide had painted watercolours and these were now displayed on the walls of the vicarage in little gold-edged frames. Usually she chose as her subjects flowering apple trees and pretty gardens and distant hillsides, and there was never a human being to be seen anywhere. But she also produced some blood-red sunsets that my father admired enormously. 'Look at that sky!' he'd say. 'Only a truly passionate woman could paint a sky like that!'

My mother was made furious by such praise. She despised Adelaide's sunsets as much as she despised her apple trees and there was no affection between the two women, who were unlikely rivals, both in their art and in their jealous love of my father.

I wasn't interested in my grandmother's paintings, it was her hair that fascinated me. She had lost almost all the hair on the top of her head and she concealed this loss under a little cap woven out of a switch of auburn hair, which must once, long ago, have been her own. This precarious deception was held more or less in place with a collection of kirby grips, but it looked so odd and unconvincing that I found it difficult not to stare.

'Some women lose their hair as they get older,' she said, her voice punctuated by little sighs, 'but I have been lucky that way.'

Now that I think of it, hair was the strongest connection between us. As soon as I crossed the threshold into her house, Adelaide would grasp me by the shoulders and steer me upstairs into the room where I always slept. The wallpaper was covered with row upon row of little roses behind bars and a terrifying portrait of Jesus as the light of the world hung just above the single bed I was to occupy.

'Aah!' said Adelaide and from out of a drawer she produced a heavy silver-backed hair brush, which she clonked rhythmically against my skull as she brushed my hair with its soft bristles. 'Aah! That's better!'

○ ○ ◉ ○ ○

My grandfather's name was Eliel and he was as dark as Adelaide was pale. He had been born on the tiny island of Praslin in the Indian Ocean, but he never said so to me, even though I would have loved to ask him about the birds and fishes he had seen.

Eliel was the son of a missionary who had declared that his task in life was to 'stamp out copulation' among the natives of Praslin and as a result of his efforts the family had to leave the island in a hurry because a sorcerer tried to kill them all with a voodoo spell. That was when they moved to the much larger island of Mauritius.

Eliel's mother was what was called 'a woman of colour'. I have never seen a photograph of her, so I don't know how strong the colour was, or whether Indian or African blood ran in her veins, but I do know that Eliel was said to be the darkest of her children, so much so that he was ostracized by his own siblings and forbidden to accompany them when they went out on social occasions.

At the age of eighteen, Eliel set off for England, where he took his training as a parish priest in the Anglican Church. He brought almost nothing of his past with him: no portraits of relatives; no clocks or teapots; just a couple of books that had been presented to him at school and a tiny photograph of a bungalow emerging out of a tangle of high trees, the word *Chamarel* written beneath it.

He never went back to his island homes and he seemed to have broken all contact with his family, but what he kept was a hatred of the 'dark-skinned races', the belief that intermarriage was more dangerous than 'a hundred atomic bombs' and some very odd ideas about sin and sexuality.

My father told me many stories about his own childhood and he wrote about it as well in a book called *Clip of Steel*. He told me how he had been beaten with a leather belt that had a heavy metal buckle and how at night Eliel would come up the stairs to the bedroom where he slept, carrying a piece of cotton wool and a bowl containing a mixture of bleach and lemon. 'Too dark, too dark,' said Eliel gently, as he washed his son's face with the stinging liquid.

Worst of all was the terrible metal contraption designed to control wet dreams, which had been especially ordered from a supplier in Mauritius. It was strapped across the boy's naked groin at night, and if he had an erection it would clamp down on his penis, thus waking him out of his state of sin. I didn't like these stories and tried to avoid thinking about them, although I could reassure myself with the knowledge that one day, when my father was being beaten, he seized the leather belt with its metal buckle and struck his father with it and after that he was never beaten again. Later, just

before he left home, he got a loaded rifle and made all the plans for a simple patricide, but he changed his mind at the last minute.

'What about Granny?' I would say. 'Didn't she stop him? Didn't she want to protect you?'

'She did her best,' said my father confidently, but I was not convinced.

⊙ ⊙ ⊙ ⊙ ⊙

It was with such images going round in my head that I would watch my grandmother and her cap of loose hair, and my grandfather and his gleaming dog collar as the three crucial days of Christmas passed in a dream of slowness.

If the weather was mild, we could walk around the garden and look at the carefully pruned rose bushes. If it was cold, we could sit on chairs in the sitting room and watch the fire burning in the grate, or sit on chairs in the dining room and work at the food on our plates. Then it was back to the sitting room for a little glass of something before bed.

I can still see that room and my grandfather in his armchair looking saintly and my father in the chair opposite him, looking both terrified and terrifying, his mouth locked in a dreadful grin. My grandmother didn't do much sitting, she was always walking in or walking out and carrying something as she went. 'Aah!' she said, as she passed by.

My mother tried to make herself useful as a way of escaping from the gloom, but every time she offered to do something to help, her offer was firmly rejected. So she had to sit in a chair and look miserable. I wished my grandparents had a dog. When my father was a child they had a fox terrier they called Pox, until someone told them it was not a suitable name for a dog. I thought a lot about Pox and how I would scratch his tummy and take him for walks, and he would be my devoted friend and companion for as long as our visit lasted.

I am not sure what rituals we followed on Christmas Day, but I think the Old Bs, as we called them behind their backs, went to church, while the three of us stayed behind to keep an eye on the turkey. My grandmother had a horror of undercooked meat, so the turkey had been quietly boiled in a big pot overnight, before it was ready to be moved to the oven first thing in the morning. It was served in a state of pale and steaming deliquescence at about two o'clock in the afternoon. Stewed prunes for pudding, or at least I can't remember anything else. And nothing as frivolous as crackers or jokes.

'Very delicious, Mummy,' said my father, wiping his fixed grin with his napkin.

'Yes, delicious. Thank you Adelaide,' said my mother unhappily.

'Aah!' said my grandmother, rising to her feet as she received these offerings of praise. 'Don't you think Julia's hair looks so much nicer when it has been properly brushed?'

And everyone agreed on that too.

⊙ ⊙ ◉ ⊙ ⊙

'God, I hate that bastard,' said my father, once the farewells had been completed and we were driving away, but now he spoke more in relief than anger. My mother began to talk a bit as well, saying how disgusting the turkey had been and how she had scraped some blue mould from the stewed prunes, but she had to be careful to avoid saying anything negative about Adelaide, for fear of making my father suddenly defensive. And she had better not say much about Eliel, because that was bound to rekindle his childhood rage. I sat in the back, firmly positioned on the penny under its brown paper bag and I watched their silhouettes.

Once we were further from Hove and nearer to London, my father would cheer up and begin to sing hymns in a loud and tuneless voice. I suppose it was an act of exorcism. The hymn he liked best for such an occasion was always

> Oh Sacred Head sore wounded,
> Defiled and put to scorn.
> Oh Kingly Head surrounded
> With mocking crown of thorn.

I liked it too and would sing it with him, doing the *pom-pom-pom* bits between the verses that were supposed to take the place of the church organ.

◎ ◎ ◉ ◎ ◎

March 1999

I realize that Rosalie sees death as a challenge, it's like a difficult climb and she is going to do it as well as she can.

She is quite decided. She wants no treatment and she wants to come and stay with me here, for as long as it takes.

She told the doctor and he was very relieved. He lost his formal manner and gave her a hug and wished her all the best and she told him what lovely eyes he had. 'Thank you,' he said, rather taken aback, but pleased too.

She's terribly excited about coming, 'We will have fun!' she keeps saying and I think she might be right. It seems absurd, but I'm really looking forward to spending this time with her.

I'm setting up what's called a Care-in-the-Community programme. One of the nurses who will come visiting was my midwife when my son was born at the farm. What an odd thought!

(Fax to Herman)

The Story of Boonie and Tuggie

My mother said I was more like her sister than her daughter. She said it as if this was a good and comfortable thing to be, but already when I was still quite young I knew her sister was dead and it was very disconcerting to be seen standing in the shoes of a dead relative. I also knew that not only had she died, she had taken her own life, using her father's gun one morning early in the family garden, just after the Second World War had been declared.

My mother told me how she and her sister used to fight. These fights usually started in the morning before breakfast and they were without rules or restraints. The two girls would pull each other's hair and use their finger-nails trying to draw blood, and all the time their father would stand and watch and shout encouragement, as if he had set two cockerels together in a ring. He only wanted my mother's sister to win and she usually did because she was two years older, which made her bigger and stronger. I found the stories of these fights much more frightening than my father's childhood battles, because of what happened in the end.

⊙ ⊙ ◉ ⊙ ⊙

My mother's sister was born in October 1914. My grandparents had been married for less than a year, after a wild romance which urged them on in spite of family disapproval of the match and she was the fruit of their love for each other. They did find it a pity that she wasn't a boy, especially her father found it a pity, but never mind, it couldn't be helped. They gave her the name of Vivienne, but when she was little she referred to herself as Boon and so she became known as Boonie.

Shortly after the birth, her father went off to fight as an officer in the First World War and when he returned on sick leave fifteen months later he was quite changed. His experience of the trenches had turned him from a cheerful and fresh-faced youth into a querulous middle-aged man. He burst into tears every time a door banged shut or there was some other sudden noise and he didn't dare to go to funerals, for fear that he might break down and make a fool of himself. The marriage faltered and never regained the passion it had once known.

My mother was born in November 1916, a witness to the unhappiness of her parents. She was christened Rosalie, but because she was plump her father called her Guts and this nickname was later turned back to front and she became known as Tug or Tuggie.

⊙ ⊙ ◉ ⊙ ⊙

This is the story of Boonie and Tuggie. In all the photographs you can hardly believe they are sisters, because even when they have been dressed in identical costumes they look completely different.

Boonie had a narrow body and skinny legs. She had straight dark hair, slightly buck teeth and she was short-sighted. She always appears nervous and awkward and as a young child she often looks really frightened of something.

Tuggie was all curves and curls and as soft and delectable as a ripe fruit. She had perfect teeth and a generous smile, and there was an expression of hungry longing in her widely spaced eyes. If she was rather insecure, then she was also brave and determined at the same time.

Their father loved Boonie and he didn't love Tuggie. Maybe that was because of what happened to him in the war, or maybe there were other reasons, but anyway he favoured his older daughter and showered her with affection. He also treated her like the son he wished she were, so that when she was little she was given woodworking sets and clockwork trains to play with, and when she was older she was taken out on hunting and fishing expeditions and was given a horse of her own, because she was such a good rider.

Tuggie was given dolls and fluffy toys. When she was little she was told she was a coward and a cry-baby, and as she got bigger she was told she was fat and stupid. Her father and Boonie ganged up against her and if they went out on one of their expeditions, they always left her behind because she'd only get in the way. It would have been easier if Tuggie's mother had told her how lovely she was and had tried to protect her from being bullied, but Tuggie's mother made it clear right from the start that she didn't like her second child, not one bit.

Tuggie felt that life was unfair and all her memories of childhood were to do with this sense of unfairness. When she was a tiny baby, a nursemaid had started to wash her with a sponge dipped into boiling water and that left a thick and shiny scar on her chest which never disappeared. When she was five and the family was living in Burma, she had woken from a terrible nightmare, but instead of comforting her, her father picked her up and dangled her over the veranda, saying that if she didn't shut up immediately he'd throw her to the snakes. Back in England, he taught her to swim by taking her to the end of the pier at Weymouth and tossing her into the sea. He laughed as he watched her struggling and spluttering in the water below and once he felt the lesson had been successful, he lowered a rope down, so that she could pull herself out.

⊙ ⊙ ◉ ⊙ ⊙

Boonie and Tuggie's mother came from a wealthy background. This was thanks to her great-uncle, Thomas Holloway, who was the manufacturer of Holloway's little pink pills, which cured all ills and made him one of the richest men in Victorian England. The possibility of having access to this wealth lay in the hands of Boonie and Tuggie's powerful, chain-smoking grandmother, Anne Driver-Holloway, but Anne Driver-Holloway had disinherited her daughter when she insisted on marrying a man she had been told not to marry.

In spite of being disinherited, Boonie and Tuggie's mother still had lots of jewellery and silver teapots and a legacy from a distant relative, which provided enough income to support her entire family, but she had lost the big money that should have been hers. This meant that after the passion of love had faded and gone cold, she was furious with her husband. She felt he had ruined her life.

⊙ ⊙ ◉ ⊙ ⊙

Boonie and Tuggie's mother made sure that they always lived quite close to the town of Weymouth, where her father occupied a pillared and turreted mansion on the seafront. He was quite friendly towards her and her family and they went to see him most weekends, but he had no financial power: it was her mother who held the purse strings. Her mother had a separate house near Ascot, complete with forty-five rooms of various shapes and sizes, but she never invited her disobedient daughter to visit her. There was, however, a gathering of the entire family every Christmas, in Weymouth. Boonie and Tuggie's mother must have felt the salt rubbing into her wounded soul when she sat at the festive table with her four brothers and sisters who had not been disinherited and who would one day become the possessors of all the worldly goods that lay around them. Already she had started to make lists of the houses and paintings, the fixtures and furnishings in the Weymouth house and the Ascot house and what it must be worth, and these lists grew and proliferated over the years. She also made careful drawings of ancestral coats of arms and sprawling family trees, which connected her back through

the centuries, via the bloodline of obscure lords and ladies, until she became a direct descendant of William the Conqueror.

⊚ ⊚ ⊙ ⊚ ⊚

Boonie and Tuggie's father was of Huguenot origin, but, although he could claim the title of Count de Meric, he had no family money. He worked for two years doing something for the railways in Burma and he was a tea planter for three years in Ceylon, but in England he was a gentleman of leisure.

He looked after the flowers in the herbaceous borders of a succession of rented houses and he planted an asparagus bed and tended his fruit trees, which he guarded with a fierce pride. He played tennis and went hunting, shooting and fishing. But there was a problem: he and his wife were not considered wealthy enough to mix in the social circles where they felt they belonged and they were too riddled with snobbery to want to mix with anyone who was beneath them on the social ladder.

The girls lived a very isolated and lonely life. They were taught the basic skills of reading, writing and arithmetic by young and not very knowledgeable governesses who never stayed with them for longer than a few months. They were forbidden to speak to the village children and they had no friends among the children of the more wealthy families. Tuggie remembered the gardener who used to take her and her sister behind the potting sheds to show them his cock and let them touch it and feel it stirring. She spoke of this years later as if it had been an act of kindness on his part, because at least he was friendly and took an interest in them. And there was a nice woman in the post office who let them have a cup of tea and a bun with her and her children in their front room, but they mustn't say anything about it to their parents or there would be trouble.

When Boonie was fifteen and Tuggie was thirteen, a stash of love letters written by their father and addressed to the latest governess was discovered. There were dramatic scenes, the governess was dismissed and the two girls were bundled off to a tiny boarding school, while their parents went to Ceylon to recover from the scandal.

The parents stayed away for three years. During term-time Boonie and

Tuggie were in the company of some forty other girls between the ages of eleven and eighteen, and during holidays they were farmed out to stay with an assortment of family acquaintances.

The school had a big effect on both of them. Boonie had always been the favoured one and the winner of battles, but now that she was on her own and unprotected by her father she lost courage, became dangerously shy and did badly at all her lessons.

For the fat and neglected Tuggie school was heaven. She became very sociable and full of laughter and quick to learn. As she explained it in a letter she wrote later, a letter she kept in her black briefcase:

> Boonie found book work very difficult. At school she had friends, but she was very secretive about these friendships and guarded them from me. We were both changing and we quarrelled frequently. Our ideas were developing along opposite lines.

As soon as she had finished school, Tuggie was eager to see the world. She wanted to be a painter and when her father refused to pay for her to go to art school she simply set off for London on her own. She trained in shorthand and typing and got herself a job at the Admiralty. She discovered that even if her father said she was ugly, she was attractive to other men and she started to fill her diaries with the little stars of her conquests. Throughout 1937 and 1938 she wrote lots of poetry:

> Passion's tongues of fire
> Licked me to a keen desire;
> Forced my trembling breasts
> To upward turn into the air.

> Filled with abandon
> The pride of possession,
> Complete relaxation,
> Deep satisfaction,
> I ruffled my hair
> And laid myself bare
> In his arms.

Meanwhile, Boonie had returned home to her parents and the tedium of their lives. She was very reclusive and by now she only dressed in man's clothes. According to Tuggie, she told her that the 'idea of marriage was distasteful to her, she dreaded the responsibility of running a home, she never wanted children and men were to be avoided because they all wanted the same thing'.

In 1937, when she was twenty-three, Boonie got a job working in a

stables down in Devon. She was clearly delighted with this proof of independence and she wrote lots of letters to Tuggie, full of talk about how jolly everything was:

Darling Tuggie,

Thank you *very much indeed* for the ripping bedside lamp. It's much nicer having something that wasn't on my list and it really is useful and I need it awfully in the early mornings as I have to fumble so for matches. I really do love it and the dog on it is sweet. I had some damn fine presents. The Higgins family gave me a new hot-water bottle, mine leaks. Winnie gave me a topping yellow tie . . . I am writing this at 11.15 p.m., while listening to my wireless.

In June 1939, she wrote to say she'd had an accident with a horse:

Dearest Tuggie,

. . . At the moment I am out for a count. When I was grooming last evening, Clinker low-kicked a fly on his tummy and somehow my head was between his leg and the fly and I got it on my nose and that rather knocked me out a bit. Everybody has been topping and insisted on my staying in bed all day. I've never been cared for so much in my life . . . Four young things went off and bought me a lemon as a joke and a large bunch of grapes and some Kia-Ora orange squash and a couple of papers. Mr and Mrs Charleston gave me some cigarettes and a brass tray.

She seemed to recover, but then she developed glandular fever and was so unwell she was sent back home. Not long after she arrived, war was declared and the stables were closed down. Her mother was often away, in which case she was in the house on her own with her father.

Boonie became listless and depressed, she was very thin and she felt she was losing her memory. Her eyesight seemed to be getting worse, there was something wrong with her teeth and her skin was bad. The idea of the war horrified her. She imagined 'terror in the streets and bombs falling' and she was obsessed with rationing and the danger of starvation. She became convinced that both her parents would be killed and she would never be able to survive without them.

She tried to tell Tuggie her fears but the old rivalry, combined with the differences of their personalities and knowledge of the world, led to a complete lack of understanding. As Tuggie explained it,

> I tried to revive the happy spirit she had lost, but examples from my own life were not sufficiently in harmony with her own ideas to give her much encouragement.

In a letter dated September 1939 Tuggie wrote:

> Boon dear,
>
> Don't worry about your memory, mine is shocking but it doesn't bother me. I never remember anything, I just invent . . . That man Alexi is proving a bit of a nuisance. He still has it in his head that I am the only thing that makes his life worth living and that one day he will marry me. Some hope! I suppose I must be a fickle fiend . . . I have had another flash in the pan during the last fortnight, a young journalist aged twenty-three, father out in Africa. He has proved a soothing tonic after the Ronald upset. Actually he is far fonder of me than I of him . . .

Two months later, towards the end of November, she wrote again:

> Boonie dear, do please stop looking for misery and trouble. People who really suffer always manage to smile and those with long dismal faces are invariably those who have no real trouble . . . As for rationing, you will be no worse off than anyone else . . . Keep your chin up and I'll look for a changed person when I come home for Xmas.
>
> Did you manage to go to the all-ranks dance? I should go whenever

you can and even get drunk for the evening (sound advice from a younger sister!). Keep your end up! Your loving Tuggie.

PS If you don't agree with me, write and say so and tell me your principles of living.

They were all together for Christmas and everything seemed fine. Tuggie was ready to return to London on Boxing Day. Her parents took her to the station and then Boonie suddenly arrived just as the train was leaving, and she ran down the platform and waved goodbye.

Tuggie was woken by a telephone call at 7.40 a.m. the next morning. Her mother said she must come home at once. 'Boonie is dead!' she said.

Tuggie caught the 9.30 from Waterloo Station. She described the journey and her arrival in scribbled pencil notes on a few sheets of loose paper.

Tried to read. Listened to arguments of sailors. Stopped at all stations. Very cold. Snow at first, then misty fog. Mummy and Mrs Bacon at the station. Ma told me the truth and I broke down. She was wonderful and drove home calmly. Boonie had left her room between 4 and 6 a.m., wandered into the garden and shot herself with Daddy's gun, in the head, just outside the coal cellar. Ma found the note she had written at 11 p.m. and sent P out to find her. She was only in pyjamas and dressing gown at 7.30 when he came across her cold and dead.

Ma and I went straight to the Bacons. Pa was there, very white and still . . . We stayed a while and then came back for tea. All three of us broke down and went over every little detail, trying to see what we could have done, or why she had done this thing.

In her suicide note addressed to 'Darling Ma and Pa', Boonie didn't give much of an explanation. She said the melancholia was getting her down and Christmas was grand, but she had been a 'wet blanket':

Everything has been *very* comfortable for me up to now, but that's no good . . . Tuggie has at least made a life for herself, even though you do despise her. God knows, I've never done anything for myself. The rotten part is that I look vaguely intelligent and the answer is *I'm not*. I've discussed this depression over and over with Tuggie and she's tried to help me, no one can, it's myself and it can't be cured . . . I'm no use to anyone . . . All love, Boonie.

Tuggie had suddenly become the only child. She returned to London and continued writing poetry and going to parties and making love and painting pictures. She wrote, 'An Outline of What I Imagine Were the Causes of My Sister's Suicide', piecing together the accident with the horse, the glandular fever, the war and adding one extra factor. She had reason to believe that Boonie might have been pregnant. According to her mother, she had missed her last three periods and had been asking questions about babies and contraception.

Surely this was why she had been depressed and unwell and worried about the future! She had mentioned a stable boy she liked, who had gone to the war, so he was the one! What a tragedy, then, that she hadn't confided in her younger sister who could easily have arranged an abortion in London and then everything would have been fine. Problem solved.

Tuggie sent a copy of her outline, including the pregnancy theory, to her mother. It was sent back with the bit about pregnancy underlined and a note in the margin saying, *Cut this out for all times and* destroy *this part! . . . Say nothing to Pa!*

Tuggie saw her parents occasionally, but the relationship between the three of them was never friendly. In 1941 she had lunch with them and told them that she thought Communism was a good thing. She received a letter from her mother saying:

> What has made you turn away from your social standing in life? Unless you
> tell Daddy you have changed your views, I cannot give you a home here . . .
> even if you fall ill, I cannot have you here.

In 1945 Tuggie wrote to say she was in love and planning to marry a schoolteacher called Thomas Blackburn, just as soon as his divorce had come through. Her mother replied:

> You say you are going 'for a holiday' with him. Are you having others in the

party? Though I know you would not what is called 'go off the rails' with a man, the outside world always looks for the worst.

My grandmother lived into her late eighties, but my grandfather died in 1952, when he was sixty-two. I only remember seeing him once, when he came to visit us at Warwick Road and I was sitting on the grass in a park and he prodded me with the end of his walking stick as if I were a worm, and when I cried he laughed.

I often asked my mother why she thought Boonie killed herself and she always told me it was because her parents would have rejected her and thrown her out of the house if they had known that she was pregnant. 'But let's not think about it,' my mother would say hopefully. 'I've got you now. And you're just like a sister for me.'

And so the story stayed locked in my mind, until that last month when my mother was ill. One night, emerging out of a deep sleep, she said something that made me rethink everything, because it seemed to imply that there had been a much more disturbing and complicated bond between Boonie and Tuggie and their father.

⊙ ⊙ ◉ ⊙ ⊙

March 1999

My mother is dying. This fact is running parallel to my life.

I'll collect her from the hospital this afternoon and bring her home.

I've prepared my daughter's room for her. I heaved out a heavy table to make more space and I've just put up some old photographs and some recent photographs on a shelf – eighty-two years of her story and our intertwined story.

I've hung some of her paintings on the wall: a beautiful tangled forest that she did in 1943 and two thin naked female figures, against a red background, which might also have been done during the war, but there's no date. And I've framed a recent watercolour of a red amaryllis flower, blowing its own trumpet as it were. The room looks lovely.

(Fax to Herman)

☙ II ❧

Moonlight in the Garden

My father had enjoyed teaching at the grammar school in London. The regularity of the life suited him and no matter what was happening at home, he managed to correct school work and prepare classes, and each day he arrived on time, wearing a suit.

Then in December 1955, when he accepted the rather nebulous post of Gregory Fellow of Poetry and we moved to Leeds, everything changed. As a Gregory Fellow he was provided with enough money to live on and a house that was twice the size of our flat in London, along with a garden that looked as big as a park, but there were no more daily obligations to hold him steady and that was the problem. He just had to talk to students, if they felt like talking to him, and he could write if he felt like writing. It meant that whatever tenuous safety nets had previously held the weeks together quickly fell away, and as a result both my father and his family life became much more dangerous and chaotic than ever before.

⊙ ⊙ ◉ ⊙ ⊙

In one of his notebooks my father was making plans to write a fictional account based on the two years we spent in Leeds. 'Keep the garden background,' he wrote.

> The screaming swifts. Do the party. Alan Davie necking with R[osalie] and the statement of R's affair . . . gradual weaning from his wife and the holiday in Cornwall with P . . . The return. The effect on R. The terrible night. Moonlight in the garden.

The garden had fruit bushes and apple trees, and there was an old air-raid shelter from the last war dug into the lawn, with grass growing on its rounded roof and steps that led down into a damp and brick-lined underground cave. I went inside it just once, with a torch to guide me, and I found a tin helmet lying among the rubble on the floor. The helmet was as quiet and cold as a dead tortoise, but still I was afraid to pick it up because it reminded me of the helmet that my father had told me about, the one that was still hot and contained a bit of its owner's head.

The garden also had a thick privet hedge where I would hunt for caterpillars pretending to be twigs. There was a swing fixed to one of the spreading branches of a large tree and if you stood beside the tree you could see my bedroom window and my parents' bedroom window and the bubbly glass of the bathroom window. The bathroom door was fitted with that same bubbly glass, so if someone was in the bath, you could just make out a vague blur of pink flesh on the other side.

I wonder if the party my father speaks of in his notes is the same one that remains so clearly in my mind. My parents had lots of parties while we were in Leeds, but this was the first that I was aware of.

I remember standing on a bend in the stairs, from where you could look down at the room below. One of my mother's new paintings had just been hung there. It showed a boy child, wearing shorts, standing on a table with his mouth open in a cry and his arms stretched out, as if in supplication. A naked woman with her head bowed was on one side of the table and a man wearing a suit and with a curiously closed expression on his face was on the other. A jumble of wild brushstrokes lay all around them. I thought it very unfair to make the child stand on the table like that.

Anyway, there I was on the staircase, next to the painting and looking down at a sea of faces in the studio-sitting room beneath me. There was a lot of jostling of bodies close together and the clink of glasses and sometimes a solitary voice would emerge from the general babble with a shout or a sudden laugh. Bottles of wine and whisky stood in great droves on the table that usually held tubes of paint and jars of brushes, and I could see my mother dancing with a man with a long red beard. Her earrings were shining and she wiggled her bottom in time to the music and then she and the man kissed. I couldn't see my father.

I watched until I was tired of watching and then I went to bed. The front door kept banging shut as people began to leave, then my mother came softly into my room and stood beside my bed so that I could smell her perfume. She asked if I was asleep. 'Daddy is very drunk,' she said. 'Don't worry. I'm going to have a bath.'

I heard her locking the bathroom door and then there was the sound of water, followed by the slow and heavy tread of my father coming up the stairs. He was muttering to himself like an old man and making the clock-chiming cough that always meant trouble. He knocked quite politely on the bathroom door. 'Let me in, darling, I need to talk to you!'

The water in the bath stirred, but my mother didn't reply.

My father changed tone, I knew he would. 'Open the door, you bitch! You whore's melt!' he said. *Whore's melt* was the insult he used most often at that time, but I have never understood what a 'melt' might be. He began to thump with his fists on the glass.

The water in the bath stirred again. I heard my father moving about and then he was carrying something heavy, which knocked against the wall as he passed.

'Kiss him, would you? I'll show you how to kiss!' and he let out a sort of Viking warrior cry. There was a crashing, crunching, collapsing sound that rang through the whole house and, with the practical logic of childhood, I understood that a bomb must have chosen just this moment to drop on our bathroom. When the bomb was silent I could hear noises, but they were not human noises, so perhaps a wild animal had burst through the ceiling and was now devouring my parents.

I ran to find them. The door was wide open and its glass pane had been smashed. I saw my mother next to the bathtub. I couldn't see her face because she was struggling to put on her nightdress, which was caught in a drift of thin nylon round her head. Her big, soft, wet body was covered in little threads of bright blood. And there was my father, sitting in a heap on the floor, nursing a bleeding hand and groaning. He seemed lost in thought and didn't notice me. Sharp shards of glass were scattered all around him.

89

'Quick!' said my mother, in her nightdress now and the blood staining through in little patterns. 'Quick, darling, we must get away!'

She grabbed me by the hand. We ran downstairs, past the boy child on the table. As we got through the front door we could hear my father stumbling after us.

We ran up the street, under the orange gaze of the street lamps, our bare feet thumping on the cold grey stone of the pavement. I was very afraid I might tread on some dog shit or on the gobbets of phlegm I was always so careful to avoid when I made my way to and from my new school, but there was no time now for such scruples.

At the top of our street we turned right and continued to run. I wondered if anyone was watching us and whether we looked like ghosts in our nighties.

We stopped at the house belonging to Nibs Dalwood. He was the Gregory Fellow of Sculpture and his wife Mary taught French at the university. They had two daughters a bit younger than me and I hoped they wouldn't wake up.

My mother rang the bell and pounded on the door.

'Help!' she cried. 'For God's sake help!'

Suddenly we were being bustled up two flights of stairs and into a room I had never seen before. The door closed and a key turned in the lock. In my memory we were in the dark, but maybe that is not so.

By now my father had arrived.

'Where have you hidden her! Bring her to me at once, before I smash this fucking house to pieces!'

And then he was outside the room in which my mother and I were hiding and he was banging on the door, but he was already calming down. I heard Mary calling him 'Tom dear' and offering him a cup of coffee, and there was some hushed conversation and he was apparently gone. I imagine that either Nibs or Mary walked him back to our house.

My mother and I slept side by side in a little bed and in the morning I went to school in some borrowed clothes and she returned home. 'I need to talk things over with Daddy,' she said vaguely.

◎ ◎ ◉ ◎ ◎

It was after the breaking of the bathroom door that I started to pray. I had learnt a new prayer at school and it had a ring of power and authority to it which impressed me. *Lighten our darkness we beseech Thee oh Lord and by Thy great mercy defend us from all perils and dangers of this night. Amen.*

I prayed every night in my room, repeating the prayer over and over like a whizzing mantra. And if things in the house were very bad I would creep out into the dark garden and kneel on the gravel path that led to the air-raid shelter, until I could feel the sharp stones hollowing little pockets into my skin. Sometimes it was even necessary to kneel right beside the open mouth of the air-raid shelter, making myself brave enough to feel its cold breath creeping around me.

The prayer was the first stage of the process. When I had done enough *lighten our darknesses* I would press my clenched fists into my closed eyes until colours began to explode before me. Then, with any luck, I would be rewarded with a vision of the Holy Family. They always looked the same: the three of them sitting comfortably side by side on a cloud, dressed in robes of red, yellow and blue. I held them there before me in a tight knot of deity, until my eyes ached and I felt giddy and slightly sick.

It must have been around this time that I had a dream about rats. I had entered a shed and it was filled with big rats that looked just like the rat in my mother's painting. They clambered over me and I could see their teeth and feel their sharp feet on my body.

I told my mother about the dream, expecting her sympathy, but she said that everything we see in a dream is a part of ourselves. 'The rats are you,' she explained sternly. I was shocked by this revelation and decided to share no more of my dreams.

◦ ◦ ◉ ◦ ◦

One day in 1956 my mother told me that my father was having 'an affair' with a woman called Patricia. I didn't know what the word meant. 'It means he loves her and he doesn't love me,' she said, 'and he sleeps in her bed and has sex with her, but I suppose you don't know what that means either.'

Patricia's name began to go backwards and forwards across Great-Aunt Molly's round table.

'I'm going to see Patricia!'

'Have you been with Patricia?'

'I love Patricia!'

'I hate Patricia!'

Then suddenly there was not only Patricia, there was also someone called Peter. Now my mother could say, 'If you go to Patricia, I'll go to Peter!' and if my father was feeling calm he would grind his teeth and fold over his bottom lip, and if he was not feeling calm he would take a swipe at her with his fist.

I asked both parents about these two new presences in our lives; people I had never met but whom I already found extremely dangerous. My father said very little about his Patricia, except that she was 'a bloody good poet'. My mother was more informative. She told me that Peter was a kind man who loved her and 'Maybe Mummy will marry him and then you can have a new daddy.'

I have never seen a photograph of Peter and, apart from the fact that he was also a painter, I know nothing about him. But in my mother's black leather briefcase there is a single letter from him. He begs her, *for our sake, as well as your own, do not let* him *hurt you, as I fear he may well do.*

He invites her to come and live with him in his attic studio room in Wakefield, where he feels sure they will be happy ever after. Reading the letter I was startled to realize that my existence was not part of the plan, so I suppose I was to stay with my father and perhaps Patricia would come and join us, from time to time.

○ ○ ◉ ○ ○

These troubles weighed heavily on both my parents and they were busy with thoughts of divorce. 'Which one of us would you chose?' they kept asking me in private.

'You!' I answered, with utter sincerity, to each of them in turn.

During the month of April my father wrote a letter to my mother, which she kept in her black briefcase, alongside the love letter from Peter:

I believe the tension arises from us both being neurotic people . . . After all your past is not too easy either . . . I don't believe in divorces, but would grant you one if you so wish, but I would defend it in order to maintain the custody of Julia and my solicitor tells me I have a strongish case, on the grounds of Provocation.

My father also wrote an undated letter to his parents, which for some odd reason my mother had kept as well. In it he explained his theory that my mother had been too subservient to him, but now she had 'swung the other way and has had a nervous breakdown'.

I knew nothing more about this breakdown until I found a very battered 1956 Letts diary. It's A4 size, but my mother has only used a handful of pages in the month of May. It seems that she is lying in bed while she is writing and she has just swallowed some sleeping pills, with the thought of maybe swallowing a few more later. Her handwriting drifts and shakes, and her thoughts ramble. She writes that she can't go on like this, the pain is too great.

When I began to read her words, I found my heart racing with apprehension. 'What about me?' I wanted to ask. 'What about me, your nine-year-old daughter, how will she manage if you swallow any more of those pills?' Then on the third page of her outpouring of despair, my mother calmed down a bit. *Julia is very understanding*, she wrote, *but she is still too young to really help me.*

⊙ ⊙ ◉ ⊙ ⊙

It was because of all these troubles that my mother decided to take me on a holiday to Ireland, so that she could think things over. It was the first time we had been away on our own together.

We stayed in a big empty house, in walking distance of the pretty Bay of Killiney. My mother explained that the man called Peter, who might become my daddy, was living somewhere close by, and one day she announced that she needed to spend some time alone with him and she was sure I'd understand.

So I went to stay with a girl called Aideen, whom I had never met before. Aideen lived in a cottage with an immensely old grandmother who spent all day and all night propped up on a line of pillows in a large double bed, watching television, smoking cigarettes and drinking whisky.

We had fun. The three of us sat in bed together, mesmerized by the flickering black-and-white television screen for hours on end. We watched the Grand National and we each chose the horse that we wanted to win. When my horse was the first to reach the finishing line, the grandmother crowed in her bed like a cockerel announcing the laying of an egg. 'You are blessed with good luck!' she announced prophetically. 'It will follow you for all the days of your life!' I was delighted by this news and I clung to the idea of possessing good luck, as if it were an amulet I could hang round my neck.

⊙ ⊙ ◉ ⊙ ⊙

My mother arrived to collect me. She took me back to the empty house and told me that Peter loved her very much, but he was a bore and so she had decided to have another try with my father. She was in a very odd mood. I remember we went for a swim and I had forgotten to bring my knickers and had to walk back to the house with a bare bottom under my skirt. We were going up some steps and there were lots of people around. 'Julia's got no knickers on! Julia's got no knickers on!' sang my mother at the top of her voice, laughing at my angry embarrassment.

My father welcomed us home with smiles and embraces, and my mother smiled back at him, though perhaps a little cautiously. The marriage was declared saved and for a while my parents were often side by side in the same bed in the morning, and at weekends I would go and lie between them, enjoying the quiet and breathing in the sweet musty smell of their sheets.

Because of the reconciliation, Patricia tried to take her own life, using a handful of my father's pills. The phone started ringing like some wild bird in the middle of the night and it was a London hospital telling my father that he must come at once. And so, in spite of my mother's entreaties, he set off in the car and returned two days later looking very solemn.

Patricia had been saved in time, but my father was very impressed by the whole business. He wrote a poem about it called 'Felo da Se', opening with the lines:

> 'Thirty,' the doctor said, 'three grains each one.
> 'That's quite a lot of sodium amytal.'

⊙ ⊙ ◉ ⊙ ⊙

March 1999

It's ten a.m. Rosalie is here with me. They gave her a blood transfusion before leaving the hospital and as a result she is very chirpy and beaming with an extraordinary contentment.

She looks radiant. It's hard to believe anything is wrong with her. As soon as she arrived she began pottering around the garden looking at things and then she wanted to go for a drive by the sea and oh she'd love a swim and the water must be quite warm by now and what about her cats, were they all right by themselves and had I seen her address book, she had so many letters to write.

At the end of the day, I went to bed exhausted and I could hear her still rummaging about downstairs. She's still fast asleep now though.

(Fax to Herman)

⤜⚬ 12 ⚬⤛

Don't Worry, Darling

In December 1957 we left our house in Leeds and set off back to London. Just before getting into the car, I picked a little pink rose from a bush that grew beside the front gate and carried it clenched between my fingers throughout the journey. I remember thinking that the rose had something to do with memory and a time that would never return.

Not long ago I went back to that house: number thirteen, on the left, at the end of a cul-de-sac. The house is now a student residence and when I knocked on the door a sleepy young man let me in and told me I was welcome to wander around. All the rooms had been divided up and even the wide staircase had disappeared.

In the garden the big tree with the swing had been cut down and there was no trace of the air-raid shelter or the privet hedge. But beside the front gate I was confronted by the same pink roses I knew from long ago: whirls of crumpled petals and a familiar soft perfume that hadn't changed at all.

⊙ ⊙ ⊙ ⊙ ⊙

The journey to London was hard work. My parents argued, their voices rising and falling, and my father emphasized his points by stamping his foot on the clutch while accelerating, so that the car lurched forward making heavy grinding noises, as if it too were involved in the quarrel. I held on to my rose.

As we entered north London my father suddenly announced, 'Then I'll go and stay with Patricia!'

This surprised me. I thought Patricia had disa
ever since the night on which she swallowed the thir
was still with us.

I expected my mother to reply with 'Then I'll g
make my own way to our new and empty house, bt
long and hard, 'I can't bear it! I can't bear it any longer
the car door, to throw herself at the mercy of the pas

My father jammed on the brakes and lit a cigaret
out and after a weighty pause we continued to dri
streets until we reached our destination. It was in Putney, close to the heath
and the tube station. My father had bought it with an inheritance from
grandmother Adelaide, who had died a little while before, leaving her steely
blue eyes to science.

⊙ ⊙ ◉ ⊙ ⊙

The house was called Cambria Lodge. It was broad and solid and looked
more like a government institution than a home. It was built from yellowish
London brick and grey stone steps led up to a turquoise front door, with two
stone flowerpots standing guard, one on either side. When these were stolen
a few months later they left pale square patches to mark the places from
which they had been plucked, like scars on the skin.

Cambria Lodge had twelve rooms, but six of them were occupied by a
white-haired sitting tenant called Miss Glazier. She had a separate entrance
and she lived on her own with Snowy, her white Persian cat. Miss Glazier
had Parkinson's disease, which made walking difficult and gave her voice a
ghostly wavering edge.

My father had his study in an upstairs room. It was next to Miss
Glazier's territory, but divided from her by a thin plywood barricade.
Whenever he went out he tried to remember to put on a record of
Beethoven's Ninth Symphony, playing it very loud and close to the partition-
ing wall. 'That will drive her away!' he said, rubbing his hands together as
he always did when he was pleased with himself.

He told me he'd appreciate it if I were to ring Miss Glazier's doorbell

te at night. He felt he couldn't do it himself; it wouldn't be good
putation as a teacher if someone saw him. I quite enjoyed the task.
ss on the white china button in its brass surround and hide behind a
rel bush, waiting until a waif-like figure finally appeared and the trembling
voice called out, 'Who's there? Is anyone there?'

My father was delighted by my work. 'Thanks so much, darling,' he'd
say, making me feel I had performed some charitable deed on his behalf. 'The
house will be worth lots more once the old bat has gone!'

○ ○ ◉ ○ ○

The wallpaper in my mother's studio, which was also our sitting room,
had printed black and gold feathers floating across it, as if two huge birds
had been fighting. My mother's paintings hung from the picture rail.
The year before we left Leeds she had stopped doing figurative work and had
gone abstract. The result was the same sense of anger and fear, but now it was
without form: violent squares clashed with other squares, circles spiralled
into a crowded distance of brushstrokes, colours dripped and blurred and fell
upon each other. The paintings seemed like a noise, like someone screaming.

A few years later, when I was on the edge of leaving home so dramatically,
my mother changed her style again and started making imagined landscapes
of smooth, monochrome hills rolling into the far distance, and after that she
went geometric, marking out carefully measured and controlled patterns of
grids, which she filled in with tensely vibrating colours.

'I've done a new painting,' she'd say, on the rare occasions when we met.
'So, what do you think of it?' and I would answer with talk about interesting
balances of energy, and say things about preferring this one to that one, all
the time avoiding any mention of what I really felt.

In the last years of her life, when she had moved to a cottage near the sea
in Suffolk and I was living with my family quite close by, she began to make
much quieter studies of the natural world: trees and fields, flowers and jugs
and fruit, and sometimes a naked figure from a life class. I told myself that
the anger and the pain had gone, but I wasn't convinced and sometimes I'd
see it breaking through.

⊙ ⊙ ⊙ ⊙ ⊙

Now that we were back in London my father returned to his old teaching job at the grammar school and that kept him steady during the day, but the nights and especially the weekends were getting wilder and wilder. He was drinking a lot, but I think the real cause of the trouble was the sodium amytal. He had made friends with two doctors from the local surgery and now he was getting three different prescriptions written out for him and taking as many as twelve pills a day.

Looking back on it now, it was all very theatrical. My father would come back in the evening and I'd hear his cough as he walked into the garden. The two of them would start to fight almost immediately; there was a lot of groaning and wailing and crashing of crockery and furniture, and a lot of curiously choreographed movements, as if they were enacting an ancient dance.

I was on the alert at all times, bristling with a sense of duty and responsibility. I don't think I slept much at night, or if I did, I was quickly awake again once the cries and shouts had reached a certain level of desperation. Then I would go to defend my mother, the sword of righteousness in one hand and the shield of protectiveness in the other. If I held back for too long, my mother would always come and fetch me, because she knew my father

wouldn't hurt her with me standing between them. She'd hold me by the shoulders and my father would weave around us like a boxer, with that baffled look in his eyes because I was in the way.

But he was getting madder, even I could see that. One night my mother came to fetch me and she said she was really very afraid. She took me into the spare bedroom where she had been attempting to sleep and she held me tight in her arms. My father was crashing about in his study and then he came coughing and muttering towards us, calling her name as he approached.

He entered the room and I could hardly recognize him. He had turned into one of those werewolves he had told me about, creatures who step out of their human skin when the moon is full. His shoulders were hunched up and his neck was craning forward at a funny angle, and his whole body was shaking as if he had been electrocuted. His face was grey and sweaty, but it was his eyes that really frightened me because they were uninhabited.

My mother held me even tighter, her body wet with fear. 'Oh Tommy, you do look tired,' she said tentatively to this hunched and snarling creature.

'Don't worry, darling, he won't hurt us!' she said to me, but without much confidence.

'*Darling!*' said my father, mimicking her voice and laughing as if he had just made a good joke. He moved close to the bed and he bent forward and placed his hands on the pillow on either side of our two heads, and he lowered his face until it was floating just above us. His eyes were bloodshot and his breath stank of rotten fruit. I kept very still. 'Darling!' he said again and then, to my amazement, he didn't kill us both, but he stumbled off into the hall.

I realized then that I could no longer single-handedly save my mother with my sheepdog efforts at protection. We both needed help, so we had better both explain our needs to that white-bearded, blue-robed figure whom I had conjured up so often when we were in Leeds.

I told my mother that I had a prayer we must recite together now and with any luck it would do the trick. So she and I lay side by side in a hot bed and I recited my prayer, *Lighten our darkness we beseech Thee oh Lord and by Thy great mercy defend us from all perils and dangers of this night.*

My mother repeated it after me, word by word in a shaky voice, but even as she spoke I realized she was doing it for my sake and not in order to summon up the help of the Almighty and, with that, a terrible desolation enveloped me. I could feel the power and the energy of the prayer draining away like water from a basin when you pull out the plug and I knew I could never ever use it again.

'He's quiet,' said my mother, the prayer already forgotten. 'He'll come to bed with me now. Perhaps I can persuade him to make love and then he'll fall asleep. You can stay here if you don't feel like going back to your own room.'

◦ ◦ ◉ ◦ ◦

In the mornings after any one of these dramas my father was always full of remorse and apologies. He said he couldn't remember anything of what had happened on the night before and so he would beg to be told and as each of his deeds was recounted to him he would be overcome by shame and surprise in equal measure. 'Oh my God! No! It can't be true! Surely not! How terrible! It's all black! Black amnesia! Black despair! Oh forgive me! I beg you to forgive me!'

He never tried to explain the fights between himself and my mother, but he did write numerous poems about what was happening and sometimes he would read these to me and I would listen to the music of complex words and be comforted, in a way.

> They hadn't noticed her coming, too busy with loud
> Out-goings, that savage night, his wife and he . . .
> And then they turned and saw her balanced there
> Upon the spinning rim of their nightmare.

And sometimes he would sob in silence and I would sit and hold his shoulders and feel sorry for him, even though he smelt of rotten fruit and his hands were shaking and I knew he had just made himself sick in the basin, because I had heard retching sounds tearing through the house.

With any luck he would cheer up and, instead of talk, he would tell me a story, something about Loki who stole the fire from the god Odin, or Persephone eating the pomegranate seeds as she was leaving Hades and wasn't that a pity because it meant she had to go back there again and again as the years rolled into each other. He liked reading great chunks of the Bible to me, especially the Psalms of David and the terrible sufferings of Job, and then perhaps he'd teach me a new poem.

In Leeds he had taught me verse after verse of 'Simon Legree' by Vachel Lindsay, in which the slave owner who beat poor Uncle Tom to death went down to the Devil where the two of them drank *blood and burning turpentine*. He was also keen on a poem about Queen Jezebel, who was thrown out of a window and trampled to death:

> Beneath the feet of the horses that beat,
> The life out of Jezebel.

I met someone who told me he was once at our house in Leeds when I was asked to do a recitation of this poem. He said I stood on Aunt Molly's table, just like the boy in my mother's painting, and everyone laughed and clapped their hands in delight as I struggled with the rudeness of the opening lines:

> God bless that Jewish woman,
> Queen Jezebel, the bitch!
> She plucked the clothes from her shoulder bones
> Down to her spent tits.

By the time I was ten, my father had taught me Macbeth's dagger scene and Othello's murder speech, the one about plucking the rose and putting out the light, as well as a lot of Yeats and Dylan Thomas. I'd be in the bath and he'd sit on the lavatory seat and I could learn things so easily that after a couple of repetitions I was ready and we could recite together:

> Dead men naked they shall be one
> With the man in the wind and the west moon . . .
> Though they go mad, they shall be sane,
> Though they sink through the sea they shall rise again,

Though lovers be lost love shall not,
And Death shall have no dominion.

❍ ❍ ◉ ❍ ❍

March 1999

*All is well. People come and go. Rosalie is right at the centre of the hive of
activity. 'Oh I am being spoilt,' she says. 'Everyone is so kind.'*

*Both my kids have arrived for the holidays and we had scrambled eggs
with smoked salmon for breakfast, very posh. Rosalie joined us, but she is much
more tired today and she went back to bed almost at once, exhausted by the
effort of getting up. She keeps telling me how much she is enjoying herself, even
though she is dying, and that made us laugh because it sounded like such a silly
joke. We take such a ridiculous pleasure from getting on well together. Gentle
words, a hug, a meeting of the eyes.*

(Fax to Herman)

❧ 13 ❧

The Facts of Life

During the first three years that we lived in Putney, from when I was nine to twelve, my closest relationships were with all sorts of animals. I had a few friends, but if one of them came to our house I was so terrified they might see or hear a fight between my parents that I couldn't concentrate on talk or games. And if ever I let a friend stay the night, I had to try to persuade them to fall asleep before the troubles started. It was impossible to explain any of this; it felt like my own private shame. But animals were different. I could tell them everything and feel relaxed in the silence of their company.

⊙ ⊙ ⊙ ⊙ ⊙

In my bedroom I had a little aquarium filled with a variety of tropical fish and after I had lost faith in the power of prayer I would kneel in front of this shimmering kingdom and find calm from the fact of staring at the movement of fishes.

I had another tank that was occupied by a colony of stick insects. They clung in silence and virtual immobility to the bunches of fresh privet leaves that I gave them to eat and I would sit beside them and watch the delicate movement of their jaws. They laid eggs, which hatched into tiny replicas of themselves and eventually the larger members of the tribe dropped dead while the smaller ones grew large. I would lift a stick insect out of the tank, for its stillness and the sensation of its clawed feet on my skin. Occasionally a little army of them escaped and lived a fugitive life in my bedroom curtains.

In the spring my father and I would set off for Richmond Park with a couple of empty jam jars and we'd collect a few pairs of solemnly mating toads which in those days still gathered in heaps along the edges of certain ponds. The toads remained stuck to each other during their jam-jar journey and then I would release them into a little artificial pond I had in the garden. It was not an ideal environment and the male always disappeared as soon as his piggyback ride was over, leaving the female to walk in lugubrious circles in the shallow water, spinning her long line of slimy eggs. Then she too would vanish, abandoning her as yet unborn family, and I would watch over the hatching of tadpoles and their gradual shift from a life in the water to a life in the breathing air.

There were other creatures to distract me from my endless preoccupation with my parents. At school I spent as much time as possible looking after the guinea pigs that were kept in cages down by the tennis court. When I had been with them I would make a point of not washing my hands, so I could have the sweet smell of their fur on my skin all through the day. I learnt everything I wanted to know about sex and the facts of life through watching them mating and giving birth to their tiny babies, which emerged with eyes wide open and flurries of brightly coloured fur.

At home, as well as the two aquariums, I had a neutered marmalade cat called Pedro, but he was not to be trusted and if I lowered my face into the softness of his tummy, he was liable to grip my scalp with his sharp claws. I longed for a dog and eventually got one, which proved to be a nightmare of unsuitability, but before then, when I was ten, I became the proud owner of a bushbaby, one of those tiny and delicate members of the lemur or half-ape family, which had been plucked from the forests of Madagascar and deposited in Harrods pet department in London.

The bushbaby was given to me by a woman called Erica Marx. She ran the Hand and Flower Press and had published some of my father's poems. She came to tea and talked to me in a very friendly way, and she asked me what I liked and didn't like and I explained that I loved animals above all else. A few days later she sent me a letter in which she told me to go to Harrods and choose myself a pet, any pet I wanted and not to mind about the price, because she was paying for it.

So I entered that mesmerizing paradise of the pet department and after a bit of uncertainty over a boa constrictor and a mongoose, I chose a bushbaby, with round nocturnal eyes and delicate hands, each finger tipped with a perfect nail. I brought him home and called him Congo.

Congo lived in a little room next to my bedroom and he slept in one of my father's cloth caps, which hung on a door on top of one of my mother's fur coats – not the leopard skin, which she kept in her cupboard – this coat had been made out of some fluffy and beige-coloured creature whose identity I could never work out.

Congo was the first real love of my life. It was like acquiring a sibling: the little brother who had been lost on the mountainside, or the other one, who never even began to be a little brother because of the mumps I gave to my father.

Now, when I came home from school, my fear of what dramas might take place that night was balanced by the anticipation of being in the company of my bushbaby. He'd wake up from his daylight sleep as soon as he heard me and throughout the afternoon and into the evening the two of us were together in a strange capsule of intimacy and contentment. He'd sit on my shoulder and he'd lift my hair with his little hands, explore my ear with his nose, climb softly over my face, examining my eyes, my nostrils, licking at the corners of my mouth.

In my mother's studio he would leap from my hand to the top of the easel and from there he could rise in a great arc of energy to land on the narrow edge of the picture rail. Like a tiny kangaroo, he'd bounce on his long hind legs, round and round the upper layer of the room and, best of all, when I called him he'd stop at the sound of my voice and leap back to land on my shoulder, or my head, or on the hand I held out to him. His body was so light that it was the warmth of him I felt, rather than the weight.

I had Congo for almost a year and then he died. He caught a chill while we were away on holiday and when I was told that he had gone I felt as if I had lost my brother, my lover, my closest friend. I made him a coffin out of an empty dried milk tin and buried him in a rose bed with a ceremony of flowers and hymns and a loud recitation of Dylan Thomas's 'Death Shall Have No Dominion'.

⊙ ⊙ ◉ ⊙ ⊙

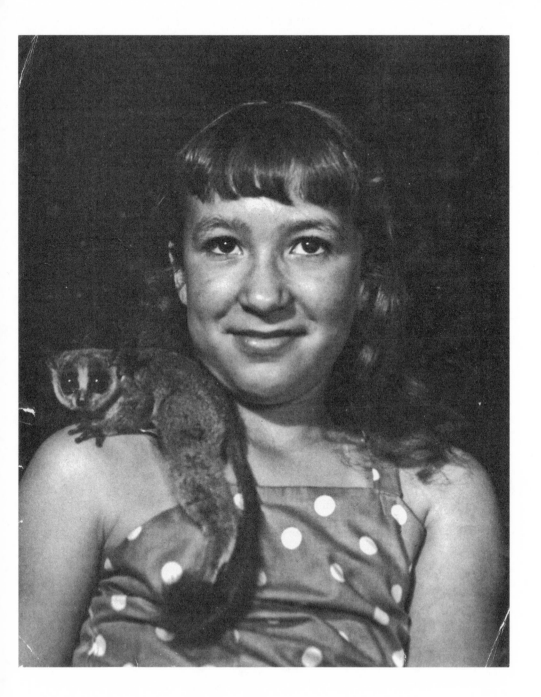

Congo's death marked the end of something for me. I suppose I felt he had betrayed me by abandoning me without any warning, and on top of that I was growing up and floating on the edge of adolescence. It was in the summer and not long after the ceremony of the funeral that I stood in a thin T-shirt by the window in my parents' bedroom one morning, with the sunlight streaming through the glass, when my father turned to my mother and said, 'Jesus! The girl's got tits!'

And it was true, the nipples of my breasts were just beginning to swell.

⊙ ⊙ ◉ ⊙ ⊙

I had often seen my parents naked. I had watched my father's cock in the bath, fascinated by the way it floated like seaweed in the water. I had looked at my mother's body, the triangle of pubic hair, the weight of her breasts, the scarred stretchmarks on her belly and thighs as if someone had cut her with a little knife, but until then I had not been aware of the idea of nakedness.

After his revelation about my tits, my father stopped teaching me poems while I lay in the bath; he locked the door when he was in there and he kept muttering the word 'puberty' at me, as if that explained something. Now he taught me poems when we were out walking together on Putney Heath, or on car journeys. There was one about the Hiroshima bomb which began with the lines:

> Come closer, see the newly-born disease,
> I am Akitchi Kubiyama, stranger,
> Akitchi Kubiyama, Japanese.

And there was 'Red Hanrahan's Song About Ireland', by Yeats, which I recited with passionate authority for a school poetry competition, although the audience response was very muted:

> Like heavy flooded waters our bodies and our blood;
> But purer than the tall candle, before the Holy Rood
> Is Cathleen, the daughter of Houlihan.

⊙ ⊙ ◉ ⊙ ⊙

But for my mother the tiny rounding of my eleven-year-old nipples created a different awakening. It was as if she had been waiting impatiently for this moment and now she was eager to share with me everything she knew about sex. Whenever she was sure we were on our own, she'd get a secretive smile on her face and off she'd go. 'Do you know the facts of life, darling? Do you know how babies are made? Do you know what men *do*?'

At first I found the information both funny and fascinating, and I was proud to be the only one of my friends to know such things and eager to share my knowledge. We had the usual problems of incredulity: surely the Queen would never take her knickers off and what happens if a man needs to do a pee at the same moment that he is making a baby. We used our imagination to work things out in a satisfactory way.

But having started on the subject of sex, my mother found it impossible to stop. She told me that men put their cocks into women in order to make babies, but it was also to achieve something called orgasm. And what an orgasm felt like and how these days she only pretended to have one with my

father, because he was so often drunk or violent and she no longer felt any pleasure.

She'd go through her black leather briefcase, searching for more stories to tell. 'Oh look, here's Mummy with nothing on! That was taken by a boyfriend before I met your father. We did it on the floor, just after he had made the picture! And here's a photograph of my friend Friedl. She was a writer, but she's dead now. During the war she lived with Elias Canetti and the only sort of sex Canetti was interested in was fellatio, putting his cock into her mouth. Imagine that! Your father doesn't even want me to touch his cock, because of the horrible thing that was strapped on to him when he was a boy and started having wet dreams.

'Oh, but silly me! Perhaps you don't even know about wet dreams? Well, I'll tell you . . .'

I was afraid of all this talk, without understanding the nature of my fear. And I suppose my mother smelt my fear and it made her aggressive.

Once, when she was getting out of the bath, she told me she had something called piles, caused by the effort of pushing me into the world.

'What are piles?' I asked, aware as I spoke that she was looking eager, which meant this was dangerous territory.

'Piles?' she said, with an edge of triumph in her voice. 'These are piles!' and with that she turned round and bent over in front of me, parting the soft expanse of her buttocks quite close to my face.

⊙ ⊙ ⊚ ⊙ ⊙

After she had explained everything she could think of explaining on the subject of heterosexual behaviour, my mother moved to homosexuality. She wasn't much interested in male homosexuals, as if she believed they had a little aberration that could be quickly solved by a night with a good woman, but she was fascinated by lesbians.

I was still at the Junior School, so I was just eleven, when my mother decided the time had come to introduce me to something very special. We were in her studio and she pulled open the bottom drawer in Aunt Molly's chest of drawers – the one that had brass lions' heads holding brass rings in their mouths instead of handles. She rummaged around until she had uncovered an orange-and-black object that lay hidden in a nest of old under-wear. The black part was a shiny, knobbed truncheon with a little hole at its tip and the orange part was an orange sack, as hard as a football, its surface covered in little bobbles. It looked like some terrible reptile. 'This', said my mother proudly, 'is a dildo. It was given to me a long time ago by a lesbian!' She explained that lesbians pushed dildos up each other's fannies because they didn't like men.

'You can fill this bit with warm water if you want to,' she said and giggled, before returning the reptile to its nest.

'Do we know any lesbians?' I asked, suddenly unsure of the world around me.

'Oh yes, we know lots, because a lot of them are artists. Artists are rebels against all conventions, you see.'

'But how can you be sure if someone is one?'

'That's easy. They have short hair and they never wear make-up and usually they live with another woman, whom they call a *friend*. Your art teacher Miss Wyatt and your headmistress Miss Sawyer are a lesbian couple,' said my mother, to prove her point.

It was true that both Miss Sawyer and Miss Wyatt had short hair and they lived together, but I found it a terrible pity that they were lesbians because I liked them and they had always been kind to me. But now the image of the dildo would get in the way every time they spoke to me and especially if they said something nice.

The other lesbian was my father's publisher, Erica Marx, the woman who had given me the bushbaby. I remember looking back at my meeting with her and being suddenly afraid of her. 'I would like to be your friend,' she had said in her letter. Perhaps that was why she had given me Congo.

I asked my mother if her sister Boonie had been a lesbian, because she certainly looked like a man in all the photographs I had seen of her. But my mother didn't like the question and became rather vague. 'Boonie had crushes on the older girls at school,' she said, 'we all did, because there were no men around. But then she got pregnant, didn't she, so of course she can't have been a lesbian! What a silly thing to say!'

Apart from my fears of lesbians and what they might want to do with me, I tried not to think of my naked mother pretending to have orgasms, or of my naked father not wanting his cock touched because of his childhood. But words such as dildo and fellatio were so odd and so different from any other words I knew that I couldn't help thinking about them sometimes, no matter how hard I tried.

○ ○ ◉ ○ ○

March 1999

I woke crying in the night, with the thought of all the muddle of the past that has haunted us for so long. I went down to Rosalie's room and she was awake. I sat beside her and she started talking, very softly, her voice gentle.

She said, 'I know nothing about your childhood, or maybe I have forgotten everything I knew.'

She began to ask me all sorts of questions, simple things like 'Were you there when Tommy and I had that quarrel? And were you very afraid? You must have been quite lonely. How odd that I'd never thought of that before!'

And sometimes, with a shy laugh, she said, 'And where was I? What on earth did I think I was doing? I was in such a rush, wasn't I! And very busy trying to find myself a new man, of course. Oh well, never mind, it's all water under the bridge now, isn't it?'

(From Julia's Notebook)

❧ 14 ❧

Having a Dog

Early in 1961, when I was still twelve, my parents gave me a black spaniel puppy. They had the idea that he would serve as a good friend and companion for me if the family fell apart, although as it turned out, he was one of the last straws in the falling. I called him Jason, even though there was nothing golden about his fleece.

Jason was genetically programmed to be a willing and obedient gun dog and he had a natural instinct for a rather exaggerated subservience. Without

a word of command he'd shadow so closely behind me when I went out walking with him that I was afraid of knocking his soft muzzle with the heel of my shoe. And if I threw him a stick or a ball, he'd lollop off and bring it back and drop it at my feet, then he'd sit down on his stub of a tail and wait for further instruction, a look of inconsolable sorrow in his red-rimmed eyes. 'I don't trust that bloody dog,' said my father, as Jason wriggled with hopeful enthusiasm under his scrutiny.

My father had been brought up with sharp-nosed terriers, independent creatures that caught rats between their teeth and had no interest in such words as 'fetch', 'drop' or 'heel'. He made it clear that he found Jason's personality difficult to get used to and after a rather awkward attempt to be friendly to this new member of the household he could no longer contain his dislike.

To remedy the situation he tried to turn the cocker spaniel into a fox terrier. This meant that when Jason brought him a stick between the dewlapped folds of his lips, my father cursed the poor creature if he dropped it and began to teach him to hold the stick tight and growl if anyone tried to take it from him. And if Jason pottered at his heels like a solemn Mohammedan wife my father would shout at him and kick him away, telling him to learn independence.

After a while the anti-Pavlov treatment took root, but rather than being transformed into a new breed of dog, Jason became a very angry and neurotic spaniel, filled with a passionate hatred of my father. He would growl when he saw him come into a room and threaten to bite if he was approached more closely, and when the two of them went to Putney Heath by car, Jason would sit on the back seat and mutter curses throughout the journey. Now he was prepared to fight for the possession of sticks and pebbles, or anything else that he thought might be taken from him, and his red eyes that had looked so sad were blood-tinged with rage and paranoia.

My mother defended Jason, whom she saw as a fellow victim of my father's aggression, and she and the dog had a certain conspiratorial bond. For my part I disowned him and kept my distance from him. In some way I think I blamed him for having been so easily corrupted and made vicious.

It all came to a head one Sunday lunch. There we were, the three of us, gathered in the dark basement kitchen for a family occasion and three stuffed lambs' hearts were roasting quietly in the oven. There was a lot of tension in the air, but there was nothing new in that, and we were used to it. For some reason the telephone kept ringing and my mother kept answering it in a curiously unreal and cheerful tone of voice. And, as my father pointed out later, she kept on saying, 'Jolly good!'

'Oh jolly good! How nice to hear from you! Yes, we're all jolly good, thanks! Well, that's jolly good! Bye-bye!'

Jason was under the table looking dangerous and my father was sitting at the table and grinding his teeth. 'Jolly good, jolly good, jolly good!' he said, doing a simpering imitation of my mother's positive approach. 'There is nothing at all jolly good, as far as I can tell, and if I hear you say jolly good one more time I shall go mad!'

Like poor old Desdemona with the handkerchief, my mother was stuck in a circle of repetition. She opened the oven door, brought the dish of hearts to the table, set them down and said, 'Oh jolly good, they do look nice!'

My father bent forward, lifted the dish in both hands and – never mind how hot it was – hurled the hearts across the table in the direction of my mother's face. They missed their mark and fell in a splatter on the floor.

Jason jumped into action and seized a heart between his teeth, while producing a horrible gurgling growl to indicate that he wanted to be left alone.

My father lunged at the dog and the dog released the heart for enough of a moment to sink his teeth into my father's trouser leg, but drawing no blood.

With a cry of fury, my father picked up a heavy mahogany doorstop, a curious lump of carved wood that must once have been part of some forgotten piece of furniture. He raised this weight above his head and prepared to smash it down on the dog's skull.

My mother screamed but kept her distance and, much to my surprise, I was suddenly back in my knight-in-shining-armour mode. I charged at my father and pummelled him with my fists. He was so surprised that he dropped the doorstop on his foot, crying out in shock and pain, because he broke a toe in the process.

Lunch was over. The dog finished the hearts, my father retired to his study, I went to my room to weep and my mother got on the telephone. 'I can't stand it any longer and now he's trying to kill the dog,' I heard her say, and for once I agreed with her.

⊙ ⊙ ◉ ⊙ ⊙

We muddled on, but in the winter of that year my mother told me she was planning to divorce my father for mental cruelty. She had been doing a lot more talking on the telephone, sometimes behind closed doors, and she said everyone agreed it was the only thing to do. My father was mad and drunk, he had tried to kill Jason and she hated him. We would all be much happier without him.

I noticed that once she had made up her mind, something began to change in her face. Her jaw got stronger and she looked angry instead of afraid. She banged doors a lot and had her curly hair permed into even tighter curls, and she made her eyebrows darker with a new black pencil. She had stopped asking if I wanted to live with her, because she said she knew I did, and my father had stopped asking me which one of them I would choose if choice became necessary.

I know from one of my mother's tiny diaries that on 8 February 1962 she came to collect me from school. She said she had told my father that she was leaving him and taking me with her and he was very angry, so we would have to go into hiding for a while, until he had found somewhere else to live.

She had the car full of a jumbled collection of shoes and socks and knickers, flannels and toothbrushes, hot-water bottles and thermos flasks, sketch pads and watercolour paints, and she said she had put Jason in a kennel because she didn't want my father to murder him, but Pedro the cat and the tropical fish were his responsibility, so if they died, I could blame him. I don't know if I still had any stick insects or if they had expired en masse, as they did from time to time, and then I had to start again. Or maybe I had given up on stick insects at this stage.

My mother had arranged for the two of us to stay in the house of a painter called Willie Barnes Graham. I knew that she was another lesbian, but she was away in Cornwall for a while, so that was all right. The house was white and beautiful with something of the feeling of a church. I was given a front-door key and warned to be very careful, in case my father decided to follow me from school in order to snatch me while I was trying to open the door. And if my mother went out at night I had to lock the door from inside and not open it on any account, because it might be my father. The hallway was very narrow and the staircase was very steep. My mother and I slept in a double bed in a room that looked out at the yellow-grey water of the Thames through a big window.

⊙ ⊙ ◉ ⊙ ⊙

After a couple of weeks we returned home to Cambria Lodge. My father had gone, but the house was haunted by his absence. Every room looked sad, even though nothing much had been removed and the cat and the tropical fish were healthy and well, and Jason, when he was collected, seemed slightly less neurotic than before.

The long coils of nylon rope had gone from the room where I had kept my bushbaby, and the gilded Tibetan Buddha, which had sat on a little plinth with his eyes closed and his right hand raised in benediction, was no longer keeping watch in my parents' bedroom. My father's grubby anorak, which made him look like a tramp, and his black coat, which made him look like an undertaker, were not hanging on their hooks waiting to see which one was to be chosen.

I went up to his study. He had removed the photograph of William Blake's death mask from the wall and he had taken all the books from the bookcase, along with a bright-yellow clay figure of a kangaroo carrying a baby kangaroo in its pouch, which I had made at school and given to him as a present. He had left his work table, covered in beer stains, standing in front of the window and gazing out at the magnolia tree in the garden below, but the Olympia typewriter, its keys worn like steps from the hammering of his fingers and with a bell that had rung out a sharp warning cry every time he completed a new line, that had gone. And all the poems and scattered words on sheets of paper had been swept up, making the room strangely silent. There were a few empty bottles of beer and wine in a corner and an ashtray overflowing with cigarette butts, and that was it, apart from the yellow pee stains in the sink.

My mother said I should use the study as my bedroom. It would be nice and quiet and out of the way, which meant that we could both have friends to stay without disturbing each other. And I could have the double bed that she and my father had slept in, because she was getting a new one.

And so, like a hermit crab, I moved into the uninhabited shell my father had so recently abandoned. I left the table where it was and when I sat on the chair and looked out into the garden it was as if my father were staring through my eyes. The heavy mattress on its metal base, but without the wooden frame, which we couldn't get up the stairs, was positioned in a corner of the room and when I lay on its bumpy surface I could feel the indentations of the two bodies of my parents lying there with me.

After a while I tried to take more possession of this room that didn't seem to belong to me. I scrubbed the sink and painted the walls dark purple and my bedside cupboard black, and chose new curtains with dark-red stripes. The room had taken on the persona of a sleazy nightclub, but I felt like the tenant and my father remained in charge.

⊙ ⊙ ◉ ⊙ ⊙

By now my mother had moved into my old room, which was next to her studio. She got herself new curtains and a new double bed. She put my single bed into the room in which she and my father had slept and quarrelled and made love, and this room was now ready to be rented out to the first in a line of single male lodgers.

⊙ ⊙ ◉ ⊙ ⊙

March 1999

We've got a mistle thrush in the garden. It's bigger and more speckled than an ordinary thrush, although ordinary thrushes are not ordinary any more.

Last night I dreamt of the Cambria Lodge garden and it was full of beautiful overgrown apple trees, the garden thick with criss-crossing branches, all covered in white and pale-green lichens.

Rosalie is much weaker today. It's as if the pot is emptying and there's nothing to fill it with. She wanted to go to her house, so I drove her there. She was very timorous and uncertain as she walked through the door, then she lay down on the sofa and stared around with a look of wide-eyed perplexity. The cats came to greet her, which was nice, but after a little while she became restless and said she wanted to leave because she felt like a stranger here. She felt she was looking at rooms in which a stranger had been living.

(Fax to Herman)

Altered Houses

When my mother declared that the marriage was over, my father was quick to take action. The story goes that he telephoned three lady friends. The first was away on holiday and would be back in a week, the second said she'd like a couple of days to decide whether he could move in with her and the third, Peggy, was quick to say yes to everything.

This meant that by the time my mother and I had emerged from hiding and returned to Cambria Lodge, my father was living with Peggy in her flat in north London.

'Peggy is my landlady,' he said to me, rather disingenuously, 'and she is very kind. You'll like her two children immensely. The girl's two years younger than you and quite bright. Italian father, but he died young –

Huntington's disease – and she misses him, poor thing! Not so sure about the boy. He's eighteen, spent most of his childhood in Sweden with his father. Got a bit of an Oedipal if you ask me. And he takes drugs. But don't worry, he and I get along fine.'

A ready-made family was waiting for me and I had always wanted a brother and sister. I was eager to get to know them.

'I'm going to have lunch with them today,' I told my mother.

'You don't need to!' she said,

bristling with indignation. 'We've only just divorced the bastard and he doesn't really want to see you. He's inviting you because he feels guilty. And Peggy's a bitch. Called herself my friend and advised me to go ahead with the divorce. "Nobody could bear to live with a man like that," she said and now she's gone and snatched him! Please stay and have lunch with me. I'll be all on my own because Bob is out and he won't be back until late!'

⊙ ⊙ ◉ ⊙ ⊙

Bob was our new lodger. He was in his mid thirties and he looked like an overgrown Boy Scout. He had straw-coloured hair, a sharp nose and a thin mouth. He laughed a lot, which was something I wasn't used to, and he had quick gestures and a tendency to snatch hold of things and people. He was always cheerful and practical and I was sure he was the kind of person who would know exactly what to do if we were caught in a flood, or the house was burning down, or war was declared.

My mother told me that she was in love with Bob and she was quite sure he wanted to marry her. I wished he would, not just because he was so practical, but also because he was friendly and he never got drunk and he didn't shout or swear. When we all sat round the table at supper time he would tell silly jokes about dogs or foreigners and I thought the jokes were wonderful, even if I failed to understand why they were supposed to be funny.

Bob was often at home because he still hadn't got the job he wanted as an architect and when I got back from school he'd welcome me with a spiky hug. One day he asked if I would like to be an aeroplane.

'Of course I would,' I replied, with no idea what the metamorphosis involved.

He took hold of my hand and ankle and spun me round and round. I had never known that adults could be such fun.

But then my mother came into the garden and saw me spinning. 'What on earth is going on?' she said. 'Put her down at once and don't ever, ever do that with her again!'

'Can't I be an aeroplane?' I asked, startled by her anger.

'The girl is thirteen years old,' said my mother, addressing Bob and ignoring my question. 'You must not touch her!'

Bob was not a quarreller, so he shrugged his shoulders and we had no more aeroplanes.

◦ ◦ ◉ ◦ ◦

I realized that my mother was getting increasingly jumpy. Bob took her to the opera and he helped her frame some paintings for an exhibition, and he went on telling jokes and being cheerful, but there was no more talk of marriage and he wasn't even sleeping in her new double bed. He made a series of photographs of her in her studio, and looking at them now I can see the angry disappointment in her eyes. 'After all, I'm forty-four,' she said to me, as if she were talking to herself, 'I haven't got much time to waste.'

The three of us had Christmas together in the changed house. The turkey was cooking and I was laying the table and then Bob was there, grinning and holding two presents.

'This is for you!' he said and gave me a little package.

'This is for you!' he said and gave my mother a bigger package.

I unwrapped mine and it contained a little bottle of perfume, Je Reviens, by Worth.

My mother unwrapped hers and it contained a book called *How to Live with a Neurotic Dog.*

I don't think I'd ever seen her so angry. 'There has been a mistake!' she said. 'Julia, give me my perfume, at once!'

'No, no,' said Bob, laughing his schoolboy laugh. 'It's for her. I thought she might like it. After all, she's becoming a young woman.'

I took the perfume up to my room and I kept the bottle after it was empty because it was a symbol of something, but I didn't know of what. When I left home my mother found it and put it on her dressing table. It was odd seeing it there. I asked her once where she had got it from and she said someone had given it to her ages ago, but she couldn't remember who.

Bob left us just a few weeks after Christmas and by then we had another lodger. This was Paul, who arrived from Switzerland with a private income, several very good-quality suits and a broken heart.

⊙ ⊙ ◉ ⊙ ⊙

But before Paul comes to join us, let me go and have lunch with my father and his new family, in spite of what my mother said about his reasons for inviting me.

Peggy was there to welcome me. She was wearing a wonderful skirt that rustled as she walked and a green shirt, which she said was made of shot silk. Her hair was black, her lipstick was red, there was a big amethyst ring on her finger and she looked radiant and happy.

I was intrigued by the furniture in her flat. I was used to living among ancestral cast-offs: mahogany chests and cupboards and faded carpets, which had all tumbled down to us from dead relatives. Peggy was surrounded by modernity. She had a lamp that sprouted a cluster of orange lampshades that could be moved in different directions. She had chairs with shiny metal legs and a table with a luminous green laminated top. She had an espresso machine that made spluttering noises when it was switched on and cups that were only big enough to hold a boiled egg, for the espresso coffee. Even her knives and forks were like nothing I had ever seen before.

She introduced me to her daughter Catherine, who was very pretty but much too shy to speak. Then I met her son Michael, who was tall and thin with curly blond hair and a nose with a bump in it. He smoked a pipe and spoke English with a very formal accent, like a character from an old film.

My father walked in looking both sheepish and jolly. I noticed that he touched Peggy's hand as he walked past her and she followed him with her eyes.

I enjoyed the formality of the occasion and when I went home I told my mother what fun it had been and that Peggy was a very kind landlady.

'Landlady, my arse!' said my mother with a snort of indignation. 'We're going ahead with the divorce on the grounds of adultery now. My lawyer says it's easier than mental cruelty. All that's needed is a private detective to collect evidence that they are sleeping together.'

My father always said that he was very happy with Peggy and I think he was telling the truth. There was a bond of understanding between them, even during the worst times, and they could talk about literature and Peggy was very well informed on European history and had read Henry James and Thomas Mann. Right from the start she was very clear in saying that if my father so much as looked at another woman she would leave him at once, and that seemed to work.

The only problem as far as I was concerned was that Peggy often got as drunk as my father did, and then she lost all her fear and hurled abuse at him as well as glasses and teapots. She'd often end up with bruises and a black eye for her pains, but I was impressed by her determination, which made for a different sort of violence.

The honeymoon between my father and Peggy's two children didn't last long. Within a few weeks my father had accused Michael of stealing some groceries and selling them to get money for drugs, and he said that Michael should be kept away from Peggy, because 'the Oedipal was getting out of hand'. The two men had a terrible fight in the street and the police were called. After that Michael moved to a flat in Notting Hill Gate.

'He has married a black prostitute in a voodoo ceremony,' said my father smugly. 'Now we can only expect the worst!'

⊙ ⊙ ◉ ⊙ ⊙

My father didn't stay in north London for long. He bought a little house in Putney, only a ten-minute walk from Cambria Lodge, for himself and Peggy and Catherine. I suppose it suited his need for habit and familiarity. It meant he could take the same walks across Putney Heath and into Richmond Park, and go to the same pubs and catch the same bus to the teacher-training college in Chelsea where he now had a new job teaching English literature. But it also made it possible for him to make regular impromptu visits, keeping a proprietorial eye on me and my mother, and checking up on how things were going.

My father had a small, claustrophobic garden of which he was immensely proud. He wrote a poem celebrating the stone lion's head he had bought in a junk shop and placed on the summit of a tiny rockery made out of a pile of building rubble; it was as if he was describing an ancient monument in the grounds of an ancestral castle.

He was keen to praise Peggy's skills as a gardener and in response to this praise Peggy bought dozens of plastic sacks containing Irish peat; these sacks lay around the garden in brightly coloured heaps, as if they had been abandoned during a dustmen's strike. Peggy used the peat to plant lots of geraniums in plastic flowerpots. My father's job was to mow the tiny lawn and to trim the pyracantha bush, which produced a proliferation of orange berries. He wrote a poem about that as well, filled with the imagery of flames.

⊙ ⊙ ◉ ⊙ ⊙

Peggy's daughter Catherine was two years younger than me, so she must have been eleven when I first met her. My father had wooed her with fairy stories and presents, but after she saw him getting drunk she became very frightened of him and tried to avoid being in the same room as him, especially in the evenings. I found it difficult to make approaches to her, partly because she seemed so young and innocent, and also because I was ashamed that she had inherited my father but didn't have reams of poetry to recite, like a magical incantation that would quieten his soul.

Eventually Catherine rebelled in the only possible way she could. She kept her room and her person meticulously tidy, banged doors loudly when she heard a wine bottle being opened and made tut-tut noises if an obscenity was uttered or the talk turned to my father's favourite topic of death and William Blake, or Freud and the traumas of childhood. She became a Girl Guide and a member of the local church, and she would rise to her feet and give a loyal salute if Her Majesty the Queen appeared on television.

◎ ◎ ◉ ◎ ◎

Now that he was round the corner, my father wanted me to become a regular visitor. I did my best, but it was not easy.

'Thought you'd like to come to supper tomorrow,' he said. 'Peggy would appreciate it. She's invited her drug addict son and his black voodoo bride, who's making a living for both of them on the streets of Notting Hill. Catherine won't be here – she avoids social gatherings – but you might find it fun.'

I was not sure about the fun, but I said I'd come. I liked Michael and I wanted to meet his wife.

I can't remember anything about the meal, but I can recall the five of us gathered in the sitting room. Michael was on a sofa with his wife Cynthia very close to him on one side and Peggy on the other, and I sat at their feet on the floor. My father was in the only armchair, facing us all and looking dangerous.

Michael had his mother's deep-set grey eyes, but he didn't look like my idea of a heroin addict. Cynthia was luxuriously black and sexy, and she had one of those tight womanly bodies that seemed to be pumped full of liquid. Her lipstick was as bright as Peggy's, but, again, she didn't look like my idea of a prostitute.

The conversation was awkward and the evening was short-lived. My father must have made an insulting remark about race, or sex, or drugs, causing Michael and Cynthia to rise to their feet and walk out, with Peggy following them tearfully to the door. But just before the eruption, Cynthia had looked at me and called me 'honeychild', giving me a wonderfully warm smile; at that moment, if she had asked me to come and live with her and her husband, I would have moved in the next day.

I did go and see them, just once. Cynthia was heavily pregnant by then and the flat was very dimly lit and scented with joss sticks. They seemed distracted and unhappy, and the marriage fell apart shortly after the birth of their son. Then there was some trouble with the police and Michael avoided a jail sentence by escaping to Sweden with the baby, but that meant he could never return to England. A year or two later he took his own life.

I always felt that my father was partly responsible for Michael's death; after all, he'd been horrible to him and had chased him out of the house. And I suppose because he was *my* father, I felt it was a bit my fault as well.

Going through my father's notebooks just now, I found a very sinister dreamlike sequence in which he describes Michael at a party, *dressed as a woman, but with jackboots and a wig and having a rather sinister conversation with Francis Bacon, whom he calls 'Master'*. I would have liked to ask him what on earth that was supposed to mean, but it's too late now.

◦ ◦ ◉ ◦ ◦

March 1999

So many people keep phoning and I am not clear enough to be brief with them, so I get caught up in long conversations. Some are nice, others are filled with ambivalence and fear. One man, whom Rosalie has known for ages, said to her, 'You are my first terminal friend and I am finding it very difficult to cope!' She was rather shocked by the remark.

How strange, Herman, the coincidence of circumstance that brought you and me back into contact, just three days before all this started. Maybe there's a guardian angel keeping an eye on us.

(Fax to Herman)

❦ 16 ❦

Father Comes to Tea

The doorbell rings and before I can get there to see who it is, the door opens and in steps my father, who still has his own key. Without a moment's hesitation he goes to the big chest where the Burmese gong stands waiting to call people to dinner and he picks up any letters that have been left lying there. He puts on his spectacles to examine these letters more carefully, although he doesn't usually open anything that is not addressed to him personally.

Calling out 'Hello, it's me!' he begins to move as smoothly as a vacuum cleaner from room to room. He casts his eye over cluttered tables and unmade beds. He opens the bathroom cupboard and counts the tooth-brushes, checking if there are any interesting pills that he can stuff in his pocket – he cannot resist pills. He is like a private detective, except that there is nothing private about the way he does his work. Perhaps he is more like a rent collector visiting tenants who are behind with the rent.

I come down the stairs from the room that was once his study and by now he is in my mother's studio.

'Hello, darling,' he says. He has opened my mother's writing desk and is going through the recent letters she keeps in a little pigeon-hole there. He pauses to give me a kiss on the cheek.

I can smell that he hasn't been drinking and his hands aren't shaking, so that's good. In fact, he tends to stay away from Cambria Lodge when he has been drinking and he looks rather smug because he knows he is sober.

'Your mother had someone to stay last night, didn't she?' he says and it's true, although I have no idea how he has found out. 'Who was that then, hmm? Hope it wasn't that ugly chap with the sandals she met at Finch's last week. I wouldn't be surprised if he walks off with the clock and her wallet.

And why did Bob leave in such a hurry? What's his game? She implied there was a little romance on the cards, but I never believed it. He can't be more that thirty-five if he's a day and anyway, isn't he still married?'

The as yet unstolen clock punctuates my father's commentary by striking the hour in a sharp and authoritative tone, while staring at us through its glass dome. I hate the clock and sometimes long to hurl it across the room.

My father looks at a new abstract painting on the easel, putting his nose close to its violent surface. 'Told her she should stay figurative. She managed some good work while she was with me, but this stuff's meaningless. How's she doing, darling? Not being too difficult, I hope? That Bob seemed like quite a nice chap, but I don't like the look of Paul, the new one. Oh, and when you see her, tell her I need to talk about money, she's got much more of the stuff than me these days.'

'Yes, Bob was nice,' I say, 'and Paul is very grumpy and hardly speaks to us, and Mummy and I keep quarrelling. We have dreadful quarrels and . . .'

But I can tell that my father is not listening. He takes off his spectacles and looks at me as if he is seeing me for the first time. I feel shy under his scrutiny. I am wearing a lot of pancake make-up on my face, but I imagine he can see how tired I am beneath the pasty surface. I also imagine that he won't approve of the dress I am wearing because it is very short and very tight.

'You look well,' he says hopefully, adding as always, 'looked perfectly dreadful last time I saw you . . . As I said to Peggy, "The girl needs to take a Mogadon at night with some hot milk. That would help her." Peggy agreed, she swears by the stuff. Or I could let you have a mild barbiturate like Sonoril. I've got some on me now, as it happens. That would calm you down. Can't spare any amytal, though, haven't got enough for myself since that new doctor took over in the surgery. Told her it's crucial for the poetry and *I* can decide how many I need, but she's a stickler for the rules.'

'I don't want any Mogadon or the other stuff, thanks,' I say. Then, 'I call him Sandals, the man who is sort of the new lodger at the moment, because he always wears sandals, even when it's raining.'

What I don't say is that I don't like Sandals and I don't trust him. It's got nothing to do with him wanting to steal the clock or my mother's wallet, it's the way he keeps staring at me with his bottom lip hanging down and now he has taken to calling me 'the little Lolita' which makes my mother really angry with him.

I've just finished reading *Lolita, light of my life, fire of my loins*, in order to find out what Sandals is talking about. Lolita was twelve when Humbert Humbert fell in love with her.

'Have you read Nabokov?' I ask my father, as a way of approaching the subject that is worrying me.

'Stuck-up little shit!' replies my father decisively. 'Critics love him because he's so full of himself, just like they are. *Speak, Memory* wasn't bad; *Lolita* is pure filth. A dirty old man lusting after a teenage girl, I ask you! Yeats understood the sexual act when he said, *and did after stretch and yawn*, now *that's* what I call erotic writing! None of Nabokov's phornography!'

'Pornography,' I say, correcting him.

'Just what I said, phornography!'

He sets off down to the kitchen and I follow at his heels, a bit like Jason, who is wisely keeping out of sight during this visit. He takes the biscuit tin from the shelf, opens it and lifts out a handful of digestive biscuits, eating them in quick succession while reading an electricity bill.

'Must be leaving the lights on all night!' he says.

'Would you like a cup of tea, Daddy?' I ask him, still feeling a bit like Jason.

'Beer!' he replies and finds a bottle in the cupboard. He pours it into a mug and the froth spills on to the carpet. He tramples the froth underfoot, 'to get rid of the bubbles,' he says, smiling.

⊙ ⊙ ◉ ⊙ ⊙

Here comes my mother.

Every time she meets her ex, she becomes very passive and subservient. She keeps asking for his approval, even though she will curse him behind his back once he has gone.

'Oh hello, Tommy dear! I've been making a new painting and I'd love to show it to you, if you've got a moment. Has Julia given you something to drink? Ah yes, she has. That's good. I've just bought myself a jumper, it's nice, isn't it, but I wish I could lose a bit of weight. Peggy never has that problem, does she?'

'Peggy has a lovely body,' says my father. 'I was reading your electricity bill. How do you manage to use so much? You must be keeping the house piping hot all through the night!'

Before my mother can think up a reply, our new lodger walks in. He sees my father and I can tell he wants to walk out again at once, but it's too late. I find it absurd how everyone in this house is afraid of my father and equally absurd how much pleasure he takes from their fear.

'Good afternoon, Thomas,' says Paul, and he gives a little Germanic nod of the head.

'Good afternoon, Herr Stalder,' says my father. I am suddenly afraid he is going to do a Nazi salute as a joke.

'Well, darling,' he says, turning his back on the lodger and his ex-wife as if they didn't exist. 'Must be off. Give us a call, we're always delighted to see you.'

⊙ ⊙ ◉ ⊙ ⊙

March 1999

Rosalie is getting more and more sleepy. I suppose the effect of the blood transfusion is wearing off. But the talk and the bonus of laughter continue and she still says she enjoys dying.

She asked me about my father this evening. 'You loved him, didn't you?' she said.

And then very dreamily, 'I suppose he must be dead too.'

It's more than twenty years now since he died and yet it's the first time I've heard her speak of him with gentleness in her voice.

I said, 'Yes, he most probably is dead.' I didn't want to be too definite in my answer, the border between life and death seems so vague at the moment.

There is a full moon laughing at me through the window. I have been reading the poems of Basho.

> *Dying cricket*
> *How full of life*
> *His song*

(Fax to Herman)

❧ 17 ❧

Talking Dirty

I've said a bit about Paul, the lodger with the broken heart and the very white dressing gown, but the more I read from the entries in my diary during the year or so that he lived with us, the more I see what a big part he played in the sexual tangles that were taking shape between me and my mother. The business with Paul was a prelude for what was to follow later.

He arrived some time in 1963, when I was fourteen. His suits impressed me because they fitted his wide, muscular body so precisely and even I could tell that they were very expensive. His shoes gleamed and he had gold cufflinks and a gold tooth, which flashed when he smiled one of his tight smiles, or let out a sharp laugh that made him jerk his head back at an angle to his shoulders. He smelt of Old Spice aftershave and Gauloises cigarettes, and although he didn't smell of sweat he was always slightly damp, his face glistening as if he had just been involved in a fight. He often mopped his brow with a white handkerchief, which he kept in his breast pocket. He spoke English with a strong German-Swiss accent and scrambled grammar, but he didn't like to have his mistakes corrected.

For the first few months Paul remained in his room for most of the day with the curtains drawn. But since this room was only separated from the studio-sitting room by a door of panelled glass, his existence was not very private. I'd hear him stirring on his unmade bed, and then there would be the sound of a match striking, or a drink being poured into a glass, or the page of a magazine turning. He never played music or listened to the radio.

Sometimes during those early days he would agree to join us for supper and he'd sit at the round table, scowling in silence with his elbows clenched against his sides. If I or my mother plucked up the courage to ask him a question, he'd bark a brief reply and then snap his mouth shut, the way that frogs do when they have caught a fly.

'So where were you today, Paul?' said my mother, offering him a plate piled high with food. 'Girlfriend? You can always bring them back here if you want to!'

Paul remained firmly silent.

'Maybe you were counting frenchies in the river?'

'Frenchies?' said Paul, genuinely perplexed.

'Condoms!' said my mother, delighted to have got a dialogue started. 'Julia counted one hundred and twenty-three used condoms in the river when she was walking Jason in Wandsworth Park. Didn't you, darling? Think of that, one hundred and twenty-three tuppenny uprights as we used to call them!'

'Shut up, Mummy, you are embarrassing him!' I said, creaking with embarrassment myself.

'I do not know the word tuppenny upright,' said Paul, although he obviously guessed the meaning. 'Thank you for supper,' he added, balancing a clean knife and fork on top of the untouched roast potatoes and the meat and the vegetables. 'Good night, ladies.'

And with that he wiped his mouth with his own white napkin and rose to his feet. He clicked his heels together and inclined his head into a little nod. 'I am needing to make a phone call. You will be out of the room until when I say I am finished, yes?'

'Switzerland?' asked my mother.

'It is none of your business,' said Paul, and with that he left the kitchen, banging the door behind him.

He didn't reappear for three days.

'He is very depressed,' said my mother. 'I know because I am also very depressed. I think he's lonely.'

'I think he's a phoney bastard!' I said.

'You are too young to understand him,' replied my mother.

◦ ◦ ◉ ◦ ◦

I didn't trust Paul. According to my diary he was often drunk and when he was drunk, or 'a little tipsy' as he preferred to call it, he wanted to ask me questions about sex and what I did with boys. Once he cornered me in the hall and pressed his body against me. 'Aha, my beauty!' he said, breathing into my face. 'I think you want to kiss me.'

I pushed him away in disgust. I told my mother that he had been making advances to me and that I didn't like the way he stared at me. I was frightened of what he might try to do, especially if he had been drinking.

'You must have done *something* to make him behave like that!' she said. 'You'd better keep out of his way in future. Particularly because I like Paul very much and I'd like to have an affair with him. He's just my type.'

'But Mummy, he's twelve years younger than you!'

'A man like him needs an older woman, someone who has a lot of sexual experience. I bet I could teach him a thing or two!'

I wrote in my diary that I wished my mother would find a *lodger/lover who was mad about her and thought of me as a nice daughter*, but I knew that Paul was not a good candidate. I also knew that from now on I couldn't say anything to her about him flirting with me because it would only make her jealous and then I would feel guilty.

On that same day, 4 April 1964, I also told my diary that I had written quite a good essay on 'Exploring the Past' and I had watched the tropical fish for what seemed like hours. I had just bought a new Siamese Fighter, a male with pink and purple trailing fins. I'd put a little mirror into the tank and when he saw his own reflection he believed he was confronting a rival male and his fins would go stiff with rage, while his colours became even more intense.

⊚ ⊚ ◉ ⊚ ⊚

After a while Paul began to venture out. He told us he had enrolled at the London School of Economics and was attending lectures and seminars, but my mother was sure he only went out to pick up prostitutes in Soho.

I wanted to know more about this stranger in our house, so I went into his empty room to search for evidence. It was in a terrible mess: overflowing ashtrays and glasses half full of brandy. Although his suits and shirts were carefully hung up, all his underwear was scattered across the floor. His unmade bed gave the impression of having been thrashed about in and there was a tottering pile of *Playboys* and other girlie magazines on the floor next to the bed.

I looked at the centrefold women in some of the *Playboys*, amazed by the shining solidity of their hair and breasts and buttocks, but the other magazines made me nervous: women with their legs splayed apart, revealing pink vaginas that looked as soft and wet as shellfish. I had examined my own vagina with a mirror, but not in such bright detail. All the women in the photographs were on their own, there were no men around.

In the bookcase, which had been mine when this was my room, Paul had several green paperbacks in the Traveller's Companion series, printed in Paris. There was one called *The House of Borgia*, which I took down from the shelf because I had read about the Borgias when I studied the Italian Renaissance at school. I opened the book at random and was confronted by a steamy world in which hot cocks were being thrust into brothers and sisters, sons and daughters, and the terrible matriarch Lucretia Borgia was at the centre of it all. I closed the book in a hurry, my heart pounding from horrified curiosity and from fear that Paul might suddenly arrive and find me there.

⊙ ⊙ ◉ ⊙ ⊙

My mother also went exploring in Paul's room when she knew he was out, but she told me of her adventures, while I kept silent about mine.

She said, 'I was looking at his sheets. I think he spends all day masturbating in bed. And I've stolen one of his magazines. I wonder if he'll dare to ask me where it is.'

It was late in the evening and we were sitting in front of the gas fire in my room. I was in my nightdress, Paul was out and my mother was bored.

She looked at me with the peculiar intensity that always presaged a talk about sex. 'You do know what masturbation is, don't you, darling?'

'Yes I do. You told me about it ages ago.'

'And do you masturbate?'

'No, Mummy, I don't.'

'That's very odd. I masturbate every night if I haven't got a man with me. So why don't you? Has no one told you how? Would you like Mummy to teach you?'

'That's disgusting!' I said, suddenly very afraid.

She stared at me, still smiling, and then it was as if a mist passed over her eyes. 'God, you're such a prude!' she said and stomped off down the stairs.

⊙ ⊙ ◉ ⊙ ⊙

Paul enjoyed the tension between me and my mother and did his best to make it worse. He'd watch us playing chess together, making comments as our pieces struggled on the tiny battlefield, and then he'd play the winner.

I had the sense that he was always much more rude to my mother when I was around and she, in turn, would be very rude to me. 'We were doing very well, until you came in!' she'd say, or, 'Can't you see you're not wanted here?'

And that was a cue for Paul to disagree. 'Oh, but she is wanted! She is wanted very much! She brightens the heart of an old man like me!' And with that he'd twinkle with delight like a Christmas tree, as the tears welled in my mother's eyes.

⊙ ⊙ ◉ ⊙ ⊙

My mother had made it very clear that any older man who spoke to me and showed interest in me was only using talk as sexual foreplay. 'Surely you're not that naïve! They don't want to talk to you, they just want to fuck you!'

In response to her certainties, I became increasingly determined to impress grown-up men with the sophistication of my fifteen-year-old mind. In Paul's company I'd ignore his rude jokes and his long stares and ask him what he thought of Nietzsche, Existentialism, the Theatre of the Absurd, Monotheism. He'd laugh and try to change the subject, but if I stuck to my guns he'd tell me things as well; so I learnt about the Boston Tea Party and the start of the American War of Independence, the politics of Western capitalism, the implications of the collapse of the Weimar Republic. When he said I must read *The Rise and Fall of the Third Reich* I went out and bought it and worked my way through all fourteen hundred and thirty-six pages. When he said it was essential to know Graham Greene's novels, I read them all, one after another.

◎ ◎ ◉ ◎ ◎

In May 1964, at school, we were asked to write an essay on 'Someone I Know' and I chose Paul as the subject of my study. I have lost all of the essay, apart from a single page that I found among some letters, but that one page gives an idea of how earnestly I took on my self-appointed task:

> Paul's face was oval-shaped and crowned by soft baby-blond hair. His features were small and compact and would have been more suited to a fragile child or a timid intellectual . . .
>
> When he first arrived we knew nothing about him and he maintained a remoteness verging on hostility. But he could not control his moods and depressions, which would reverberate around the house . . .

Paul began to talk to me about his problems. He told me he sometimes wanted to kill himself because life was meaningless and with the practical honesty of the young, I asked why he didn't do it, if that was what he really felt. He told me how much he hated his wealthy father and I asked why he accepted money from him then, and he had no answer to my harshness. But he went on talking, snatching conversations with me whenever he could get me on my own. 'I have a problem with women,' he said one day when we were in the kitchen. 'You know what a hard-on is? Of course you do, because you are very wise. My problem is that since I lost Merrit, I can no longer get a hard-on and without that, what can a man do, eh?' He turned to look at his own reflection in the mirror and punched himself under the chin. 'But, when I talk to you, I get a hard-on! Still, I am an honourable Swiss gentleman, no? I don't rape you, which you might not like, and I don't seduce you, which your mother might not like. But I go hard with the sound of your voice and that fills me with hope!'

I listened to him because I felt like an adult when he was talking to me, because I was flattered by the attention and because it made me feel more powerful in the battle with my mother who I knew wanted these kinds of conversations for herself. But I was frightened all the same, so I balanced my fear by filling my diary with my thoughts about Paul and details of all our meetings and conversations.

On 21 April 1964 my mother was out at work and I was at home revising for a school exam. *Paul came trotting up to my room cos he was bored. We listened to Elvis the Pelvis and he asked if he could make me up to 'look wicked'.* I said he could and so he set to work: rubbing rouge into my cheeks, drawing black lines of kohl round my eyes and colouring my lips with a bright-red lipstick. He was delighted with the result and said that now I looked like *a little tart,* and he taught me the words of a song, which we sang together,

> I wish I were a fascinating bitch,
> I'd never be poor, I'd always be rich,
> I'd sleep all day and work all night,
> And live in a house with a little red light.
>
> And then one day I'd take a vacation
> And drive my customers to masturbation,
> I wish I were a fascinating bitch,
> Instead of a bastard child!

On Friday, 5 June Paul came up to my room at 1.30 in the morning when I was fast asleep. He switched on the main light, knelt beside my bed, pulled back the covers and kissed me on the shoulder. I was naked under the blankets and I kept very still. His breath smelt of overripe plums.

'We are having a party my beauty!' he said by way of explanation. 'You must come and join us. I'll make you drunk and cook you an omelette *à la française!*'

I waited until he had left the room, then I got up and put on my dressing gown. I could hear music and laughter in the studio. A little crowd of men and women had come back with my mother after closing time at the pub. A man called Ken, whom I had met before, was there with his girlfriend.

Set — woke at 1-30 by Paul —
switched on the light, [...] &
gave me an "uncle" kiss on
my shoulder — I was very sleepy
& naked — though decent —
heard sounds & got up — laughter
& music — people — down to
few around adults — Thought
John [...] for entering — record
[...] & people — [...] studio —
[...] but was very nice — a girl
apparently I was told a
Cinderella — & very charming —
down to the kitchen —
I [...] up for a Paul
omelette — me with 2 beans

Brian was flirty with one man
to my embarrassment Paul
[...] to get [...]

Back to bed at 2-30
couldn't go to sleep into
dark [...]

[...] on to become —
[...] came the following
day with a most "happy
[...] one he pissed [...]

Ken was dark and elegant, and I thought he was beautiful and looked like the villain in a Hollywood movie. There were two other men, both with beards, and one of them, whose name was Brian, had been sleeping with my mother during the last week or so.

Brian now lurched to his feet and pulled me towards him. 'Ah! Here is little Cinderella! Cinders has come to the Ball and never mind what the wicked sisters might say!'

I struggled free and went down to the kitchen. Paul was making the omelette, surrounded by a haze of blue smoke.

'Drink some brandy! You must swallow it quickly, like this, and then it won't burn your throat! We don't need the party, we have each other, yes?' and he did his open-mouthed grin.

I went back to bed at 2.30 and the next morning I moved from room to room *like a zoo keeper*, as I told my diary, bringing black coffee to the guests who had stayed the night.

Paul said he had a hangover and was in need of love and sympathy, so I lit him a cigarette and poured some brandy into his coffee. My mother was in bed with bearded Brian and there was no answer when I knocked gently on their door, so I left them undisturbed.

Hollywood Ken was in the front room and he tried to grapple me into bed with him, next to his sleeping girlfriend. 'Come here, my pet,' he said 'and don't mind her, she's a fucking virgin!' and he laughed at his own joke.

'I'm also a virgin,' I said, with an edge of formality.

'Not for long, petal! Did your mother tell you I'm going to be your new lodger. I'm renting this room from today. I know lots of famous people who'd love to meet you. We'll have such fun, you and me!'

In the studio I found a man called Robin who had gone to sleep on the chaise-longue. He said he was cold and needed a blanket. I heard Paul calling for me: 'Help, I am dying! More cigarettes! More brandy! It is an emergency!'

The party continued throughout the weekend and on Monday morning I was late for morning assembly at school. 'Dear God,' I thought, 'let there be no more drunken nights and no more old men leering at me and grabbing hold of me and no more talk of hard-ons and doing it, for the sake of Thy only Son, our Saviour Jesus Christ Our Lord, Amen.'

But when I came home that afternoon the house was in a panic. Ken had disappeared and his girlfriend was sitting on the floor sobbing. Paul was comforting her with brandy. It seemed that Ken had stolen some money and perhaps some items of value but no one could work out what was missing.

'He only came here to rob us!' said my mother, who was also in tears.

'And to seduce your daughter!' added Paul. 'But we all are busy with that, are we not?'

'Shut up, damn you!' said my mother and before the conversation could develop I went upstairs to do my homework.

⊙ ⊙ ◉ ⊙ ⊙

And then one evening towards the end of July, Paul was back in my room. I told him that my mother treated me as her rival and I hated her and I hated him and I hated everyone and I didn't know what to do.

Paul looked sad and serious. He said I was too young to cry, too young to solve other people's problems. 'I don't want a quarrel between you and your mother,' he said, 'but I know what I do want,' and he began to giggle.

I told him he had to be serious. I told him that I understood him much better than he realized and that I had been studying him for ages and had kept an account of all our conversations in my diary. I showed him the diary and began to read from one of the entries.

Paul was furious. He snatched the book from me and looked at the open page, his face getting redder and redder. 'You have no right! You have no right to try to control me in this way! You are taking the piss and I do not like that!'

And then he began to tear out the pages. He started on 19 June and he went on tearing until he reached 10 July, ripping through five or ten days at a go, until almost an entire month lay fluttering at his feet. He scrumpled the pages up and placed them on the little flagstone in front of the gas fire. He lit the heap with a match and I watched as the lined sheets of paper curled and darkened and turned into fragments of ash.

'Never, never do that again!' Paul shouted, waving his index finger at me as if it were a gun. Then he stormed out.

I am looking at the diary now, its spine broken from that long-ago violence. All the pages are lose from 3 June through to 16 July and the torn edge that marks where the other pages once were still gives me a shock of fear.

I didn't write much for the days that followed, except on 17 July *I talked a bit to poor sad Paul* and on 23 July, when my mother and I were getting ready to go on holiday, *I said goodbye to Paul and asked him not to be any sadder than he had to be and he kissed me on both cheeks and I kissed him on the cheek too.*

By the time we came back from our holiday at the end of August, Paul had moved out of Cambria Lodge and returned to Switzerland.

◦ ◦ ◉ ◦ ◦

March 1999

I sat beside Rosalie while she ate supper in bed: a bowl of bright-green spinach soup, followed by stewed prunes. She fell asleep very fast, as soon as she had finished eating.

I went to check that she was all right at around two in the morning because I had heard her stirring.

I lay down beside her. She gave me a sleepy smile and then she said, ' "Two little babes in a bed!" That's what my father used to say when he got into bed with my sister! He never got into bed with me!'

I was completely taken aback, but before I could respond she was asleep again, her breathing very deep and slow.

I thought of asking her to tell me more when she woke, but don't think I can. Anyway, she has probably said enough, just in those few words.

(Fax to Herman)

Uncle Guy

My mother did have some relations – a few cousins, uncles and nieces – but she never spoke of them and I don't think there was even an exchange of Christmas cards. So, as far as I was concerned, after the death of her sister in 1939 and her father in 1951, her entire family consisted of her mother, Blanche.

Blanche never came to see us, but my mother would visit her a couple of times a year and sometimes she'd take me along. As we drove towards our destination, her face would begin to look different, because she'd press her lips so tightly together. When we arrived, she'd comb her hair into flattened respectability and say, 'Come on, then, let's get it over with!'

Blanche was always carefully powdered and permed, with diamond rings on her fingers, strings of pearls round her neck and an unexpected cleavage, which revealed the soft plunge of her breasts. She carried a walking stick, which I longed to own because its ivory handle was carved into the shape of a duck's head, with very real-looking golden-brown eyes.

She'd welcome us with a look of regal disdain and condescension, as if we had come to beg favours she was unwilling to grant, and the look was swiftly followed by a flurry of criticism. 'Hello, Rosalie, I see you've put on weight again. Your hair is a mess, you really should do something about it. Oh, you've brought Julia; she looks more and more like her father. Her shoes could do with some polish.'

Blanche never spoke directly to me and so I was left to fend for myself. She had a yellow Labrador called Shway and I'd sit on the floor beside him and search his thick coat for fleas, until the formality of lunch was ready to begin. After Shway died, she got herself a miniature papillon called Butchy, but she usually carried him lodged between her cleavage like a hairy brooch and on the rare occasions when he was allowed to put his feet on the ground he tended to yap if approached and bite if touched. From then on I took a book with me.

I was startled by the change that came over my mother during these visits; there was no belching or farting, no telling of inappropriate jokes while staring defiantly into the shocked silence she had created around her. Instead it was all 'Yes, Mummy' and 'No, Mummy', as she did her best to be friendly and polite and lovable, trying not to show it when she was hurt by a particularly sharp comment. I saw her transformed into a little girl who was much younger than me, a little girl who longed for a word of approval.

On our way back we would always go for a walk in the woods somewhere, even if it was raining, and apart from my mother saying 'Well, that's done then!' there was no mention of where we had been and what had transpired.

○ ○ ◉ ○ ○

And then, in the summer of 1963, during the time that Paul was first living with us, in the middle of all the drink and parties and wild nights and tearful mornings, my mother suddenly announced that someone I had never heard of – her Uncle Guy – was coming to stay.

He arrived like a creature from another planet and stayed for eight weeks. A curious hush descended on the house from the day he walked through the front door until the day when he packed his bags and left. For me it was a brief oasis of calm.

Uncle Guy was Blanche's younger brother. Born in the 1890s he, like her, had been brought up in a remote and rarefied social stratosphere: a world of davenports and ormolus and Chippendale furniture; a world in which Poussin's *Shepherd and Shepherdess* looked down on the diners in the dining room and a dark *Annunciation*, wrongly attributed to Rembrandt, did its best to ignore the cigar smoke and the clink of glasses in the gentlemen's drawing room.

Uncle Guy was thin and willowy, and he wore soft clothes that flapped when he walked. He was devastatingly polite and he had a number of little feminine gestures, which I liked. He would lift the little finger of his right hand when drinking tea from one of our chipped china mugs and press the tips of his fingers together and smile conspiratorially when he wanted to show that he was thinking something over. He also had a rather skittish wrist flick and a wonderfully elegant way of sitting in a chair, leaning his chin on the palm of his hand and blinking, to show that he was nice as well as friendly.

He loved to talk, just so long as the talk was light and harmless. He told me about the tedium of his early life and what it was like to have nothing to do from one year to the next, apart from sitting straight and behaving oneself and trying to learn a better hand at golf and tennis, and to be less nervous when holding a gun or a fishing rod, or sitting on the back of a large horse. 'Oh, I was so *bored*!' he'd say, mopping his upper lip with his napkin. 'But I was fond of our Dalmatians. We had two beautiful Dalmatian dogs, which ran beside the carriage at night, so the driver could see his way in the dark, don't you know, and they were absolute poppets!

'Then I joined the Scots Guards and life picked up, picked up considerably. But my true calling was as an aide-de-camp. Funny title, *n'est ce pas?* I worked for the Governors of Kenya, Ceylon and Bermuda. Most of my duties involved arranging one thing or another: flowers, parties, little outings. Your grandfather said I was nothing but a glorified butler! Most unfair, especially since he was Prince Consort to your grandmother and never earned a penny in his life! Apart from the five years he spent in Burma and Ceylon, if you call that work.'

In the late 1950s Uncle Guy took early retirement and bought himself a house in Malta. There the social arrangements he was so good at continued to flourish and he shared domestic duties with a succession of gardeners: 'Such sweet boys! Absolute darlings, all of them!'

In 1963 he was diagnosed with throat cancer and told that if he wanted the best treatment he must go to the Chester Beatty Hospital in London. And that was why he came to stay with us. 'I shudder to think what it would have been like if I'd had to go to some dingy hotel in South Kensington,' he said.

His voice was very whispery, but that must have been because of the cancer. 'Can't sing like I used to, such a pity, but would do you a tinkle on the piano if you had one here. Jazz is my speciality, don't you know.'

He always wore his shirts open at the neck with a bright-red handkerchief tied round his throat. I thought this was in order to look dashing, but it must have been to hide the unsightly redness on his skin, caused by the radiotherapy treatment he was receiving.

Every morning during the week he'd set off for hospital around ten o'clock and be back in time for a glass of sherry before lunch. Then an afternoon nap and he was ready for tea and biscuits, closely followed by another glass of sherry in advance of supper.

My mother and Uncle Guy spoke a lot about 'the family'. I began to realize that they weren't referring to the changing and uncertain nucleus of individuals who sat round the table at Cambria Lodge or at my father's house a few streets away, but to an invisible army of blood relatives about whom I knew absolutely nothing. Suddenly we were drinking tea out of dear Aunt Ethel's silver teapot, which emerged from the dark cupboard where it had been hiding and took its place on a cork mat on the table. And we were drinking sherry from little glasses that were awfully like the ones that 'Cuthy

had at Weymouth', and wondering vaguely who had the Poussin now. My mother and Uncle Guy smiled at each other when they raised their glasses and said things like 'chin-chin' or 'bottoms up'.

⊙ ⊙ ◉ ⊙ ⊙

When the four of us sat round the dining-room table in the evening, my mother was a demure hostess, while Paul appropriated the unlikely role of pater familias, telling me to wash my hands and sit up straight and taking on the duty of carving the meat and pouring out the wine into well-polished glasses.

'Good evening, Guy. I trust you passed a pleasant day, yes?'

'Most agreeable, Paul, thank you. Usual stuff. Beastly hospital. But lovely weather, don't you think? Simply glorious!'

'Glorious!' echoed my mother, looking as though she might suggest that we all 'thank the Lord for what we are about to receive, amen', before beginning to eat, instead of launching full-tilt into the food on her plate without any all-clear signal needed.

Chatter chatter, clatter clatter and nobody transgressed the rules. Paul tended to talk about current political issues and Guy listened attentively even though he declared he hadn't a clue about politics: 'A great advantage for those of us who worked in government circles!'

'How was school today, my dear?'

'Very nice, thank you, Uncle Guy. We played tennis in the afternoon.'

'Ah, your grandmother and I used to be a jolly good doubles pair. She had a fiendish backhand! Hear she's got herself a Boyfriend. Foreign Office chap called Seymour-Williams. Longing to look him over if I get the chance!'

I knew that Blanche had recently started an affair with a widower, the only eligible male in the rather grand old people's residence where she was now living.

She had written my mother a letter in which she said how much fun Seymour-Williams was in bed: 'much better than your father!' she added, although there was a little potency problem and she wished she hadn't sold the rhinoceros horn paperweight, which might have done the trick, ground into a powder and drunk with milk. (I remembered that rhinoceros horn on its silver base. Blanche also had a hypnotically sinister elephant's foot, which had been hollowed out and given an ivory base, thus transforming it into an umbrella stand.)

'Oh yes,' said my mother, when Uncle Guy asked her about the Boyfriend. 'I hear he's absolutely sweet! Would you like some lamb, Guy dear? It should be nice and tender. And some for you Paul? Julia?'

Clatter clatter, chatter chatter. How I wished that all mealtimes could be so smooth, so harmonious and peaceful.

Because of the trouble with his throat, Uncle Guy had to eat with a teaspoon and it wasn't an easy process. 'Absolutely delicious!' he'd say wistfully, lifting the little spoon towards his mouth and gazing nervously at its contents. 'Can't taste a thing though!' and with a sigh he'd settle the teaspoon back in its place and put the tips of his fingers together to show he was deep in thought and had no time to eat anything more.

As his stay went on, Uncle Guy's afternoon naps got longer, his voice got more whispery, his neck got redder and his clothes flapped alarmingly around the narrow bones of his arms and legs. But his conversation remained unfailingly cheerful until the day he left to catch a plane that would carry him back home.

On 8 October he sent my mother a letter from 18 Buskett Road, Rabat, Malta.

My dear Rosalie,

Two Maltese from here came to meet me at the airport and also my Naval Surgeon. He is to check me each month and report back to London.

What a life! I still eat with a teaspoon, quite maddening! I am told it will take time. I found my garden really beautiful: the garden boy has been every week and sometimes more, bless him! Temperature here around 70F, however no blankets as yet on one's bed . . .

How is Julia? My love to her and remember me please to Paul. I hope he is fit and flourishing. Not much news as my life is still rather a routine and the wretched complaint makes speaking difficult. I am fed up with it!

Love to all of you. Au Revoir. Guy.

He died just before Christmas of that same year. One of his garden boys wrote to tell us the news. My mother showed me the letter, but I don't think she cried. It was as if Uncle Guy was a distant relative she hadn't seen since childhood. I don't think I cried either.

◦ ◦ ◉ ◦ ◦

March 1999

At six in the morning Rosalie rang the little bell I have given her, to save her the effort of calling out. I came to see what was the matter and she looked at me with her gentle face and said, 'It's all sleep,' and then she was asleep again. The doctor is coming today to see how things are going.

I have been looking at a photograph of my shell-shocked grandfather and wondering if he really did have the habit of climbing into bed with his eldest daughter, while his youngest daughter was somewhere in the room as a silent witness.

(From Julia's Notebook)

⋘ 19 ⋙

Driving to Majorca

My mother and I had three summer holidays together in the village of Deia in Majorca. For the first one, when I was nearly thirteen, we started in the same pension together, but then she said it would be better if she stayed somewhere else, so that she could be more independent and if she had a chance of going to bed with someone I wouldn't get in the way.

She went to bed with quite a few men during that first holiday. There was a black American writer, but her period started while they were making love and he didn't like that one bit.

'He was really angry,' my mother told me. 'He thought I should have warned him, but it was the sex that brought it on so suddenly. I threw the sheets in the bath and left before dawn. Perhaps you heard me come in.'

Then there was an American Abstract Expressionist painter, but that didn't last. 'They're all after the young girls!' said my mother despairingly, seeing him at another table in the café, deep in conversation with a teenager from Paris. The teenager had a room next to mine and the night before I had been kept awake by the methodical creak of the bedsprings and the sound of a rather worried man's voice saying, '*Viens, chérie! Viens! Viens!*'

My mother discussed the problem of men with her friend Binky, who had a terrible smoker's cough and a way of rolling her tongue round her lips while she was talking. 'We'd better get hold of the young ones then!' said Binky. 'Fight for our rights and fuck the kids!'

It seemed like a good joke at the time, until I met Binky's eldest son and we went swimming one moonlit night, the phosphorescence scattering its little fires on the surface of the water. We stood naked and shivering on the beach in the half-dark and he began to cry. I asked what was the matter and he said, 'I can't touch you! I can't touch any woman because I fucked my own mother, one night when we were both too drunk to care!'

⊙ ⊙ ⊙ ⊙ ⊙

I started keeping a diary in 1964, so the only written account I have is of our third and last holiday in Deia.

My mother and I had got used to the life in the village by then. She had learnt how to smoke dope, although it made her giggle uncontrollably. A group of friends had given me lessons on how to inhale cigarette smoke deep into the lungs, so now I was able to smoke dope as well. I drank a lot of wine and spirits, but I avoided taking LSD or any of the other drugs that were on offer.

That year we were leaving London on 23 July. I was taking a friend called Vivien with me, and my mother was accompanied by a man called Ian who had answered an advertisement she had put in the paper for someone who would like to share the driving through France and Spain and then share a holiday too. I suppose she and Ian must have met and assessed each other before setting off, even though it was obvious from the start that they weren't going to get along.

Ian was tall and plain, with thin hair and a strangely featureless face. He kept his shirt well tucked into his slacks and he polished his shoes and maintained a disconcertingly cheery manner at all times. He had been in the army until he took early retirement and he had recently lost his wife and step-son in a car accident. This tragic bereavement was the reason why he had decided he needed an adventurous holiday. 'Pastures new, that sort of thing!' he said hopefully, but without much conviction.

In my diary I recorded that he arrived at our house at seven o'clock in the evening. He was *slightly drunk* and he looked *pale and worried*. I don't know if he slept with my mother on the night before our departure, but the two of them certainly started the journey as if they were a couple. They even bickered like a couple.

We were planning to drive to Barcelona where we would take the ferry to Majorca. All four of us and our luggage had to fit into the limited space of my mother's Wolseley and there was a quarrel about Ian's suitcase, because it was clearly bigger than everyone else's.

'You don't seem to realize that we are going to a very bohemian Mediterranean village,' said my mother. 'People there hardly wear any clothes, so you simply don't need all this stuff! Jesus! I imagine you've even packed a pair of pyjamas!'

◦ ◦ ◉ ◦ ◦

My mother had sprained her ankle just a few days before our departure and it was still very swollen, so Ian was responsible for all the driving. My mother thought he drove much too fast and she sucked in her breath and fussed whenever he overtook another car.

We spent the first night in a pension just outside Chartres. My mother took me to one side and asked if I had noticed that Ian kept one hand in his trouser pocket while he was driving. 'He's masturbating!' she said.

I conveyed this information to Vivien and from then on the two of us in the back seat kept a careful watch on the movement of the hand in the pocket. We thought my mother might be right, but we weren't entirely sure.

A thunderstorm broke as we entered Chartres, but we managed to visit the cathedral. I was hugely impressed by the tall stone figures who guarded the great entrance porch with such stern authority and then, when we stepped across the threshold, the vision of the great rose window, bright with fragmented colours, swept me back into my old fervour of religious belief. *I would like to stay here for ever and dedicate myself to God,* I wrote with solemn conviction, before my mind was diverted and I turned my attention to other things.

Later that day we had a picnic of fruit and cheese by the side of a road, but there were flies everywhere and I thought there must be a rubbish heap nearby. We were close to a field of ripe sweetcorn waving sharp leaves into the sky and my mother, who always believed in living off the land, rushed off to pick some.

'But that is common theft!' said Ian when she returned triumphantly with a noisy bundle of corn.

'You're so narrow-minded,' she said and unpeeled one of the cobs. That reminded her of the joke about the young woman in a train who was preparing to eat a banana. 'Slowly, slowly, she peeled back the skin and then, suddenly, she bit off the tip of the banana and all the men in the train who were watching her said "Ouch!" and clutched at their cocks.'

Ian didn't find the joke funny.

⊙ ⊙ ◉ ⊙ ⊙

We stayed the night in a village called Argenton (if I can read my own writing). Ian drank a lot of wine and began to say how much he missed his wife, the tears welling in his eyes. My mother tried to get him to change the subject, but then he remembered that he missed his stepson as well and the evening became increasingly gloomy.

Vivien and I were not very nice to Ian, partly because we didn't think we liked him and also because he kept criticizing us. He told us that our hair was a mess, asked why on earth we put that ghastly black stuff round our eyes and said we shouldn't be smoking, not at our age. We discussed his faults when we were in bed that night. We also talked about how far we had gone with boys on a scale of ten and how soixante-neuf got its name and about the exciting thudding of desire when you kissed someone.

◦ ◦ ◉ ◦ ◦

The countryside was flat and hot. Miles and miles of cornfields and long avenues of plane trees with white bands painted on their trunks. The three of us women ganged up against Ian because he kept insisting on doing all the talking even though his French was awful and he found it funny to call the local people 'the natives'. He was determined to increase the average distance covered each day during our journey and so he delayed stopping to find somewhere to stay until late in the evening. When we protested, Ian said rather primly, 'I once flew seventeen hours in a bomber.' He and my mother were still sharing a bedroom, but she told me in a loud voice that they were no longer having sex.

We drove to the medieval fortress town of Albi to see the cathedral there, and I wrote a careful description of a painting of Hell in which the sinners were nailed to a spiked wheel and the blood gushed from their bodies in little fountains. We also had time for a Toulouse-Lautrec exhibition and I made a note that *his tarts are never cruel.*

Our next stop was Foix. My mother had often spoken of Foix: her Huguenot ancestors had once been the owners of the great castle that dominated the town, before they were forced to flee from persecution. They had carried a chiming clock with them when they fled, the same clock that now stood on our chest of drawers in Putney. My mother was eager to view the old family seat and to introduce herself to its new incumbents.

'*Je suis Rosalie de Meric,*' she announced to the woman who sold entrance tickets for the castle. '*Mon père était le Cont de Meric. Je voudrais parler avec quelqu'un.*'

The ticket lady was not impressed. No excited phone calls were made and no distant relative appeared to welcome us with offers of a private tour of the property. The people behind us in the queue became impatient and we left without seeing anything.

Finally we reached Barcelona and got the night ferry to Majorca. In the morning we drove the last lap of our journey along the rocky coastline, past Valldemossa where Chopin and George Sand had spent such a difficult winter, and then at last the road made a long swoop to the right and there was the village of Deia cradled by a ridge of biscuit-coloured mountains and facing the sparkling sea. Ian and my mother went up the hill to their pension and Vivien and I moved into ours. I washed my hair, but *it looked frightful* and I was in despair.

On Monday, 27 July we made our way down the narrow path through the olive groves and settled ourselves on the beach in the bright sunshine. Several of my mother's women friends were there and they all stripped to the waist, unashamed of their hanging breasts. Virien and I looked at them in horror and kept the tops of our tiny bikinis firmly in place. *They all looked haggard*, I wrote in my diary. *I never realized that Binky was so randy.*

That year I spent a lot of time with two new friends: an English prostitute called Sally, and Barry, her homosexual friend. Barry had enormous front teeth, black-rimmed spectacles and a great wave of floppy hair. Whenever we were in a public space together, he kept disappearing in order to engage in some brief sexual congress with a man who had caught his eye, only to reappear a few minutes later, rumpled and triumphant and ready for more of the same. All sorts of unlikely men were eager for one of these encounters and Sally would get very jealous of the speed and regularity of Barry's conquests.

⊙ ⊙ ◉ ⊙ ⊙

So here we are and it's 3 August, and tonight we are all going to a fancy dress party. Vivien has decided she wants to appear as Aphrodite and she even went by bus to Palma to buy some material for her diaphanous robe. I have no clear idea who I wish to be, but I plan to wear a few silk scarves.

Suddenly Barry bursts into our room in the pension to have what he calls some *girlie talk*. He tells me he just wants to *be himself* this evening and asks if I have any Tampax which he can use as earrings. I give him two and he pulls them out of their cardboard sheathes and colours them with a smudge of my red lipstick before dangling them over his large ears. He has already put on lots of Sally's make-up and tied his floppy hair into a ponytail. He takes off all his clothes and practises what he calls his Salome dance, tucking his cock between his legs and doing a sort of shimmy, then releasing his cock and shaking it about to make us laugh. Sally comes in without knocking. She has collected a bunch of ivy leaves and she wants to sew them on to her tiny bra and even tinier knickers. I try to help, but I am not much good at sewing.

My mother arrives and the room is getting crowded. She says she plans to wear one of her own pink nylon nightdresses with nothing on underneath and she will call herself *La Concierge à Minuit*. I tell her she is too old to parade her nakedness like that and we shout at each other and she stomps off back to her pension to get ready. I have no idea what has happened to Ian. I think he must have tired of these pastures new and caught a plane back to England.

Now the party is just beginning. My mother is already a bit drunk and when someone tells her he's thirsty, she pulls out one of her breasts and offers it to him. Several people tell me how lucky I am to have such a liberated mother and I smile and nod and keep silent, but when I get back to the pension in the early hours of the morning, I pour out a scribbled account of my thoughts about the evening:

> I hated the party. Ma got drunk and Sally and Barry were too high to care. Mummy was watching them all. Sally peed through her pants and did an erotic dance. The party broke up at 1 a.m. when the Fascist Police arrived with guns. We shook with fear in a room upstairs, 'dressed' in blankets. Ma kept on shouting and laughing . . . Sally disappeared and then at 3 a.m. we heard horrid sobbing and coughing noises in the street outside the pension and found her completely broken and dishevelled, having been sick while being raped by that man called Snooky.

○ ○ ◉ ○ ○

March 1999

Sometimes a sense of isolation, as I watch over this process of dying. But always there's Rosalie's unexpected gift of calm and acceptance, which makes everything all right.

I dreamt that I had a guinea pig living under my jumper, moving from back to sleeve, from front to side. It was a rather reassuring presence. We used to have them free-ranging in the garden when we lived on the farm.

(From Julia's Notebook)

Driving Back from Majorca

My mother was filled – I am tempted to say fuelled – by a competitive enthusiasm. She would challenge someone to a game of chess or draughts and be prepared to cheat in order to win; she saw nothing wrong in that. If a car overtook her when she was driving, she'd shout, 'You bastard! I'll show you!' and give chase, struggling to get ahead and waving in cheerful defiance if she succeeded.

Her enthusiasm could be very charming. Just as she had climbed the steepest granite rocks on that first weekend with my father, she would also go for a walk in a thunderstorm or a swim in the coldest of seas without a moment of hesitation. She swam in the North Sea in the month of October, just eighteen months before her death, and the only problem was that she kept losing her balance when she was knocked by a wave, so my son had to help her out. As a younger woman she'd never say no to a party or an unfamiliar drug or the offer of a sexual encounter; she once answered a rather dubious lonely

hearts advertisement and was perplexed when a gentleman arrived at the front door with a suitcase that contained nothing but a length of rope. 'He tied me to the bed before we made love,' she said. 'He found it fun, but I didn't really enjoy it.'

She was a wild and humorous and exciting woman to be with. She could be too aggressive and too overtly sexual, but many people enjoyed her company enormously and she got on especially well with insecure young men. They would confide their most private secrets to her, while she listened without comment and blinked her green eyes.

◎ ◎ ◉ ◎ ◎

Richard, an American painter whose leg had been withered by childhood polio, was just such a young man. He had recently finished his art school training and had come to Europe because of all sorts of troubles with his conservative family and with the US government and with drugs. He was also eager to find his own soul and he turned up in Deia, busy with the search.

Richard had a soft voice and a gentle handsome face and I thought he looked like the photograph of Jack Kerouac on the back of my copy of *On the Road*. I was so impressed by him that I was unable to say a word in his presence and I felt faint if he so much as looked in my direction. My mother got on with him at once and the two of them would talk about painting and childhood traumas, and they'd go sketching together.

My sense of the injustice of this situation came to a head at my sixteenth birthday party. I had the use of the house of one of my mother's women friends and I had invited anyone who wanted to come. We played Little Richard records and someone had a copy of 'Twist and Shout' by the Beatles and *the noise was fantastic and everyone screamed and yelled*. I wore a tiny red dress and danced as if my life depended on it. Sally did a strip, but everyone laughed at her and she suddenly seemed infinitely old, even though she can't have been more than twenty-five.

My mother had come along, '*to make sure everything was all right*'. She leant against a wall with a fixed smile on her face and a drink in one hand

and a joint in the other. She watched Sally doing her strip and me dancing the twist, and she watched all the other young people immersed in this world of loud music and dim lights. She came up to me and said, 'It's not fair! No one wants to dance with me! I feel left out!'

'You're too old, go away and leave us alone!' I replied, shouting through the noise. 'You look at us as if you're watching animals at the zoo!'

With those words, I released the catch that had been holding my mother back. She went and fetched Richard, who had been busy in a stoned conversation on the other side of the room. Holding him tightly by the hand, she grabbed hold of the hand of the boy I had been dancing with. She stood in front of me, flanked by the two of them. 'You are my witnesses!' she said, her voice breaking with emotion. 'Julia has told me I am not wanted here! Is she right? Do you think I should leave and go out into the night on my own, just because my daughter is so beastly to me?'

By now she was weeping openly and Richard, who could hardly stand, wrapped her in his arms and the two of them almost fell over. 'I love you,' he said. 'We all love you!'

'You see!' My mother turned to me in triumph. 'They want me to stay, even if you don't!'

I left at 2.30 a.m. in the dark and alone, I wrote, and I poured out my rage and despair into the pages of my diary.

◦ ◦ ◉ ◦ ◦

A few days later Richard was involved in a car crash. He and some friends had been driving very fast along the winding coast road and had hit a wall. No one was badly hurt, but the car was ruined. This meant he couldn't go to Morocco as he had been planning. 'Come back with us to London,' said my mother. 'I have a spare room you can rent.' So that was decided.

On 31 August the three of us were getting ready to leave. In my diary I wrote, *Slept till lunchtime and set off in rush and panic.* And then the pages remain blank until 3 October.

But I remember that journey back very vividly. I was sure that I was in love with Richard but I felt shy and unattractive and incapable of communicating with him. I had headaches and stomachaches and a weal on my leg where I had been stung by a jellyfish. I kept bursting into tears and then feeling even more unattractive with a snuffly nose and swollen eyes.

My mother and Richard sat side by side in the front of the car, talking to each other about painting and their childhoods, and I sat in the back and felt sick and lonely. When we stopped for the night, I said I didn't want to join them for a meal, so I wept in a dark room and they went out drinking and came back late.

Once we had got home, Richard moved into the little front room where Uncle Guy had stayed. He smoked a lot of dope and read books and made wild drawings on big sheets of flimsy paper.

I would sometimes knock on his door when I knew my mother was not in the house. I'd ask if he minded if I joined him for a while, then I'd sit in silence and watch him working, or present a little prepared speech about a book I had been reading, or about something important that I wanted to discuss. I remember asking him if he thought it was possible for a man and a woman to make love without being in love.

He gazed at me with his Jack Kerouac eyes and laughed, but there was no cruelty in his laugh. He said, 'Yes, it is possible. You don't need to be in love to do it. That's a pity, isn't it?'

Made brave by this conversation, I told him how frightened I was of so many things and he said, 'There is nothing to fear, except fear itself.' I wrote his words down on the cupboard by my bed and that seemed to help.

⊙ ⊙ ◉ ⊙ ⊙

During those months at the end of 1964, Barry and Sally were back in London. They tried to persuade me to sell my virginity, while I still had it to sell. Sally explained that she had spoken to someone, 'a harmless old man', who would pay me one thousand pounds for that little thing I would otherwise give away for nothing. I didn't like the idea, but I enjoyed talking to my two new friends.

Mostly we spoke on the telephone, but they came to the house a few times and once I went to see Sally at her flat in Mayfair. She showed me her collection of whips and masks and also a low glass table which she said was part of the job as well. She explained that some of her clients, the ones who paid the most, liked her to squat on the table and do a shit, while they lay underneath and watched. I found it a very odd idea.

While I was at her flat one of her clients arrived unexpectedly. He was a pleasant-looking middle-aged man in a suit and I wondered if he was a glass-table customer. When he saw that Sally was busy having tea with me, he said, 'Never mind, I'll come back later.'

Then two Americans phoned. They were staying at the Ritz and they wanted a bit of company. Sally took me along and the four of us ate lobsters and she put a handful of silver-plated cutlery in her handbag. The talk turned more and more to sex and I found the atmosphere a bit tense. One of the men asked how old I was. 'Fifteen,' I replied, aware that Sally was giving me a look of disapproval because I was about to spoil the fun.

'Jesus!' said the man. 'This girl's a minor! Get her out of here!' He ordered a taxi to take me home and, as a parting thought, gave me an illustrated book on sex techniques. 'You can learn a few things now and do them later,' he said in his best paternal manner.

⊙ ⊙ ◉ ⊙ ⊙

I stopped seeing Sally and Barry after that and I lost my virginity, unpaid, at a party in Cambria Lodge on 3 October. My mother was out for the night, but she had left her friend Beryl to keep an eye on things. Beryl got very drunk and walked from room to room, frightening people with her wine-stained lips and teeth.

At around midnight I was called down to the kitchen and she was standing next to the round table wearing nothing but a pair of stripy black socks. A nervous huddle of young men were looking at her with a mixture of horror and fascination.

'Come here, little Peter Rabbits!' she said, advancing towards them and holding out her arms with the offer of an embrace. She had a milk-white body and an enormous triangle of reddish-blonde pubic hair.

We managed to fit Beryl into the striped pyjamas she had packed in her overnight bag and someone persuaded her to swallow four sleeping pills with the help of a glass of wine. She said the night was young and she only wanted to dance, but after a while she agreed to go to bed in my mother's room. Her seven-year-old daughter was already there, fast asleep.

In the early hours of the morning I went to bed with the brother of my best friend Peggy and I lost my virginity. The sexual act impressed me very much. In my diary I wrote:

> One moment I nearly cried and the next I was smiling. I felt warm inside and contented and would have slept for hours, but I was terrified of Ma coming back and finding the two of us together.

By the following evening I had become even more lyrical:

> It's raining. The night is velvet black. I would like to run naked, swim in the shallow sea, wallow in the milk of moonlight, kiss rose petals, love God and the sun, dive through cold linen, lick rough apples, ride through fire and die at peace with myself . . . I feel sad and happy and hungry and tired and depressed, and my exams are in two weeks and all I can think about is SEX.

I rambled on for a few more pages about life at school and at home, and wrote a poem called 'Kiss the Dew of the Rose'. A few lines later I described the thrill of *two bodies working together, belonging completely to each other for a few moments of something like love.*

And then, on 28 November, my account of what happened in 1964 came to an abrupt end, apart from a few drawings of naked bodies, a list of *Poems for Girls for Dad* and something which I called *My Budget.* For that I had a column for *Got* on one side of the page and a column for *Spent* on the other. In the *Got* column I included thirty shillings, which was the money I made when I sold my stepmother's ring to a man in a second-hand furniture shop in Putney High Street.

The ring was from my stepmother's previous marriage to the Italian who had died when he was still so young. She explained that she was giving it to me because she didn't want my father to see it, in case he got jealous. It was a very thick wedding ring and the gold had a wonderful reddish gleam.

I thought it was much nicer than the one my father had given to my mother, the one she still wore even though she was no longer married.

⊚ ⊚ ◉ ⊚ ⊚

March 1999

I dreamt that my father had come to live with us here.

He'd got into the food cupboard in the kitchen and he was rummaging about among the bottles.

'What are you doing?' I asked him.

'Getting drunk,' he replied rather smugly and he leered at me as he finished a bottle of sherry.

(From Julia's Notebook)

21

Lodger Number Seven

From the spring of 1961, when my parents separated, until the autumn of 1964, we'd had five lodgers staying with us, six if you include Uncle Guy. My mother had declared herself seriously in love with three of these lodgers and she had flirted with the other two to test the water, as it were, but she hadn't been to bed with any of them. I know this because every time she did go to bed with someone she wanted to tell me all about it in great detail. 'I don't love him,' she'd say, 'but it was a good fuck. You'll understand more when you're a bit older and have started having sex.'

Everything changed when Geoffrey entered our lives. 'He wants to be our next lodger and I like him very much,' said my mother. 'Keep your fingers crossed. I think he might be my Mister Right.'

⊙ ⊙ ⊚ ⊙ ⊙

I'd met Geoffrey already. On the evening of 14 March 1964, my mother had organized a little supper party. Our first lodger Bob was invited, along with his new wife, Barbara. And Geoffrey was there as well. Paul did most of the cooking because, when he was in a good mood, he liked cooking and playing the host.

I hadn't seen Bob for ages and I was disappointed by how old and awkward he seemed, but I liked Barbara who had been my babysitter for a while when we lived in Leeds.

Geoffrey arrived on his own. He wore a soft suit that had dark-green stripes in it and a curious gleam to the cloth. I wondered if it was made of silk, or a silk and wool mixture. He had big teeth and big pale hands with long fingers and very long legs, which he folded into a sort of plait when he sat down.

We were gathered round the table. I tried to signal to my mother to stop chewing her fingers – it was a habit when she was nervous and it wasn't nice to watch. But when I gave her a meaningful stare, she looked away angrily and made a point of ignoring me.

The wine flowed and Paul got drunk but not impossibly so, and Bob started saying all sorts of provocative things about the 'savages' in Africa, so everyone turned on him and accused him of being a racist and a bigot. In my diary I described his views as *untrue and unfounded* and I was clearly very shocked because until then I had always thought he was very wise.

I liked my first impression of Geoffrey. He seemed quite shy and didn't join in the general babble of talk. When he did speak he used complex words such as 'pragmatic' and 'didactic' and 'exacerbate' and although I didn't always understand what he was trying to say, I had the sense that he was being very precise. Everyone stayed until 2.30 and seemed to enjoy themselves.

◦ ◦ ◉ ◦ ◦

After we returned from our trip to Majorca Geoffrey became our new lodger. He had a full-time job at an art school where he taught interior design and a flat somewhere in north London, which he was renovating, and a cottage in Wiltshire, so he was always away at weekends and often not around much during the week either. I don't remember him eating meals with us, so maybe he never did.

But then on 6 November, the day after her forty-seventh birthday, my mother came to talk to me. She was in a state of wild excitement. She had spent the previous night with Geoffrey. The sex had been wonderful. He had told her that he had never stroked such smooth thighs in all his life.

She went away that weekend and returned on her own, still happy, still elated. But there was something important she needed to explain to me. 'I have been thinking about you and Geoffrey,' she said. 'You see, he has always been attracted to really young women; his last wife was one of his students and he told me that he'd even like to fuck his own daughter, imagine that! This means that I don't want you to have *any* contact with him. I want you to keep out of sight as much as possible when he is in the house. I'm sure you understand.'

My life at home changed abruptly. Sometimes I was there on my own in the enormous silence of the rooms, or I was there with my mother and Geoffrey and I was not supposed to be seen – and if I was, everything I did or said was watched for signs of flirtation. If Geoffrey was away without my mother, she would be worrying about where he was and what he was doing and was he with a woman perhaps. Or she would be mooning around, talking about her new love.

◦ ◦ ◉ ◦ ◦

As each weekend approached, I always tried to persuade my school friend Peggy to come and stay with me. She was the only person to whom I could reveal my sense of isolation; not that we talked about it much, but she accepted the fact

of the empty house without asking questions. Sometimes Peggy's boyfriend John came too and then the three of us would enter a private bubble from Friday night until Monday morning, making strange meals from whatever food we found in the cupboards, drinking whatever there was to drink and rattling around in a curious state of anarchy, like the last survivors of a war in a ransacked town.

If the weather was mild we'd carry the old wind-up record player out into the garden and we'd wind it up and go through my mother's 78 rpm records. We'd play 'You're the Tops' or 'Dancing Cheek to Cheek' and we'd dress up in old counterpanes and dance on the lawn. When we were tired, we'd wander through the rooms deciding which bed we wanted to sleep in, and we'd sleep together, curled up like puppies. There was no sex, we'd just lie close, our voices floating in the dark, and one by one we'd fall asleep.

If Peggy couldn't come for the weekend I'd try to arrange to stay with her. She lived in a flat with her older brother and sister and her parents, who were friendly and distant and called me 'dear'. 'Hello, dear, how are you then? Mother well? Funny weather we've been having. Shall I make you a cup of tea?'

Whenever I was at Peggy's I'd hope to get a chance to make love with her brother. Never mind that he had a steady girlfriend and I knew he didn't love me and thought I was much too young for him. Never mind, either, that his parents must have guessed what was going on.

I'd creep into his room after everyone had gone to bed and stand there, hopeful and uncertain. Sometimes he would ask me to join him. We hardly ever spoke and I had no idea what his thoughts were or what he wanted from his life, but I worshipped his quiet face and his pale body and would do anything for the brief pleasure of nakedness and intimacy.

But although Peggy did her best to accommodate me weekend after weekend, she wasn't always available. There was no one else I felt easy with, so I was quite often on my own.

I began to have bad headaches. I kept being sick and I felt as if I were falling to pieces. On 12 January I wrote in my diary that I was out shopping with Peggy when I began to cry uncontrollably. I ran home, conscious of people staring and stepping to one side to let me pass. My mother was there and wanted to know what had happened, but I pushed her away. I went back to Peggy's house and that night I dreamt that my mother had died and I felt ashamed of the dream. I confessed to my diary:

> I feel an overwhelming hatred for Mummy. Feel she has betrayed me, but I can't understand how or why . . . everything she does seems dirty, guilty, horrible . . . Why should she need me? She has found more worthwhile pastures now. I'm so rude to her, so cruel, I don't mean it, I can't understand it. I'm frightened she'll get hurt and involve me.

On 15 January my mother went to the cottage with Geoffrey as usual. When she got back late on Sunday evening, I was really ill with a high fever. I stayed in bed for a week. My father came over every day and read me his new poems and talked about poetry and books. I tried to tell him what was happening, but he was too preoccupied with his own life and could only suggest that I go to see Doctor Kollestrom.

On 20 January I was invited to have lunch in our kitchen with my mother and Geoffrey, an occasion which I described as being *tense but pleasant*. Geoffrey made no attempt to draw me into the conversation and that was a relief. I decided that he was a *very sweet man, but Mummy worships him and she wants me to like him through her and not for himself.*

By 21 January my mother must have caught whatever illness I had and she took to her bed. Geoffrey stayed away and I must have been glad to feel that I was needed. I wrote that I was *being a housewife of sorts*, trying to keep things in order and making my mother soups and cold drinks, while all the time she moved in and out of the strange delirium of a high fever. She spoke about my father as if he were still living with us and about her childhood as if her sister were still alive. I remember her saying, 'The ships have all gone out to sea' and that frightened me because I thought that maybe my dream was coming true and she was going to die.

On 12 March I was invited for the first time to stay for a weekend at the cottage with my mother and Geoffrey and his two young children, a boy of three and a girl who was just two. My mother had arranged to go ahead in her car, and Geoffrey and the kids were due to arrive later.

⊙ ⊙ ⊚ ⊙ ⊙

The cottage was made of pale stone. It stood very close to the road. The rooms were neat and ordered, and they had a special sweet smell because the windows and doors had been made from cedar wood. The floors were made from a different and much darker wood that had a soft gleam to it. There was a beautiful rug from Afghanistan on the floor and interesting books in the bookcase. An orderly line of little brown mugs hung from hooks above the sink and I was told they had been made in Japan by a famous potter called Bernard Leach. My mother warned me to be very careful with them; Leach was dead and so the mugs were irreplaceable.

I went to bed in a room with two cots in it. Geoffrey arrived long after I had gone to sleep. A light went on as he came in carrying his two wailing and sobbing children. I kept myself hidden under the blankets while he lowered one and then the other into the little cots from which they couldn't escape. They were still crying inconsolably.

As soon as the light had been switched off, I emerged from my hiding place and lifted them out. They ran about in the half-dark, shrieking like

wild animals, but eventually they calmed down. I brought them into my bed and that night we all slept together. The little girl peed on me, but I didn't dare to move in case the wild rumpus might begin again. I dreamt that someone gave me a plate of uncooked eggs, but I couldn't eat them.

The next day Geoffrey worked at his desk, drawing up plans for the layout of someone's house. My mother went out sketching and I played with the children.

> They are always crying, wetting pants, asking 'Where's Daddy? Where's Mummy?' I felt I couldn't get angry because they are not to blame . . . I wanted to soothe away all their fears. Felt increasingly guilty about unfinished essay and also increasingly tired from perpetual strain of noise and tears. Arrived back home at 11.30. Decided not to go to school in the morning. Had splitting headache and felt depressed.

I don't have any clear recollections of the months that followed, but according to my diary I didn't go back to the cottage for a long time. I seemed to be living in a floating sadness in which nothing was real or tangible. Doctor Kollestrom was kind, but he seemed to be at a loss as well. I brooded about what I called *self death*, and wrote:

> I want to end, but haven't got the energy. Nothing exists, nothing matters ... Every weekend I get overcome by a desperate feeling of isolation and rejection. I search in my mind for an answer, for a friend, but everything I find is merely superficial. I have to be fond of my mother, simply because I have nothing else in this goddamn world to cling to ... Maybe I misjudge myself, but I am sure I would never have gone off and left Mummy alone, weekend after weekend ... I can't bear to live in this house alone any more.

On 6 June I went to a party given by Beryl, she of the stripy black socks. There were some kids of my age there, but they sat around looking very solemn and serious, keeping an eye on the adults who were getting increasingly drunk and noisy.

I met a blind man, holding a glass of whisky in one hand and a white stick in the other. We talked about poetry until his wife came up and said, 'Goodness! You two are getting on well!' She leaned towards me and tried to kiss me on the lips. Then she whispered loudly in my ear, 'You can have him, ducky! He's useless in bed.' The blind man smiled when he heard her saying this and I suddenly didn't like him any more.

I went to talk to a woman called Rosalind. She was an old friend of my father's and she had always been kind to me. She once read fairy stories to me all through the night while my parents were screaming at each other in the room next door. Every time I was distracted by the noise and thought I must do something to help, she steered me back into that other world, which was also frightening but in a different way.

I told Rosalind about my battles with my mother, my loneliness, my despair. She listened carefully and seriously. She had a cascading river of reddish gold hair and huge sorrowful eyes. Her voice was as deep as the sea, but very gentle. When I had finished speaking, she paused and said very simply, 'Stick with it. You just need to keep going for another two years and then you can make a break. Unharmed!'

I wrote her words down when I got back that evening. I thought she was right. Two more years to go and then the break.

⊙ ⊙ ◉ ⊙ ⊙

Four days after that party my mother came up to my room looking very sad and grim. She told me that 'in order to purge himself from the past and to stop living a lie' Geoffrey had decided he no longer wanted to make love with her. He had assured her that they could have 'a mental relationship which is as close as the physical', but I knew that wouldn't work, even if she had been persuaded it might.

> Mother is upset. The pretty flowers and wedding bells and birdsong have all dropped and drooped, so fasten your safety belts, depressions are imminent and the clouds will be heavy and black.

In a way, the news must have pleased me because I thought it meant that Geoffrey would leave and my mother would spend more time at home and she and I could reach some sort of understanding, while I *stuck with it* until I was ready to make my break. *Unharmed.*

But nothing happened. Geoffrey still slept in my mother's bed and they both went off to the cottage most weekends. The only change was the increase of tension.

My mother now lived in a state of permanent obsessive jealousy. When Geoffrey was in the house she padded after him from room to room, telling him how unhappy she was. If he came back late from work she was convinced he had been 'doing it' with one of his students, whom she referred to as his 'dolly birds'. She opened his letters, listened to his phone conversations and became hysterical if he had contact with any woman, no matter what age she was. He responded by refusing to talk to her for days on end and if she shouted at him he would simply walk out of the house and slam the door shut after him, leaving her jabbering with desperation.

I watched from a distance. This was much more frightening than the troubles with my father, because there at least I had the power to pacify or protect. And now that the sexual bonds between my mother and Geoffrey

had been broken, she saw me more and more as a potential rival. In my diary
I described a particular quarrel which

> started about my school work and her lack of interest . . .
>
> Got on to the subject of Geoffrey and his kids and why I can't have him
> as a father figure: because she doesn't want me to have anything to do with
> him . . . In her pacifying, unfeeling, school ma'am voice, she tells me I can
> get to know him when I am 'a little older and a little wiser'. Shit to that!

◦ ◦ ◉ ◦ ◦

In the summer of 1965, my mother wanted to have some time on her own
with Geoffrey, 'to sort out the relationship'. She arranged for me and a school
friend to accompany Beryl and her young daughter on holiday in southern
Spain. We went by car and the journey took us almost a week. Every morning
Beryl bought herself a litre bottle of red wine and all through the day she
drank as she drove and the more she drank the less pressure she put on the
accelerator, so that by the evening we were travelling at around fifteen miles
per hour.

Beryl knew Spain quite well and she had three words in Spanish: *vamos
a ver* – let's see. She said this had always been enough of a response for any
situation and perhaps she was right. In Murcia a man in a café became too
eager with her. '*Vamos a ver!*' said Beryl and punched him on the nose. In the
gipsy village of Guadix we all got very drunk waiting for an impromptu
flamenco show to get started and a young girl came up to me and presented
me with a little naked baby and then walked off, as if the child was now
mine. '*Vamos a ver!*' said Beryl, snatching the sleeping baby and dumping it
in the arms of a man who was about to play the guitar.

We finally arrived at the little fishing village of Torremolinos, which was in
the process of being turned into a vast tourist resort, the concrete carcasses of
new hotels sprouting up all along the beach. In Torremolinos we stayed in a
pension and met Beryl's old friend Elpie who had just been deserted by her
husband and was very angry and keen to get laid, 'to teach that bastard a
lesson'.

Elpie took us to meet a Spanish painter called Enrique. He lived in a tiny studio apartment on a street crammed with noisy cafés. He couldn't speak a word of English, but it didn't seem to bother him and he filled our glasses and showed us his dark paintings full of mysteriously transforming figures. He was very thin with big eyes and a quick, wild laugh, and when he shook my hand and leant towards me, he smelt of honey.

As we were about to leave, my friend looked briefly at Enrique and announced she wasn't coming with us, she was staying here for the night. She returned in the morning, rumpled but pleased with herself. I was deeply impressed by such determination of purpose.

We were back in the studio the next evening and inspired, I suppose, by my friend, I let it be known that this time, I was going to stay the night with Enrique. In my memory it was just the two of us in a room smelling of turpentine and Ducados cigarettes, although in fact Elpie was there as well, having rather grumpy sex on a mattress on the floor with another Spanish painter, whose name and face I have forgotten. Such a distraction didn't bother me and by the morning I knew I had fallen in love.

I went back to the pension to collect my few belongings and moved in

with Enrique. My school friend returned to England by plane and Beryl and her daughter made the slow drive home, while I settled into my new life. One night I dreamt that my face had melted like hot wax and in the morning I went to stare into the bathroom mirror, searching for proof that I had now changed beyond recognition.

The fact of having no common language was not a problem. I liked being free of the restriction and confusion of words. I was happy to sit for hours in a vague dream watching Enrique working on a canvas and when I needed a change, I'd go and stare at the sea. I never doubted that I would stay with Enrique for the rest of my life, and maybe it was that certainty that gave me the freedom to decide to complete my school exams first. I could begin the rest of my life a bit later. By now Enrique and I could communicate enough for us to promise that we would be together again very soon and with that we said goodbye.

⊙ ⊙ ◉ ⊙ ⊙

My mother had arranged to meet me at the airport, but she was four hours late. When she finally arrived she didn't seem at all pleased to see me. She didn't ask how I was, or if I had enjoyed my holiday, but told me that Geoffrey was still at Cambria Lodge and still not having sex with her.

None of this bothered me any more. I felt like a creature from another planet. My future was securely planned and my mother's problems were no concern of mine. As proof of my love I was carrying a thin layer of my lover's sperm, stuck to my belly like egg white, and I kept postponing having a bath because I didn't want this tangible evidence of passion to be dissolved and washed away. Maybe it also felt like a protective coat, a magic charm that would keep me safe in a dangerous house.

I was back at school the day after I got home. I kept myself very busy and private and hardly spoke to my mother. Geoffrey was around, but I avoided him. In my diary I wrote that I now found him *silly, poofy, artificial and spoilt.*

But during those first few days I did have a brief and very disturbing confrontation with him. He was standing nonchalantly in the open doorway that led to my mother's studio and I had the feeling that he had been waiting for me and had planned this encounter.

He looked at me with a sad and slightly quizzical expression and he said, 'I envy you your euphoria!' He spoke very clearly but almost in a whisper, even though there was no one near. It was as if he was confiding an intimate secret. I realized that some sort of dangerous border had been crossed. It felt as though he wanted me to know that he had seen the sperm, gleaming on my belly.

◎ ◎ ◉ ◎ ◎

March 1999

Rosalie has gone to the local cottage hospital to have another blood transfusion.

The phone rang at three in the morning – how strange it is to be pulled out of deep sleep like that. A nurse said my mother was in a bit of a state and asked if I could come and be with her.

I went in at once. She'd had a nosebleed and other troubles resulting from the blood transfusion, but she was very calm and welcoming. The nurse made me a bed of cushions on the floor. Rosalie began to talk, her voice slow and quiet.

(Fax to Herman)

22

Private

I have just found another of my diaries from those last years I spent at home. It was hidden away at the bottom of a chest filled with typewritten manuscripts and research files. I must have put it there ages ago and then forgotten all about it.

It's a hard-backed blue notebook, a bit smaller than A4, and I have written my name on the cover, alongside the word PRIVATE in capital letters. On the first page I have made several attempts to draw the back view of a very thin naked man and these drawings must be the remembered image of my Spanish lover Enrique. On the second page there is a strange totem-pole doodle, done in black and green felt tip.

⊙ ⊙ ◉ ⊙ ⊙

Then it is Tuesday, 29 November 1965 and I am seventeen years old and lying in bed with a fever. I have just received a letter from Enrique telling me that he is living with another woman and so he won't be coming to live with me in England after all. I am feeling sad and lonely and odd, and I can't sleep at night, even though my mother has been giving me sleeping pills. I have found a new quotation to write on the cupboard beside my bed: *Man has places in his heart which do not exist and into them enters Suffering, in order that they might exist.*

The fever continued for ten more days and I stayed in my room with the curtains drawn and filled the pages of my diary with what I called *a continuous stream of self-interrogation.* I wrote numerous complicated letters to Enrique, which I then translated into pidgin Spanish with the aid of my

Collins Little Gem Dictionary. It was true that he and I had only spent five weeks together, but I felt that he held my life in his hands and I wanted to explain this fact to him, without being too demanding or admitting how much he had hurt me. I tended to address him in a rather grand oratorical style, but most of the letters were never sent.

Alongside the sadness and the sense of loss, my mind in the pages of this diary kept spinning with thoughts of sex. I wrote a long and lyrical description of making love, which opened with: *Do you remember the nights?*

> . . . when you thought you would die if you felt any more and you were drugged with feeling and still you felt more. And breathing was so hard and heavy and intoxicating like gas and you felt yourself falling head down, climbing so high and then the fall and when you stopped falling, he held you still.

Eventually the fever passed and by 9 January I was mending my broken heart in the arms of a young man called Theo. He was only a year older than me and he had straight black hair cut in a Beatle bob and there was something funny about his teeth, but I can't remember what; maybe a gap between the two front ones.

Theo played the guitar and sang the blues in a high nasal voice. He sat on my bed in that upstairs room with the curtains drawn and he sang,

> When you go to Tallahassee,
> Put some money in your shoes,
> Cos those Tallahassee women
> Sure gonna mess with you!

He sat there with no clothes on and his eyes closed and he sang,

> This is the story of Willy the Weeper,
> Now Willy the Weeper was a Midnight Creeper!
> He had a habit and he had it bad,
> Let me tell you 'bout a dream he had:
> Deedadadadeeda, deedadadeeda, dadadeeedadadadidada!

Theo smoked a huge amount of dope and I began smoking too. He'd turn up most evenings and we'd smoke dope and make love and smoke some more dope and make some more love and then he'd sing a bit and smoke a bit and the dawn would be lifting across the rooftops and I needed to think about getting ready for school.

Theo took me to see some friends of his who were all heroin users. As always when I was frightened of something, I tried to dilute the danger by describing it. I wrote that I saw

> One boy, no underpants, no socks, yellow concave teeth that seemed to be soft and soluble, dark folds of skin around his eyes and an apology of a smile and a whimper of a laugh. And his girlfriend who looked naked, despite her faded blue nightgown.

We all sat together in a room and I watched as a young man squirted the blood from his syringe up to the ceiling and someone made a joke about blood being wet. Then there was talk of broken needles and a guy who pumped the stuff back and forth into his arm, pump, pump, pump, for over an hour.

I came home on my own at four in the morning. I hadn't tried the heroin offered to me, but I was very stoned and my body seemed to separate itself from my mind, so that I was watching the stranger who was me pacing around my room, shivering on the floor, being sick in the basin. My heart was racing at different speeds and I was sure I was about to die. I decided that if I didn't die in the night, then I would kill myself in the morning.

But then when the morning came, instead of taking my own life, I took out my diary and wrote down what I was feeling:

> I want, need, isolation, complete solitude. Keep away, get back, leave me alone. I hate every one of you for what you are and for what I am. No wish to grow older. No wish to be. No wish. Block out feelings. Shut off emotions.

Throughout this time my mother was mostly at home, getting on with her daily life, and she apparently didn't notice anything; not the man in my room, or the sweet smell of marijuana that accompanied him, not the sound of me coming back in the early hours of the morning and pacing the floor and vomiting.

She was still very busy with Geoffrey. When he was in, she would pad after him like a puppy and when he was out – and he was often out all night – she tumbled head first into despair and she would go round and round in small circles of jealous imagination. 'Where do you think he is? Did you see how he looked at that picture in the paper of a girl in a miniskirt? Perhaps he's making love to one of his students! He might be doing it right now! Oh, I can't bear it! Do you think he loves me, I mean *really* loves me?'

And then one morning she came rushing into my room to announce that they had done it again! A few weeks later she had missed her period and was convinced she must be pregnant. 'You don't seem very happy for me!' she said. 'Don't you like the idea of having a little baby brother?'

I watched the two of them and made notes about their disparate characters, their lack of communication, their difficulties. They were very uneasy in each other's company; Geoffrey tended to become increasingly nervous and flippant, while my mother became more hopeless and helpless, groaning out loud with her longing to be loved. One day Geoffrey announced that he wanted to move to America, 'to start a new life', he said.

'But what about me?' wailed my mother, her voice rising in panic. 'Can I come too? Oh please say I can come too!'

'I'll be going on my own,' said Geoffrey and walked out of the room.

⊙ ⊙ ◉ ⊙ ⊙

I despised Geoffrey and felt he kept making a fool of himself, but my rage against my mother was growing deeper and more entrenched. Then something happened and the rage turned into a cold hatred.

Geoffrey was out for the evening and my mother was feeling desolate and abandoned. She wanted to talk to pass the time away. She told me the sex had stopped again and asked if I had any idea how important sex was to someone like her. 'That explains why I feel so insecure,' she said, a note of pleading in her voice, a dreamy look gathering in her eyes. She was sitting beside me on my bed, two girls together.

'You never tell me anything,' she said. 'I didn't even know that you had lost your virginity until a year after it happened. I have no idea what you get up to. When did you last do it? Tell me that at least!'

I was very taken aback.

'Oh, come on, darling!' She looked really hurt. 'Tell me when it was, Mummy wants to know! In the summer? Last month?'

'Four days ago,' I said, regretting my words as I spoke them.

She was startled. 'Goodness and I never knew! Did you enjoy it?'

'Yes, thank you.'

'And what sort of contraception did you use?'

I told her I had used the withdrawal method.

She let out a gasp of disbelief and looked at me as if I were on the brink of being devoured by a monster and she was the one who must rescue me. 'Withdrawal? You must be mad! You might be pregnant! We've got to do something and quick!'

She grabbed hold of my hand and led me down to the bathroom. By now the urgency had turned into a sort of hysteria. 'Get undressed!' she ordered. When I hesitated she screamed, 'Do as you are told, you stupid girl! I'll be back in a minute!'

She left the room and I took off my clothes: shoes and tights, jumper and bra, skirt and knickers, or was I wearing the jeans I had so carefully frayed round the hem at the bottom?

The bathroom was a bleak, cold place at the best of times. I stood on the cold floor, shivering and apprehensive.

I heard my mother thundering down the stairs and then she was back. I had not stood naked before her since my breasts had taken shape.

To my horror I saw she was holding that orange-and-black contraption, the thing she had shown me when I was much younger. She pulled up her sleeves in a businesslike manner. She filled the basin with warm water, then rubbed a bar of soap between her hands, turning the water milky. She separated the orange rubber ball from the black, knobbed stick, held it in the basin and squeezed it so that it made gurgling, belching noises as it filled itself with the soapy water. She fitted the two parts back together. 'Get in the bath!' she said.

I was crying now because I was very afraid. The white enamel was cold under my bare feet.

She handed the thing to me. 'Come on, stop fussing! Push it up your fanny, or do I need to do it for you? That's right, now squeeze! And again!'

I did what I was told and committed what seemed like rape upon myself, while my mother watched me, implacable and determined. Even I realized that pumping soapy water into my vagina was ridiculous; you couldn't wash sperm away such a long time after the event.

Years later, I tried to remind my mother of this incident. Her face went very blank and her jaw became set, as it did when she felt she was under attack. 'What a terrible thing to accuse me of!' she said in a wounded voice.

And I faltered and felt that perhaps I had got it wrong and this story was indeed some figment from my own cruel imagination. Until just recently, when I read the tight-lipped, angry account of what happened in the diary I had forgotten about.

That night I was again ill with a high temperature. In the morning when my mother came to see why I hadn't got up for school, I was so shocked by her face and the hostility it contained that I screamed and told her to go away and leave me alone.

She went downstairs and telephoned my father. She said I was being hysterical again and she really didn't know what to do with me. So an appointment was quickly made with Doctor Kollestrom.

I told the doctor that I thought I was splitting in half, but I don't remember if I dared to tell him about the scene in the bathroom. Even thinking of it made me ashamed. He put the tips of his fingers together and pursed his lips and coughed and nodded his head and did his best to reassure me.

I avoided having any contact with my mother for several weeks, but I began to talk to Geoffrey whenever I had the opportunity. *He needs to be understood by me*, I wrote in my diary, *because I see him trapped and humiliated by Mummy.*

⊙ ⊙ ◉ ⊙ ⊙

March 1999

Several days have passed without me being in touch.

It's been a sort of descent into Hell. Rosalie had to be rushed to the big hospital in the middle of the night because she was haemorrhaging after the blood transfusion. They filled her with drugs and rushed her along bright corridors and all sorts of strangers poked and prodded and they managed to stop the bleeding, but the drugs and all the unfamiliar faces left her in an awful panic.

They brought her back this morning and I went to see her and Natasha [my daughter] *came too. Rosalie was still very querulous and frightened. She kept saying, 'I felt so vulnerable! I felt so vulnerable!'*

She said that when she came round, she didn't know where she was or even who *she was and people kept treating her as if she were a demented old lady and she thought she had gone mad and been put in a lunatic asylum.*

We sat beside her and sang songs to her and stroked her face and her arms, and slowly she calmed down. I have promised that she won't be left alone again, not for a minute.

'Not for one minute?'

'Not for one minute!'

'Oh good,' she said, 'then everything will be fine, won't it?'

(Fax to Herman)

23

A Little Family

June 1966 and I had almost finished school, and I had a place at a university far from home, in the north of England. There was just one more summer to go and then I felt the cords would be cut and my childhood would be over. I thought of hitch-hiking through France with Peggy and some other friends, and I also thought of visiting Enrique in Spain and never mind that he was living with a new woman. But then my mother invited me to come on holiday with her and Geoffrey.

She said it was very important I come. She had realized that the reason the relationship was not going well was because Geoffrey needed a sense of family. I must be his daughter and then she could be his wife and he would feel he truly belonged with us. Bonds would be cemented, troubles would be over, the sex would return and Geoffrey would stay with her for ever and ever. 'Do it for me,' she said. 'After all, you're leaving soon. Do it to make me happy.'

And so I agreed, although I still don't quite know why, and the plans for this unlikely holiday began to take shape.

○ ○ ◉ ○ ○

My mother arranged to rent a little house on the Mediterranean island of Formentera. She said she had chosen the house because it was nice and remote and far from any villages; just right for the three of us. 'We'll get really close,' she said with confident enthusiasm.

Geoffrey's two young children, as well as his eldest son, who was a few years older than me, and his eldest daughter, who was a year younger than me, would join us later and of course they would add another dimension to this newly blossoming family.

Instead of flying, or driving straight down to Barcelona and catching a boat there, Geoffrey decided he wanted to do a great loop via Portugal. We would take the car to Portsmouth and get on board a cargo ship that stopped at Brest and Bilbao and La Coruna on the western tip of Spain and then went down

the Atlantic coast as far as Vigo. From there we would drive through the Alto Douro mountains, which he had heard were well worth seeing, before re-entering Spain, zigzagging our way to the port of Valencia and catching a boat to Ibiza and then another one to Formentera. We were going to avoid main roads and keep to the high ground whenever possible. Geoffrey expected the journey would take about two weeks, maybe a bit more.

I have no recollection of the boat trip. I don't even know if the Bay of Biscay was rough, but I remember when we stopped at La Coruna I walked past a shop that had a painted wooden saint for sale in the window. I thought how nice it would be to have such a saint standing in the corner of my room and I was startled because I wasn't imagining my room at home, but a room in the future, a place I hadn't yet seen.

In another shop I bought a watering pot made of white clay. I showed it to my mother and she said I must have chosen it because the spout was like a penis and the bit where you put the water in was just like a vagina. In that case she might as well have the pot as a present, I told her, and she kept it for all the years of her life, but who knows, maybe she forgot where it came from.

In Vigo we climbed into Geoffrey's green Austin mini-van and off we went. The weather was relentlessly hot and the back seat where I was sitting was crowded with luggage. Geoffrey said he wanted to explore the region and so we'd follow roads that weren't going anywhere in particular. I couldn't get much of a view of the landscape and I passed the time singing sad folk songs about dead lovers and broken hearts. I knew dozens of verses for dozens of songs, even though the tunes often escaped me. I was particularly fond of 'The Unquiet Grave', in which a man asks if he can climb into the coffin beside the body of his dead beloved:

> Is there any room at your head, my love?
> Is there any room at your feet?
> Is there any room about you at all,
> For me to lie down and sleep?

My mother was so eager to please that she chattered about anything that came into her head. 'Oh look, there's a man! He's doing up his flies, he must have pissed against the tree. Is that a dog in the field? No it's a bucket!'

Geoffrey insisted that he do all the driving. He smoked cigarettes, one after the other, and hardly ever spoke. The atmosphere was very tense and I kept wishing I had the courage to get out of the car and go off somewhere on my own.

⊙ ⊙ ⊚ ⊙ ⊙

One evening we were sitting in awkward silence at a restaurant when my mother suddenly began to drink a lot of wine. She drank until she had broken down some sort of emotional barrier and then she threw an empty glass at the wall, so people turned to stare. She let out a great rumbling moan: Geoffrey didn't love her any more and she couldn't bear it, the pain was too much. She asked him why he was so cruel and when he remained silent, she began to shout and weep at the same time.

I had a red notebook with me and on its first pages I described with extraordinary coldness and detachment what had happened:

> Her suffering seemed self-indulgent, her tears nothing more than indecent exposure. We are all isolated. Each one of us is drowning and cannot save the others.

Geoffrey changed after that evening. Now, whenever we stopped somewhere on our slow and laborious journey, he made a point of noticing every pretty girl who walked by and he was excessively charming to waitresses and shopkeepers and any other woman he came into contact with.

My mother was quick to respond. 'I saw how you looked at her when she asked if you wanted anything else! I saw what was going on in your mind when you paid the bill!'

I suppose that was when I began to take more notice of him. In a way, he was just like me, because everything he did or said was being given a sexual slant. I felt he was being bullied, just as I had been bullied. And probably I also wanted some of the compliments that were being handed out so freely to all the pretty girls.

In my most intense and serious manner, I began to talk to him about books. I asked if he had read the Anna Livia Plurabella speech in *Finnegans*

Wake, and what did he think of the symbolism of the whale in *Moby-Dick*? Did he prefer T.S. Eliot to W.B. Yeats? I learnt that he had just finished reading *Steppenwolf* by Hermann Hesse and this delighted me because I had just finished it too. I told him he was in many ways very like the Steppenwolf character.

A new and dangerous game began to unfold. My mother sat to one side and listened to these earnest conversations. She said she really admired me and envied me, because I knew how to talk to Geoffrey and she didn't. She also said that although I might think I was talking about literature, he was certainly only talking to me as a form of flirtation. I disagreed with her and the more I disagreed, the closer I felt to Geoffrey.

◦ ◦ ◉ ◦ ◦

In 1993, when I was trying to shake off some of the burdens of the past, I wrote to my mother to ask her how she would describe my relationship with her when I was a teenager, and her relationship with Geoffrey while he lived with us, and most especially during that interminable car journey. I threw away her reply almost at once, because it upset me, but she kept a copy of it among her papers.

In a very arch tone she told me that she and Geoffrey were always very happy together, that they had never quarrelled about anything and any minor difficulties that arose between them were diffused by what she called *sadness and hope*. She said she certainly had *no idea* that he was interested in me sexually, either before or during that fateful holiday, but of course I was very angry and unstable, so I might well have imagined such things.

But then, close to that same letter, I came across a couple of scribbled pages, written on Friends of the Samaritans headed notepaper and dated 2 June 1993. My mother was clearly busy with her own private memories of that car journey, even though she had no intention of sharing her thoughts with me.

She wrote:

It was Geoffrey's bland statement, one night in a cheap hotel, when he said, *Of course I want to fuck your daughter!* It was that remark that set me in a panic. From then on the flirtation became a frightening threat, driving me to hysterical protest.

So, there we were in the green mini-van and our journey was just beginning. In my red notebook I kept a list of the places we saw and where we stayed:

Sunday. Vigo Castle
Villa Real. Post Office
Coimbra. Slept out
Castel Blanca
Tejo
Guadalupe. Night drive via Córdoba

I only paused to describe one particular night we spent in a house in the Alto Douro mountains.

Geoffrey had kept on driving until it was very late. He finally stopped the car by a solitary house at the bottom of a steep hill. People came bursting out of the house and crowded around the car, the adults laughing like children, the children staring at us with adult solemnity. They led us into a big room lit by oil lamps, and chickens and dogs and cats milled around on the floor, which was covered in a layer of rustling straw. A long table stood in the centre of the room and there was a double bed at the far end.

A woman was lying on the bed and we were invited to go and see her. I understood that she had fallen and hurt her back. She was large and fat and about the same age as my mother, and she looked very happy, even though she was clearly in pain.

The people made gestures to ask if we were hungry and when we indicated that we were, someone grabbed a chicken and brought it to us dangling by its feet, its eyes wide with apprehension. It was placed on the table and its head was chopped off and the warm body was plucked and cut into pieces. Once the chicken had been cooked, the family gathered around to watch us eating, following each mouthful with their eyes.

Later in the night the whole family found places to sleep, the children piling into a heap on the floor covered by blankets. My mother and Geoffrey were given a bed in a cubicle built into the wall and I had a little bed in the

main room. I lay awake, listening to the movements of the house: subdued voices, bodies turning and breathing. I heard the woman with the bad back being joined by her husband and when their breath became heavy I realized that they were making love.

On the next morning I went to do a pee and was shocked to discover a flat black insect nestled among my pubic hair. Before we left my mother took a photograph of me standing by a fountain. Looking at the photograph now I can see that the water pipe resembles nothing so much as a stiff penis.

I think it was during that day's driving that a lamb jumped out from the side of the road and Geoffrey hit it, so that it was lifted up and thrown into the ditch. I shouted at him to stop the car, but he just went on. I looked back and saw the lamb's body twitching in the dust and I suddenly hated this cruel man who seemed to have his own plans and wouldn't listen to anyone.

It was then that I saw he was always watching me in the rear-view mirror. And when our eyes met he would smile.

A few nights later he and my mother made love noisily in the room next to mine. 'It's the first time in five months!' she said tearfully. 'You must be pleased for me!'

In my notebook I wrote:

Why does Mummy have to tell me how many times she had made love to
Geoffrey? Why does she have to say I want the same? Why do I flatter his
fucking ego, when I don't want to flatter? Why must I be a voyeur to
others and never true to myself?

⊙ ⊙ ◉ ⊙ ⊙

The rented house in Formentera was a low, modern building, painted white
and standing all on its own in a bare field. On the day of our arrival, two very
forlorn and mangy dogs arrived at the door, asking to be fed. I welcomed
them like old friends, christened them Perdido and Mulo and, once I had
provided them with bread and cheese, they followed me everywhere, only
distracted in their devotion when they needed to sit down and scratch.

The rest of our 'little family' was due to arrive in a couple of weeks, but
for the moment the three of us were on our own. We sat in bars and swam
in the sea and sat in more bars and drank wine and brandy, and in the
evening we gathered round the table in our holiday house and made attempts
at conversation, while the dogs waited for scraps. Sometimes we played chess.
One evening we each chose a section from one of Eliot's poems in the *Four
Quartets* and read it aloud.

I was aware that Geoffrey was slowly building up his attentions towards
me. He would light a cigarette for me without me asking for one and then
he'd lean forward and place it between my lips. He'd say little cryptic things
to me, quietly, when my mother wasn't in earshot. He said it was important
to live one's life with 'honest selfishness' and I thought I agreed, even though
I wasn't quite sure if I had understood. He said, 'What a beautiful belly you
have. How I would love to kiss it!' And I wasn't sure about that either.

My mother must have noticed what was going on because one day she
asked me if I was now aware of what she called 'my power', and how did I
intend to use it? She said that she 'admired and envied' me and that pleased
me in a way, but it also made me feel more lonely than I had imagined
possible.

Then Geoffrey asked if he could kiss me. He made the request with the same whispered intimacy as when he had said that business about envying my 'euphoria'. So I let myself be kissed, one night in the back of the car.

I can remember the awful shock of seeing his old face bearing down on me, the smudged darkness under his eyes, the lines in his cheeks and across his forehead, the triumphant way he smiled. But I felt curiously liberated by the act. Now, when my mother accused me of flirting, I no longer had to protest my innocence because I had finally done what had been expected of me. It was quite a relief.

As soon as I was back in the house, I told my red notebook what had just happened and I asked myself if this meant that I was falling in love with Geoffrey.

○ ○ ◉ ○ ○

My mother came into the room and saw me writing and she snatched the notebook and began to read it. She didn't pause over the pages in which I'd written that I wanted to die because I felt so sad and lost. She didn't notice that I also declared myself in love with Enrique and Rowland and someone called David and maybe Theo too, even though he smoked so much dope.

She went on flicking through my tangled account of the last few weeks until she found the one entry she had been looking for. In triumph she read out my own words.

I remember standing up on the wobbly bed and swaying like a snake, and like a sibyl prophesying doom, I told her that all she cared about was sex and she didn't care about me and I hated her. I told her that the only way I could have been a good daughter in her eyes was if I was a mongoloid child who could never grow up and become a woman, and with that I spat in her face. By now Geoffrey was also in the room. He stood there in the background and watched.

Next morning I packed my belongings into a straw shoulder bag and set off to see Enrique, who had no idea that he might be expecting me. In my red notebook I wondered what I would *think of all this, twenty years hence.*

○ ○ ◉ ○ ○

March 1999

Many days have passed. The sadness, the deep, profound sadness on Rosalie's face this morning. 'I'm not sure that I'm ready to die, but I have no choice,' she said.

She has the sadness of a person who is having to leave the physical world, which she has grown used to inhabiting. She also has the sadness because of all the troubles between us, the anger and pain, but there is an underlying acceptance of what is and what has been, and that is wonderful.

She gives me all the compliments that I longed for over the years. Things like how good or kind or beautiful I am. 'What a nice smile you have,' she said today. 'How odd that I never noticed it before.'

I went for a walk along the beach. The tide was low and the sea was very quiet. I found a tiny lump of amber lying there among the pebbles, bright yellow, as light as a feather and not much bigger than my thumbnail.

(From Julia's Notebook)

～ 24 ～

And Then

I arrived at the village near Malaga where Enrique was now living with his girlfriend and after a lot of searching found his house and knocked on the door. He was very surprised to see me. He let me in and sat me down in a chair and kept staring at me with wide eyes.

My Spanish had improved after a year of writing him letters, the sent and the unsent ones, but I didn't give any explanation of why I had come, or how long I wanted to stay. Instead I asked if I could see his recent paintings. So he showed them to me, heaving out the big canvases and leaning them against a blank wall. He said I was welcome to sleep on the studio floor if I wanted to and I thanked him. His girlfriend turned up and we were introduced to each other. Her name was Monica and she came from Sweden.

Every night I settled myself in a little nest of cushions and blankets, surrounded by the comforting smell of oil paint and turpentine, and every night Enrique came and lay beside me for a while and we whispered a little in the darkness and made love in almost complete silence. If Monica knew what was going on, she didn't say anything, but she told me she wasn't happy here and wanted to move to England. I said I thought she might be able to rent a room in my mother's house; in fact, she could have my room because I wouldn't be needing it any more.

During the day I went out on my own. I would sit for hours in a café, or walk through dry fields until I found a tree or a wall I could lean against. If a stranger tried to approach me, I'd glare at him and that usually worked, although a man with only one leg once crept up on me; I hadn't noticed him because I was looking at a mass of white snail shells that lay on the ground among the white pebbles. He made a loud grunting noise as he lunged at me and I was able to get up and run just in time. He stumbled in pursuit, but I was too quick for him and his solitary leg.

I took my notebook with me wherever I went. In its pages I was trying to work out what had happened between me and my mother and Geoffrey, and how I felt towards both of them, and what I must do in order to survive.

◦ ◦ ◎ ◦ ◦

I tried to put together a picture of Geoffrey, this forty-eight-year-old man who had kissed me, even though he was my mother's lover.

He'd said he was planning to write a book about the theory of design, or was it the semantics of design? He explained his ideas at great length, but I couldn't remember much, except that he believed rooms and houses and the objects they contain are an extension of who we are as individuals.

He'd praised the poems of Philip Larkin and I hated them, mostly because of a photograph I had seen of Larkin in a raincoat which I thought made him look like a dirty old man. Geoffrey was also enthusiastic about John Updike's novels and I had told him that Updike gave me the creeps, with all that smooth clever talk round dining-room tables, followed by the conquest of beautiful ladies with silky hair and silky knickers, who were then betrayed. At least we had both enjoyed *Steppenwolf* and had agreed that Geoffrey was just as troubled and tormented as the main character.

I'd asked him if he had any homosexual tendencies, because he always looked a bit what I would call 'poofy'. He told me about his friend Anthony who was also a designer and how they had been so close they were almost like lovers, even though they had never been to bed together. Several times the two of them had had affairs with the same women and had even brought up each other's children. And then a few years ago they'd had a quarrel and a falling out which had been as painful as a divorce.

He had told me that when he was my age he had been obsessed with the idea of killing himself and had got hold of a signet ring with some sort of lethal poison hidden in a secret chamber. He wore it all the time: 'It gave me a sense of freedom and independence,' he said, and I thought I understood what he meant.

I found all this very exciting, but was disappointed that he no longer had the ring. I told him I too had often thought about suicide, only I wasn't sure if I had a self to kill and that was part of my problem.

I had listened to all this with my usual earnestness, but of course it was Geoffrey's unhappiness that appealed to me most; that and his vulnerability. I could see his soul was very troubled and I thought it had a lot to do with his childhood. His father had been cold and his mother had been very demanding, and they had made him feel like an outsider. He said he often woke screaming from the same nightmares he'd had when he was a child, but with the passing of time they had become even more frightening.

As well as kissing me, Geoffrey had offered me his friendship and something he called 'moral support'. He explained this as 'the ability to give if needed and take if needed, knowing that there is no debt of obligation'. I was quickly convinced that moral support was exactly what I needed.

⊙ ⊙ ◉ ⊙ ⊙

In my memories of these weeks I had broken all contact with my mother. In my notebook I wrote that I must

> Stop all love, all feeling for Mummy, allow a complete death or I shall go mad. I'm old enough to survive without maternal protection and I have to protect myself.

So I was very surprised to find that she had several letters I'd sent to her while I was in Enrique's village and she was still on Formentera. And in those letters I don't sound very much like the determined young adult I thought I was being, but more like a frightened child, asking for help.

> *My dear Mummy,*
> *. . . I just feel so lost. Please send some sanity. I'm sorry, but I'm in a terrible state. Can't think, can't decide, talk, anything. If things go on inside me so badly, then I must come back to Formentera because I think I might break. I won't come to flirt with Geoffrey, it's just that I need friends. Both of you. If you say I can't come, I don't know what I'll do.*

Once again I must have destroyed whatever my mother sent me in reply, but she did keep a copy of one of her letters. It's a very odd document, or at least I find it so.

She described scenes from what she called *family life here*, which she thought I would have *found fascinating*: Geoffrey getting very drunk, his young children being difficult, his older children arguing and other *moods, happenings, revelations . . . material not for a novel, but for a bloody saga of five volumes*. She advised me to read a book called *Directions of Human Development* when I got back: *it makes some revealing deductions about love, dependence, security, society, morality and is clear and precise.*

She asked if I would consider talking to Doctor Kollestrom about the *Mummy, Geoffrey, Julia set-up* and reassured me, rather unconvincingly, that she wasn't putting all the blame for what had happened on my shoulders, saying,

> I know the initiative always comes from the man, but I find it hard to fight
> Geoffrey and women do tend to attack each other in triangles.

She didn't mention my request to be allowed to return to Formentera and instead offered some rather brisk comfort: *I hope you can find some measure of peace and stability in yourself, at moments of quiet.*

As a postscript, she described going for a swim to a submerged rock, half a mile out to sea, while she was *a bit high on brandy and wine*. She said that getting there was all right, but coming back was quite frightening, with the waves blowing in her face.

⊙ ⊙ ◉ ⊙ ⊙

I recently found a letter from Geoffrey folded up in the pages of my red notebook. It was also sent from Formentera and it was written in a disconcertingly jolly tone, making it sound as if he viewed the journey the three of us had just made and the consequences of that journey as a rather thrilling adventure.

He wrote to ask if I'd like to join him in Barcelona and then he and I could go back to England together, *at our pleasure*. He instructed me to ignore anything that my mother might tell me about the situation, because *the general plan is to present her at the last moment with an inescapable fait accompli.* He went on to say that the two of them were quarrelling continuously, *rows are our constant daily bread* and talking with her was *like building sandcastles,* which are washed away by the next tide.

> It is now even claimed that I promised not to write to you, whereas what I . . . Oh it is too tedious to explain. I hope you will understand, if you are being subjected to the same sort of distortions.
>
> This must be brief, R. at beach returns in a moment. So, do write, love, Geoffrey.

Reading this now I suddenly remembered that much later he told me he had wanted to write a play about our journey. He'd thought of calling it 'The Master Drives at His Pleasure'.

I don't know if I answered him in any detail, but I do know that his letter filled me with disquiet. Geoffrey was approaching me as his lover, whereas I wanted to forget the kiss and to see him more as a friend who was going to give me the moral support I so much wanted. I thought the idea of travelling alone with him back to England was ridiculous.

I stayed in Enrique's studio for a week or so, then I went to meet my friend Peggy and some others, who were having a holiday at a beach resort near Barcelona. Her brother Rowland was with them and at night I slept with him in his little single bed. I must have let my mother know where I was, because she turned up late one evening at the pension where we were all staying. She had Geoffrey's two young children in the car and she was on her way home. Geoffrey had told her that their relationship was over.

I was having a shower when she suddenly burst into the little bathroom. She pulled back the curtain and, fully clothed, stepped in under the drenching hot water. She put her face close to mine and she began screaming accusations at me, about how I had destroyed her life for ever. I remember thinking that maybe she had a knife and she was going to kill me.

My friends heard the noise and came in and grappled with her and pulled her away. They told her they would call the police if she didn't leave at once. So she left, soaking wet and shouting curses at me as she went down the steep stairs.

March 1999

Rosalie is very weak and her body won't accept another transfusion, so there's nothing to be done. Because she has no pain and no need of drugs, she drifts in and out of sleep and talk, and there is no distinction between day and night. Sometimes I lie on the cushions on the floor and listen as her voice comes and goes. She tells me not to be afraid, not to be sad, not to mind that she is dying. She tells me how happy she is that we got to know each other, just in time.

'Mother and daughter, mother and daughter,' she says, practising the words. And then, 'We have done well, haven't we? That's good!'

(From Julia's Notebook)

25

A Red Nightdress

York University had only been functioning for three years when I arrived in September 1966 as a student of English Literature. The campus looked virginal and clean and rather startled. The students and teachers moved about in a daze, like extras in a film waiting for the director to appear.

I enjoyed my first lecture, which made a connection between *Pilgrim's Progress* and the lack of progress of K in Kafka's *The Trial.* I wrote an essay about Yeats, using my father's study of the poetry and quoting whole chunks of it as if his thoughts were my own. I wrote an essay about Ibsen's *Wild Duck* and became very interested in the idea that everyone has a 'life lie' that protects them from the harshness of reality and ultimately destroys them.

I sent regular letters to my mother and she kept them all. *Dear Mummy,* I said, shortly after I had arrived, *at last we have started work and it seems very interesting, with a particular emphasis on the link between literature and the visual arts.*

During the weeks that followed I told her I'd made some good friends and lost my chequebook, my purse and then my jumper, and that my tutor didn't like the essay on Yeats because it was *far too subjective.* I was feeling ugly and uncertain, but I was doing my best, even though I wasn't sure if I could keep going for much longer.

I told her that lots of the students were taking LSD and that someone in Sociology killed himself last Saturday by jumping out of a window and a number of others were talking of leaving, so it wasn't just me who was finding things difficult.

I said, *I keep having the strangest dreams!* And I asked rather vaguely, *How*

are you and your life? Adding, *I hope you're not too sad,* although I never mentioned the possible cause of any sadness.

I also wrote to Geoffrey at his new address. His replies would be waiting for me in the college pigeon-hole and they were often lying side by side with a letter from my mother. She used small brown manila envelopes and he used long white ones. She wrote in blue biro on old pieces of lined notepaper, while he wrote in black or green ink, on sheets of onionskin paper that rustled when I picked them up. I always threw away my mother's letters as soon as I had read them, but I kept Geoffrey's until a few years ago, when I decided to have a look at them. They were all out of their envelopes and jumbled together without dates or page numbers. I read some floating paragraphs and was shocked by the tone and the things that were being said and so I threw the whole lot away, and that was that, all gone.

⊙ ⊙ ◉ ⊙ ⊙

Shortly after I had arrived at York my mother wrote to say that Monica, Enrique's girlfriend, had turned up and she was now in my room. 'It's just like having a daughter here,' she said, and I wondered what on earth that meant.

My mother also told me she had found a new lodger, a twenty-nine-year-old Dutchman called Herman. She had met him one evening at an exhibition and he was looking for somewhere to stay because he had recently separated from his American wife. 'So now he's here!' said my mother, 'and we're quite a family!'

When I got home for the Christmas holidays my mother was surprisingly friendly towards me. She told me there had been a lot of excitement in the house. 'Monica had a fling with Herman, but it didn't work out so she left, which is good because it means you can have your old room. I wasn't sure where I was going to put you otherwise. Herman's here now. I'll introduce you.'

She knocked on the new lodger's door and there he was. He had dark curly hair, twinkly eyes and a walrus moustache. I had been reading *The Tin Drum* on the train coming down from York and he looked just like Günter Grass. We shook hands and his hands were dry and warm. I noticed that he had square-tipped fingers and that his palms were criss-crossed with very deep lines, which I thought must indicate that he knew what he was doing with his life. The lines on the palms of my hands were very vague and kept breaking off at points where I knew it was important they kept going.

'My daughter would like to see your room!' said my mother as she walked straight in with a proprietorial manner. She cast her eye over the bed, the chair, a precarious tower of books and a small green typewriter. She bustled about, picking things up and examining them, making comments.

She left the room as suddenly as she entered it. Maybe she heard the phone ringing.

I stayed for a while and talked to Herman. He was wearing very strange cloth slippers that had a separate bit for the big toe. I asked where they came from and he said he had got them in Japan, when he was living there. He showed me a pair of really tiny shoes, made of black silk and embroidered with little explosions of flowers. They had been worn by a Chinese woman with bound feet. I examined his typewriter, which was called an Olivetti 32, and decided secretly that I wanted one just like it. Next to the typewriter there was the manuscript of an unpublished novel called 'The Hollow Mountain' and a little heap of short stories. 'The novel's not much good,' he said, 'but you're welcome to read the stories.' I told him I wanted to write but had never written anything apart from a private journal. I realized that there was no sexuality in our conversation, no little smiles of collusion, no hungry stares.

⊙ ⊙ ⊙ ⊙ ⊙

The friendliness with my mother was short-lived. She went rummaging through my luggage while I was out and found Geoffrey's address and phone number in my address book. She scribbled over the words and the numbers in blue biro and wrote *No!* in the margin beside the angry tangle of ink.

After that she started coming into my room at night when I was asleep. She'd sit on the edge of the bed and wake me with the sound of her weeping. Then she'd begin the interrogation: 'Why are you doing this to me? Do you realize that you have ruined my life, my happiness? Has he written to you? Show me his letters! I love him! Do you love him? Does he love you?'

I would cry and say that Geoffrey was my friend and not my lover and it was not my fault that he had gone, or I'd get angry and tell my mother that she had no business interfering with my life and I hated her.

I wrote to Geoffrey, describing these scenes to him and telling him how unhappy I was.

He wrote back, saying all this was typical of my mother's irrational behaviour and I must resist her and be strong. He told me that things were difficult for him too. The relationship with his new girlfriend wasn't going well, he had failed to get a teaching job he had applied for and he was very depressed.

I was overwhelmed with pity and a curious sense of deep personal responsibility and I filled the pages of my notebook with my earnest thoughts on the subject:

Nothing can be gained through becoming any more involved with G. considering the amount of guilt and complexity the relationship already produces, innocent though it is, but I'd be honoured to be one of his women friends in about ten years' time.

And then, one night at around eleven o'clock, I had had a bath and was about to go to bed, when my mother made some comment and I began to cry. I said I didn't know what to do. I couldn't go on any longer. I wanted to die.

My mother listened. She didn't get angry, but her face was set and determined. 'I know what you must do!' she said. She took me by the hand and led me to Herman's room. She knocked gently on the door, opened it and pushed me inside. She closed the door and went away.

He was sitting in an armchair reading. He looked up and saw me standing there in my long-sleeved red flannel nightdress. He asked what on earth was wrong and I had no words to explain the story of me and my mother and my father and Geoffrey and the other lodgers who came before Geoffrey and the muddle and sadness and fight of it all. So I let out a wail and sat on Herman's lap and buried my face into his neck and kissed him. And after a while, we went to bed.

With the first glimmering of dawn I crept back to my room. I felt like the princess in the fairy story who must not see her new husband by daylight, or else the curse would come true and they would be separated for ever.

'Well?' said my mother cheerfully over breakfast. She looked me up and down and I suddenly realized she might have been there, listening outside the door. She had told me she enjoyed listening to people making love. 'Well?'

I said nothing.

'You don't need to worry. *I* haven't slept with him, if that's what you're thinking. He's not really my type, and anyway, darling, I got him especially for you!'

The affair with Herman continued for the rest of the holidays. I would sleep with him at night, but could hardly dare to acknowledge his existence during the day. We sometimes had meals together with my mother, but I kept silent and avoided any meeting of eyes.

I went back to university for the start of the second term, but I felt so ill and mad that I thought I must give up my studies. My professor was quite helpful. He said I just needed a psychiatrist's assessment of my state of mind and then I could leave and come back in a year or so, when I felt better.

I telephoned Herman and told him I was coming down to London. I said he must understand that I couldn't live at Cambria Lodge ever again and

I needed somewhere to stay. He didn't question my desperation, but he contacted a friend of his who had an empty flat and within a few hours he let me know that it was all arranged. I could stay there for a while, until I knew what I was going to do next.

My father arranged for me to see a new psychiatrist, a gremlin of a man called Angus G. MacGregor who had his practice close to Harley Street. After a few sessions during which I was often completely silent, Doctor MacGregor felt qualified to assess my mental state. He sent a letter to the relevant authorities and this letter remained in my medical files for years, until a doctor, who was also a good friend, gave it to me, saying I might find it interesting. According to Doctor MacGregor, I had

> emerged from a disturbed family as an expert in mental ju-jitsu, but with no personal identity . . .
>
> From a diagnostic point of view she would come under the category of Personality Disorder, [but] does not now present with any symptoms . . .
>
> As you can appreciate from the above report I feel it would be in her interests to have a period of time away from the university. At this early stage I have no idea how the matter will resolve itself.

Doctor MacGregor also explained that he was attempting to show me that there were other ways of dealing with people than by manipulation, *which process she is beginning to give up with me.*

All I can remember of him, apart from the long silences, is the occasion when he demanded that I kiss him on the lips. When I tried to obey but was overcome with trembling, he kept asking, 'Why are you afraid of me? What is the meaning of this fear?'

◎ ◎ ◉ ◎ ◎

March 1999

Rosalie can't turn her head and she can only see me from one eye, so if I move out of her line of vision I disappear. Her voice has dropped to a quiet, deep monotone.

And yet none of this matters. An immense gentleness has descended on her. I suppose it was always there, but hidden under layers of fear and sadness that had turned to rage.

I brought the little piece of amber to the hospital to show it to her. She took it in her hand and lifted it slowly to her mouth. I realized she wanted to lick the taste of the sea. 'Salt!' she said and handed the yellow fragment back to me.

(From Julia's Notebook)

~~ 26 ~~

York Street

The flat was in central London and close to Baker Street. It consisted of one elegant and gloomy room and there were heavy velvet curtains that could block out every hint of daylight. The little kitchen at the back looked down into the playground of a Catholic primary school for girls and sometimes a bell would ring and a mass of little figures in identical uniforms would emerge from their classrooms, and I'd watch them milling about and listen to their seagull cries.

Herman helped me to move in. I didn't have anything apart from a few clothes and books. I had no plans and no idea how I was going to pass the time, but I was convinced that I needed to be on my own in order to find out what was happening to me. So Herman only visited me when I said I would like to be visited.

I was fine, just so long as I had company, but as soon as I was on my own, even for a few hours, I panicked. I had no sense of inhabiting my own body and I felt as if I was evaporating and would soon cease to exist. I would draw the curtains shut and stand in the darkened room with my arms held out from my sides, penguin fashion, and then I'd turn round and round, very slowly, as if I was winding up a machine. When I had made myself dizzy, I'd lie on the bed with the covers over my head and not know what to do next.

In my notebook I wrote, *I am filled with a terrible, terrible calm that won't break, but hangs, seeps, oozes through me.*

○ ○ ◉ ○ ○

For the last year or so I had avoided meeting my father, always saying that I was much too busy. I wrote to him regularly from university, telling him cheerful things about my life and clever things about the books I had been reading, but not mentioning any of my troubles. But then, back in London, I told him I needed to see him urgently. I thought I could explain my situation to him and he would be sure to understand. We talked in his study and the Tibetan Buddha on its little shelf watched us through partially closed eyes, one hand raised in benediction, the thumb and forefinger pressed together.

My father was not the slightest bit interested in my state of mind and not at all pleased that I had decided to give up my university degree. As far as he was concerned there was no room for discussion. He told me that I had destroyed all hope for the future and now I would inevitably become what he called 'a common prostitute'.

I reminded him that when he was my age he had been expelled from Cambridge, where he was not happy, and I tried to explain that I was also not happy. But he wasn't listening. He kept repeating the business of becoming 'nothing but a common prostitute' and I had a brief Dickensian image of myself walking the streets of the city and trying to inflame the desires of strangers in a voice made hoarse by poverty and unnatural acts. My father seemed to have persuaded himself that this metamorphosis had already taken place and from now on I was a fallen woman who could never rise to her feet again.

I tried my old trick and fell screaming to the floor, in the hope that this might make him more sympathetic towards me. Once again the wave of sound made me feel strong and invincible, and I remember seeing a huddle of sherry bottles that seemed to be watching me. There was a pile of manuscripts on the bottom shelf of the bookcase, next to the bottles, and I wondered if that was the autobiography my father had been writing and whether he'd change his account of his only daughter, now that she had become a common prostitute.

My father was unmoved by my screaming. 'The girl's ridiculous!' he said to himself, and he walked out of the room.

◦ ◦ ◉ ◦ ◦

A few days later I telephoned my mother. She didn't seem to mind that I had thrown away my academic future and she didn't ask why I hadn't come home. She wanted to know if I had enough money to live on, and when I told her I hadn't she said she had a job for me. She was teaching painting at an evening class in Chelsea and she needed a model.

I went for one session and earned myself five pounds. I had to stand on a platform underneath an electric heater attached to the ceiling, which made my head very hot but left the rest of me quite cold. I felt proud and ashamed of my nakedness, proud and ashamed of the muscular beauty of my body. The students were mostly old ladies and old men who wanted to do a bit of art in their spare time. When I arrived they were gossiping together like chickens, but once they had started to draw they grew silent and were very busy with their sheets of paper and their sticks of charcoal. I watched my mother moving among them, making comments on how their work was developing.

She kept a vague smile on her lips and when she said something to me, it was as if we had never met before. 'Would you mind turning round a little, that's right, now raise your arm. Good, hold it there! So, everybody, we'll do this pose as a five-minute sketch and then I'm sure our model will need a change of position. Come along then, get started!'

In my nakedness I was suddenly reminded of the time when I stood in an empty bathtub while my mother watched me. I took my five-pound fee and when I was asked if I could attend for the next session, I said no, I was much too busy.

⊙ ⊙ ◉ ⊙ ⊙

Some nights I slept with Herman and some nights I slept restlessly on my own, hemmed in by fears that gathered in a crowd around my bed. And then, almost imperceptibly, I started an affair with Geoffrey.

He invited me to have supper with him. I hadn't seen him since all the trouble in Formentera and now there he was in a rather grand restaurant, wearing a suit and smiling. I caught sight of my own face in a mirror and I looked so serious and worried that I thought I could easily pass for thirty and that pleased me.

I sat down. We drank wine by candlelight and the conversation rumbled smoothly along, and the world suddenly seemed very ordered and steady. Once the meal was over Geoffrey ordered a taxi for me and paid the driver to take me home. A week later he asked if I would like to spend a weekend with him in the cottage and I said yes, I would.

It was all so nicely familiar. The drive down, the little pale stone building, crouched close to the road. The smell of cedar wood, the rug, the scrubbed pine table, the row of brown mugs that had been made by Bernard Leach in Japan. Cigarettes and wine and a glass of brandy as a nightcap and then there I was, lying in the bed in which my mother had lain and making love to a man with whom my mother had also made love. It all seemed very straightforward and logical, and I felt the burden of blame dropping away from me. I was on a road to freedom and truth, and it didn't matter that the sexual act itself was so quiet and lacking in passion. It was just a necessary ritual.

I told Herman that I had been away with an old school friend and I went on seeing him and sleeping with him, and we were busy making plans for a long holiday to Corfu. We were going to travel there on his scooter and he had already bought me a helmet and a jacket; so a little pile of essential equipment was taking shape in the room at York Street.

I was filled with the sense that I was being carried forward by my own destiny and the despair of the previous weeks had been supplanted by a wild elation. I no longer had to think about what I was doing or why, I just needed to let it all happen. I told my notebook that I loved Herman more than ever and I was very excited by the prospect of the holiday we were about to take. I made no mention of Geoffrey by name, but rather ominously I wrote,

> The difference between these two men makes them totally separated and everything is right, each action is sincere and as near to spontaneity as possible. I have no idea what is happening or what will happen.

The day arrived on which Herman and I were setting off for Corfu. He had stayed with me overnight and had gone back to Cambria Lodge in the morning to collect a few things.

Just after he left, my first lover, Rowland, dropped by to say hello and we made love. Then a couple of hours later Geoffrey telephoned and said he needed to see me, so he turned up at the flat and I made love with him as well. I remember imagining the sperm from three different men swimming around in my body and mingling together.

I told Geoffrey I was about to go on holiday that same afternoon. He said he didn't want to stop me or influence my decision, but he knew it was a bad idea. 'The only way you can ever escape from your mother is by living with me,' he said.

⊙ ⊙ ◉ ⊙ ⊙

Geoffrey was still in my bed when the doorbell rang. I went downstairs and there was Herman, eager to be off. I hadn't anticipated what I was going to say. I hadn't even decided yet what I was going to do. But when I saw him, smiling and eager and knowing so little about me, I told him I had changed my mind. I couldn't come with him because I was going to live with Geoffrey, the man who had been my mother's lover. In fact, he was in the flat right now, waiting for me.

I could hear myself speaking and I was surprised by what sounded like the premeditated clarity of my words. Herman was terribly shocked. He said he had no idea, he couldn't believe it, why was I doing this? I remember looking at his face contorted with misery and being surprised and vaguely embarrassed.

I watched him drive off on his scooter and then I went back upstairs. I was confident that I had made the right decision. Geoffrey would know how to look after me and keep me safe. He had said this was the only way to escape from my mother and I trusted his wisdom.

⊙ ⊙ ◉ ⊙ ⊙

March 1999

I have been spending all my time in the hospital with her. During the day I lie on her bed; there's no room to lie side by side, so I lie at the opposite end and that way we can see each other. She hasn't eaten anything for almost a week, but I give her water on one of those little sponges and she sucks at it greedily. This morning I went out and bought a jar of honey and I dipped my finger in it so that she could taste the sweetness. She liked that.

She knows that I booked a flight to come and visit you in Italy on 5 April. She says she hopes she will be dead in time for me to go. 'It would be such a pity to waste the ticket.' It was another of her quiet jokes.

(Fax to Herman)

27

Certain Choices

So now, instead of going to Corfu with Herman, there was a new holiday plan. Geoffrey had rented a house on one of the Canary Islands. He said I should go there first, maybe with some friends of my own age, and then I could think things over and let him know if I really wanted him to join me.

I arranged to travel with Peggy and a couple of her friends from university. We planned to make our way in pairs down to Marseilles and then take a boat to the Canaries. Before setting off I wrote a letter to my mother, telling her that I was going to run away with Geoffrey, just as she had always said I would. I posted the letter when we had reached Dover.

Peggy and I hitch-hiked together. I don't have many recollections of the journey, except that once we had to jump from a moving car when the driver seemed to be planning to take us to some quiet place that he knew, where he could rape us at his leisure. Luckily he didn't follow us when we ran off down the road clutching our possessions, and we were not far from a little town. We spent the night in the waiting room of the railway station. I can still see the red benches we slept on and the bleak light of the morning coming in through windows smeared with grime.

In Marseilles we met up with the others and got on a big Italian cruise ship. I suppose we must have booked our tickets in advance. We sat on deckchairs and sunbathed, and the other three talked about what they were planning to do next term, but I kept silent on that. A photographer took my picture. I was wearing a very short skirt, blue with white stripes, like a butcher's apron. I leant against the white metal railing and the wind blew into my face and he told me to look sexy and then he said, '*Yes!*' But when he showed me the photograph he had made I didn't like the person I saw there, so I tore it up and threw it into the sea.

○ ○ ◉ ○ ○

We reached the island of Las Palmas and went by boat to the island of La Palma and then by bus to a house we had rented, which was not the one Geoffrey had rented. I don't know how we found the house and in my mind I can't find a single image of it, or of the village or fields that might have encompassed it. All I can see is the empty corner of a white-painted room and the straw shoulder bag that held my passport and whatever else I had brought with me, leaning against the wall.

A letter from my mother was waiting for me at the post office. She had sent it to Geoffrey's London address and he had forwarded it on. It was very odd seeing both of their handwriting on the same envelope, but I avoided thinking about it.

My mother said she was sure I must be feeling *terribly unhappy* and if I did what I said I was going to do, then I would *bear the stigma for the rest of my life*. She was wrong. I didn't feel unhappy at all, just very light-headed and unable to concentrate on anything, but I was intrigued by the word 'stigma'. It made me think of Cain, who had a horn growing out of his forehead so that everyone would see at once that he had killed his brother Abel. It also made me think of Christ and the marks of blood on his hands and feet, to show where the nails went in.

A letter from Geoffrey turned up a couple of days later. In his elegant and slightly spidery handwriting he explained that of course I could still change my mind, but I had better telephone him quickly because he was planning to leave soon. He told me the date and time of his arrival and added, *I want to be sure this is what you want.*

I read both letters quickly and vaguely, and scrunched them up and threw them away, although I did copy the bit about the stigma and *I want to be sure* into my notebook. I never considered telling Geoffrey not to come and join me and it never occurred to me to look more closely at the implications of the path I was about to follow. I felt I was doing what I had to do and I had absolutely no choice in the matter.

◎ ◎ ◉ ◎ ◎

I pottered around with my three friends for a week or so, until the day when Geoffrey was supposed to arrive. I couldn't remember what time he was due and there were no plans about where we were to meet, but I was sure I knew he was arriving on the island of Las Palmas, so I went there by boat early in the morning to surprise him.

I sat in a café by the docks and drank black coffee and a glass of brandy, and waited for several hours. Then I made some enquiries and realized that I must have come to the wrong island. On top of that, there were no boats going back to La Palma until the next day. I saw a sign pointing to the museum of local history, so I went there while I tried to decide what to do.

When I think of that long-ago museum, the mist that was enveloping me in great blanketing clouds is suddenly lifted and blown away and I can see everything with a sudden clarity. I entered a room that was bright with fluorescent lighting and filled with glass cases. Each case told something more of the story of the Beaker People, an old race who had lived on this island thousands of years before. A little notice, in English as well as Spanish, explained that the Beaker People used to bury their dead in caves close to the sea, with pots filled with food in case they were hungry and jars filled with a rough wine in case they were thirsty and extra clothes and necklaces, in case they wanted to dress up. The entrances to these caves were then carefully sealed over and they had only been uncovered very recently.

I looked at row upon row of almost identical earthenware pots, each one decorated with wavy black lines. I looked at strings of round beads made out of the same red clay and at the tattered remnants of rough pale clothes in which you could still see the pattern of the thread.

And then, in the next case, I was suddenly confronted by what was left of the Beaker People themselves. The caves were so dry and well ventilated that when the dead were laid there they went through a natural process of mummification, which turned them as hard and dark as ebony wood. There were no complete bodies, but there were arms and legs and a few broken and solemn faces on display. But what I remember most vividly were the hands: delicate and perfect hands that were so graceful and eloquent that they seemed to be creatures in their own right. The hands made me want to cry, although I wasn't sure why.

I had almost no money with me, but I did have the address of a couple of men who lived somewhere in the town. I think Geoffrey must have given it to me before I left England. So I went and found their house and, although a complete stranger, I explained my problem and asked if I could stay the night. The man said they had no spare bed, but I could sleep on the sitting-room floor if I wanted to. I suppose they gave me supper. The next morning I remember that they spent an interminable time in the bathroom, gargling and sloshing about with water. Then the three of us had breakfast on a little terrace with a view over the harbour.

I returned the way I had come. When I finally arrived back at the house there were Peggy and the others looking rather awkward, like children who had been caught stealing sweets, and there, sitting on the floor in the corner of the white and empty room, was an elegant old man with very long legs. It was like meeting Death. It made me think of that story called 'Appointment in Samara' in which a man goes on a long journey in order to avoid just such a meeting, but Death finds him anyway.

'Is this him?' I asked myself. I was not happy or sad to see him, just surprised by how enormously old he was, with such deep lines cut into his cheeks, such dark stains under his tired eyes.

◦ ◦ ◉ ◦ ◦

March 1999

Thank you so much for sending me the key to your house in Italy. It's lying quietly on the window ledge, next to the fragment of amber. Time past, time present and time future.

Rosalie asked me today if I might move into her house after she was dead, and I said I wasn't sure, but I'd keep it for a year anyway and that seemed to please her.

I told her I would paint her coffin cerulean blue. 'What a good idea,' she said. 'Cerulean blue is my favourite colour.'

(Fax to Herman)

\thicksim\!\!\!\! 28 \thicksim 28 ⊶

In the House of Aaron Juda

It was not easy, being with Geoffrey in the company of my friends. If I looked at him I was in one world and if I looked at them I was in another, and there was absolutely no connection between the two. It must have been awkward for him as well, finding himself on holiday with four fresh-faced youngsters who talked of essays and suntans and wondered about the best way to fry an egg. When I discussed the situation with Geoffrey that night, we decided to set off immediately to the place he had rented on the other side of the island's ridge.

This was a house belonging to a writer called Aaron Juda, who was the brother of a friend of Geoffrey's. As I remember it, there were big eucalyptus trees in a courtyard and stone steps leading up to a rather austere building that stood on its own, quite a distance from the village.

It was obvious that Aaron Juda didn't have much money and he wasn't very happy either. The rooms were bare and colourless and imbued with a feeling of despair. The whitewash on the walls had flaked off in patches, revealing dark archipelagos of dusty plaster; the floors were covered with a layer of cement and the mattress on the floor was covered by a thin bed-spread, which had the faintest traces of a pattern clinging to it. The kitchen table had a piece of stone under one of its legs and the seats of the rickety chairs had been repaired with pieces of string.

The owner of the house had been waging a long war against ants. All the legs of the furniture, including the table leg balanced on its stone, were stand-ing in empty tins filled with oil, and the oil was gritty with the tiny bodies of drowned ants who had started out on a doomed journey. The wooden shelves in the kitchen were also barricaded against possible invasion; they hung from ropes attached to the ceiling by hooks and each length of rope had a little paper funnel fixed round it, so that if an ant fell in, it could never climb out again.

As another aspect of this same war, there were numerous cartons of DDT in the food cupboard, tucked in among the bags of rice and beans and the tins of sardines. I once went into the garden and poured out a little mound of DDT in the middle of a line of marching ants and then I sat and watched as they continued to march, the first ones falling over and dying in their minute agony and the rest persevering on the journey, ignoring the heap of corpses that lined the way.

As well as doing battle with ants, Aaron Juda was also engaged in a fierce struggle against time. On the walls in different parts of his sad house he had counted off the passing of each week with six little upright lines and then a single diagonal stripe through the uprights. There were dozens and dozens of these desperate hieroglyphs, moving in drifts and droves across the white-wash, with a particularly dense concentration of them above the table that was used for writing. This table held a heavy black typewriter and all around it there were heaps of typewritten pages, which I supposed were part of an unfinished novel, but I never tried to read it.

The house had no electricity and I enjoyed the evening ritual of lighting the oil lamps and candles. The water came from a well in the courtyard and the lavatory was a privy in a wooden shed. The privy was just a hole cut into a well-polished plank of wood, fixed over a steep drop of some four or five metres at the bottom of which was a heap of seaweed. Every time you had finished using the lavatory, you threw in a handful of salty-smelling dried seaweed, which fluttered down as soft as feathers.

The weather was very hot and during the day Geoffrey spent a lot of time lying on the mattress and reading the books from Aaron Juda's bookcase. He found a copy of something called *Shame and the Search for Identity*, which he was already familiar with, but he said I must read it too, because it explained the difference between shame and guilt so clearly. 'You can have shame about who you are,' he said, 'but not guilt. Guilt is very narrow and destructive.'

I had no wish to read anything. In a solitary house not far from ours there lived a woman who kept a flock of white goats, so every morning before breakfast I would go and collect a can filled with frothing milk and smelling of stables. And then after breakfast I would potter off into the landscape. I never went far. I would examine the ants and beetles and butterflies in the garden and wander short distances up and down the track that led eventually to the sea. There were lots of bright-green lizards in the stone walls. When I came back I would tell Geoffrey about my small adventures and he would tell me about the books he had been reading.

We did go to the sea, but only once. It took a couple of hours to get there and when we arrived there was no one around and the little waves were lapping against a coarse black sand. I didn't like it. I felt as if we had crossed over to the Land of the Dead.

On our way back up the steep hill, we kept being overtaken by old women with short bodies and bandy legs, carrying heavy baskets on their heads and walking very fast with a curiously jerky movement that made me think of wind-up toys. We met an old man pushing a handcart on which lay the huge and glistening body of a tuna. When someone wanted to buy from him, he stopped his cart, took out a long knife and sliced a piece of bright-red meat from the side of the fish. We bought some and cooked it that night.

After about five weeks the holiday was over. We were going back to England by plane and the journey to the airport involved catching several buses. I noticed that the women who climbed on to the bus often pulled up their big skirts before settling down like hens on the hard seats, and I had the impression that they weren't wearing knickers, but I might have been wrong. I wasn't wearing a bra and the juddering movement of the bus made my breasts shake so wildly that I had to hold on to them as discreetly as possible.

And then we were in a town near the airport and we were sitting side by side on high stools in a bar drinking brandy, and I looked at our reflection in the mirror behind the bar and saw a tall old man sitting next to a very solemn young girl and both of them appeared to me as complete strangers. 'Now you see, you are becoming beautiful!' said Geoffrey, smiling proudly at me in the mirror, as if this was something he had engineered single-handedly.

I don't know if I anticipated what sort of life I would lead once I was back in London, or how Geoffrey's friends would view me, or what my parents were going to say and if I would ever see either of them again, but I did have a growing sense of dread that lay deep in the pit of my belly like a tummyache.

And then there we were 'home again, home again, jiggedy-jog!' as the old rhyme goes. Geoffrey had a ground-floor flat in a tiny Georgian house in Camden Town, which I had never seen before. I moved in with all my possessions contained in the one straw basket, which I could carry on my shoulder. I had hardly any clothes, no shoes apart from a pair of Spanish espadrilles, no coats or books, no mementoes of the past. One day I went to a second-hand clothes shop near the tube station and bought a black cotton skirt with embroidered patterns round the hem showing stylized chickens facing each other in pairs. The woman who sold it to me said it came from Romania.

Slowly I accumulated other things as well: an Afghan coat that never stopped smelling of old goat, a pair of Wellington boots that I wore through-out one winter, a black beret that I thought made me look like Colette. I went to a second-hand music shop and bought a record of work songs from Louisiana state prisons. 'You could try something a bit more cheerful, you know,' said the young man to whom I paid my money, and I went out in a huff.

○ ○ ◉ ○ ○

One day – maybe it was around Christmas – I somehow learnt that my mother was going to be away on holiday for a while, so I asked Geoffrey to take me to Cambria Lodge. We went late at night. He waited outside in his car while I walked up the familiar steps to the turquoise front door. I still had my own key. I opened the door and entered what had been my childhood home.

The house was much bigger than I had remembered it, the ceilings were higher, the staircase leading up to my old room looked vast and imposing. I went down to the dark kitchen and looked at the round table. I went into the bathroom and did a pee in the lavatory where my father used to sit with the wooden lid down when he was teaching me poems while I had a bath.

I went up to my mother's bedroom and nothing had changed there either. I went into her studio and saw the work she was doing in which three big abstract shapes floated on a violent background of brushstrokes. I went into the room where my parents used to sleep and where the lodgers had slept. Herman had moved out and there was no trace of him left behind, not even the sweet smell that clung to his hair and skin.

I was aware that all the furniture was watching me. When the glass-domed clock on the chest of drawers began to chime the hours, I expected it to cry out, 'She's here! She's here! Get her! Get her!' I thought the round table might growl a warning to the chairs and then they would crowd around me, hemming me in with their angry chatter. But everything held its breath. The house was cold and silent and empty of life.

Finally I found the courage to go to my old room. Things had been tidied up and moved around, but my clothes were still in the wardrobe and I stuffed some of them into a pillowcase. I also took the bedcover from my bed.

Just before leaving I entered my mother's studio again and I stole a little lead statuette of an old naked woman with her hands clasped together and her head bowed. It had been given to my father by the sculptor Nibs Dalwood when we were in Leeds, but my father can't have liked it much, so he had abandoned it when he moved out.

I checked that I had turned off all the lights before leaving the house and banging the heavy door shut behind me. Then Geoffrey drove me away. When we were back in his flat, I put my bedcover on the bed and placed the old woman on the marble mantelpiece in the front room, next to a big glass vase filled with dried flowers.

⊙ ⊙ ◉ ⊙ ⊙

March 1999

Rosalie on the edge, but slowly drifting away.

I lie here listening to the pattering of rain outside in the dark night. The whole sweep of time is around me. I'm still so much enjoying the unfamiliar pleasure of being welcomed, being loved, without ambivalence. To feel close and at ease in the company of my mother. The joy of companionship. She stares at me with faraway green eyes.

(From Julia's Notebook)

∼ 29 ∼

Daily Life

Geoffrey was in the process of making his flat very elegant. The light from the street outside came in the window through white roller-blinds, which were kept down, so you never saw the houses opposite, or the passing of cars and people. A modern sofa covered in white linen sat with its back to the window. He had sanded and polished the wooden floor, so it now had a warm yellow gleam. I liked to look at the floor through the thick glass surface of a low coffee table that stood beside the sofa; maybe it reminded me of looking at fish in a fish tank.

His architectural drawing desk stood in one corner of the room, with an Anglepoise lamp fixed to its side and all sorts of special pens and rulers lying in an ordered row and waiting to be used.

Not long after I arrived I sat at this desk and made drawings of little figures on a sheet of cardboard. There was a man in profile riding a hobby-horse, a Harlequin, his arms hanging limp at his thin sides, and there was Death, holding a mask on a stick in front of his own face.

I had found these images in a book about Medieval Mystery Plays. I copied them very carefully and then cut them out and coloured them in with wax crayons. It was the sort of thing you did at school when you were still too young to be taught real subjects such as History or Geography or Mathematics.

I divided Harlequin's costume into red and yellow sections. The man riding the hobby-horse had blue trousers. I made Death's featureless face white, before covering it with a black mask I had cut out separately. I then pinned these three characters on the cork board on the wall facing Geoffrey's double bed. They were my own things and I liked to sit and look at them. Sometimes I would move them about to change the relationship between them.

Geoffrey was working full time at an art school, and a few weeks after we got back I found a job that involved putting flat cardboard lampshades, plus a little metal fitment and the assembly instructions, into envelopes. That lasted for a while and then I got a job as a tea lady and switchboard operator for a documentary film company in Soho. Everyone there was very nice to me, even when the tea was cold or when I managed to disconnect important transatlantic telephone conversations by pulling out the wrong plugs on the switchboard. The company was producing a series of television films about important people in the art world and I was very impressed when Arthur Miller was on the phone, asking to speak to someone. I wore my Wellington boots to work and didn't talk much and always had lunch on my own, at the same pub near Berwick Street market.

I'd get back at around six and Geoffrey usually arrived half an hour later. We'd have a brandy and then supper with wine and then some more brandy and then we'd each take two codeine tablets before going to bed.

We made love every night, him and me, always in the dark. I no longer had orgasms; they had stopped happening without me really noticing the loss. So the world didn't spin and tumble beneath my falling body any more and instead I would breathe very fast as if I was running away from something and then suddenly the running was over and I could relax. We'd talk a bit and smoke a cigarette and then I'd fall asleep at once and Geoffrey would lie awake for much of the night. When we stayed at the cottage and the moon was full, I'd sometimes wake and see him, propped up with pillows, very still beside me, staring at the opposite wall.

I had very little contact with my parents during those first months. My mother kept silent, while my father wrote me a letter in which he said he was planning to take legal action against Geoffrey for something called 'Gross Moral Turpitude'. 'He is a teacher,' said my father, 'and as such he has a pastoral duty to behave correctly towards young people such as yourself. I've spoken to my lawyer.' I had a brief and terrifying vision of standing in the witness box, accused of being complicit in the act of moral turpitude, but nothing came of the threat.

However, I did speak to my stepmother Peggy a few times and she kept me informed about what was going on in Putney: Mother sad but managing, Father often drunk but also managing in his way.

Peggy had an old friend called Edith who she said was very keen to meet me because I was 'living out the Oedipal', as she put it. So the three of us met in Soho one lunchtime and we had a meal together in a Greek restaurant.

Edith was a large-boned woman with a small piping voice and a stubbornly jutting lower jaw that made her look ready for a fight. She was quite a few years older than Peggy and her white hair was dyed a bright orange, 'because I am in the autumn of my life', she said, when she saw me staring. We all got rather drunk on sharp-tasting Retsina and although I enjoyed the talk at first, it became rather frightening when there were too many questions about the Oedipal I was living out.

○ ○ ◉ ○ ○

Most weekends, Geoffrey and I went to the cottage in Wiltshire, taking his two young children with us. We'd set off at around ten or eleven at night, because he preferred to do the drive when the roads were more or less empty. He'd stop the car in front of the house where his ex-wife was living and I'd sit and wait in the dark while he went in. After a while, quite a long while sometimes, he'd emerge with first one child and then the other, wrapped up in blankets and eiderdowns and I'd settle them in the back seat of the car. Occasionally his ex-wife stood in the doorway as we drove off, her dark-red hair shining in the light from the hallway, but I never spoke to her or waved goodbye as we left.

The children slept in the same downstairs room where I had once slept with them, while I slept upstairs in the bed next to the bookcase, where my mother used to sleep. If I had any thoughts about this I never let them rise to the surface, but I did have very strange dreams.

Geoffrey tended to spend most of Saturday and Sunday at his desk, while I was busy with the kids. If the weather was fine we'd go out into the fields. We called it 'sploring' and we were never bored. We'd crawl about on all fours, pretending we were animals and we'd make nests in the long meadow grass and play hide and seek among the elm trees that still dominated the landscape with their magisterial presences.

When it was too cold or wet to be outside we'd construct blanket houses in the downstairs room, and I'd sing them songs and read them stories. They wanted to have the same four or five stories read over and over again, and that suited me as well because I also appreciated the reassurance of repetition. Their favourite story was called *Cat and Rat* and it told of how these two animals, who had once been such good friends, learnt to hate each other for ever after. Their favourite song was one I had learnt from an old Harry Belafonte record which I used to listen to at Cambria Lodge.

> I wonder why nobody don't like me,
> Or is it the fact that I'm ugly?
> I leave my whole-a house and go,
> My children don't want me no mo',
> Bad talk around the house they bring,

And when I talk, they start to sing,
'Mama look at Boo-boo!' they shout,
Their mama tell them, 'shut up your mout'!
Dat is your daddy!' 'Oh no!
Our daddy can't be ugly so!'

We played together like three little children and Geoffrey was our father somewhere in the background, distant and remote and always busy with grown-up tasks that must not be interrupted. The only time he emerged to be with us was when we went to the pub together, sitting outside at a trestle table drinking Scrumpy cider and eating crisps. In the evening, after I had put the children to bed and read them a final story, he and I would sit at the table and talk and I'd return to my other persona: that of a teenager who did her best to look and sound like a thirty-year-old.

Late on Sunday Geoffrey would start packing the car and getting the cottage in order before our departure. He used the fibrous outer shell of a coconut to polish the dark wood of the floors and he poured bleach on the kitchen table before scrubbing it down.

I'd entertain the children until it was time to go and he'd get very angry if any of us got in his way. Driving back in the night I supplied him with a continuous stream of lighted cigarettes and I'd sing songs to keep him awake, the same sad folk songs about unhappy lovers that I had sung when I was on my way to Formentera, all those months ago.

The children always cried a lot. They cried in the car, they cried when we arrived at the cottage and they cried when it was time to leave. Tanya, the little girl, who had her mother's dark-red hair, cried even more than her older brother, although sometimes he would join in for company's sake. She wet her bed every night and that upset her every morning, and she once became completely hysterical when she saw me cutting through the silver-foil wrapping of one of those little triangles of processed cheese. I tried to explain that I really hadn't meant to upset her, but by then it was too late: the sealed silver body of the triangle had been irrevocably divided and nothing would ever put it together again.

⊙ ⊙ ◉ ⊙ ⊙

It was a curiously detached existence, but still, I don't think I was unhappy during the first months I spent with Geoffrey. I enjoyed his company. He'd talk to me about his childhood and the work he and his friend Anthony had done on the development of radar during the war. He'd talk about girlfriends and wives and children, and about his theories on the meaning of design. He said his whole life had been a series of failures and missed opportunities, but now that he was with me he felt he was living *honestly*, which pleased him very much. He explained that he wasn't *in love* with me, but he loved me and that was important. We avoided mentioning my mother and I never asked what place she had had in his affections.

And what did I tell him about my short life? I'm not really sure. I think mostly I listened and then made comments, if I had comments to make. The regularity of the life and the sense of order and structure suited me very well. I felt more quiet, more at peace with myself than I had ever done before. I suppose I felt safe. I had after all come through something and survived.

The odd thing was, I didn't feel bound to Geoffrey in any way. I knew that as soon as I was strong enough I would leave him and set off into the world, and I was confident that when the moment came he would give me his blessing.

◎ ◎ ◉ ◎ ◎

March 1999

I lay at the end of Rosalie's bed, head to toe. She asked me in her slow deep voice what date it would be tomorrow.

'April first,' I told her.

'Well I'd better hold out till the second, no good dying an April Fool!' said my mother and one side of her mouth lifted into the idea of a smile.

(From Julia's Notebook)

30

The Year Comes Full Circle

Somebody gave me a black kitten. She was half Siamese and had a wonderfully guttural and agonized miaow and a natural fondness for travelling in buses, trains or cars. I called her Tart and the name seemed to suit her well enough.

By now half a year or so had passed and I had a new job doing picture research for a publishing company in Fitzroy Square. I'd go to work by bus with Tart sitting contentedly in the straw basket on my shoulder, observing her fellow passengers. And when I got to the office, she'd curl up and go to sleep under the table. Another girl brought in her flame-coloured dog and the two animals liked each other.

The atmosphere in that office suited me very well. There were four of us in one room and we were vague and friendly and never talked about home life, although once a woman with dark hair came to do part-time work and we got talking about sex and she said her husband tied her wrists to the metal bed frame whenever he wanted to make love to her. We all paused over our sandwiches and she fell silent and became very reticent for the rest of the week.

When Geoffrey gave me a ring, one of the other researchers said she didn't know I had a boyfriend and were we now engaged? I explained he wasn't a boyfriend, not really, and let the subject drop. And when I accompanied a photographer and one of the editors to the Isle of Wight for the day, to meet the man who had made the first prototype of the Hovercraft using a vacuum cleaner and an empty baked-bean tin, the editor asked me all sorts of questions about myself and I avoided providing any clear answers and was rather proud of my powers of evasion.

Herman was the first to get in touch. He'd been seeing my psychiatrist Doctor MacGregor, to help him through the crisis that hit him when I abandoned him so dramatically, and he said he felt much better now and he'd like to come and see *both of us*. So there he was, sitting on the white sofa, looking well and happy. He had left Cambria Lodge immediately after our separation and he was now living in the East End. He had a new job in the sculpture department of an art school, so he and Geoffrey could exchange professional chit-chat while I sat very still and kept quiet.

Enrique came as well. He was visiting London with the woman who would be his wife and an American friend whose face I can't remember so all I see of him are his wide cotton shorts and his big strong legs. The three of them were lined up on the sofa and there were several awkward silences in between the brief flurries of talk in Spanish or English.

And then my father announced that he wanted to see me. We arranged to meet in the Fitzroy Tavern after I had finished work. We sat at a table and drank beer. I was wearing my black beret and I had Tart tucked into my coat, with just her head sticking out.

My father was very friendly and not at all drunk. He talked about some lectures he'd been giving on *Wuthering Heights* and the difficulties he was having with other members of staff. He asked me how I was and I felt very strong and brave and told him I was fine. He made no mention of Geoffrey, but said he was sorry I had left Herman. 'Liked what I saw of him. Gather he was quite broken-hearted, poor chap.' When I said nothing, he didn't try to pursue that line of conversation.

A few days later he sent me a copy of a poem he had written about our meeting. He called it 'Mercy'.

> With her sailor hat and her kitten
> Tucked in a coat and warm,
> You, will You keep my daughter
> From any particular harm?
> I mean because of the habit
> Of love, and the way she has
> Of leaning upon the shoulder

Of this bent world of Yours,
As if she feared no disaster
Wound in the skein of the years,
No beaten man or woman
Crawling upon all fours,
But trusted whatever happens
Is destined to occur;
If You have need of mercy,
God, have mercy on her.

◎ ◎ ◉ ◎ ◎

I think it was Peggy who told me that my mother was renting the spare room to an American couple – she never again had single men as lodgers after I left. And she had found herself a new lover.

He was twenty-one years old which made him two years older than me and almost thirty years younger than her. His name was Jimmy and he was studying History and Economics at the London School of Economics.

One day, out of the blue, Jimmy telephoned me at the office. He introduced himself as 'a good friend of your mother's' and said we must meet. It was very important. He made it sound like a matter of life and death.

So there I was, back in the Fitzroy Tavern, with Tart in her basket.

Jimmy recognized me at once and came to introduce himself. 'Know you from your photos!' he said, chuckling with the thought of all that he knew. He had a soft round face that looked permanently perplexed and his chin was edged by a carefully sculpted beard, which did nothing to hide his extreme youthfulness. We sat down and he kept giving me long, lingering stares.

'I do realize,' he said in a rather plummy voice that imbued his words with the formality of an after-dinner speech. 'I do realize that I would not fulfil your fantasy in the way that Geoffrey clearly does, and yet I feel that you and I have a lot in common and . . . I'd like to go to bed with you. How about it?'

I asked if this was my mother's bright idea.

'Well, yes, sort of. Your mother thought you were bound to fancy me,' he said, as if he had learnt his lines by rote. 'I mean, given your history, your need for competitiveness, that sort of thing. And then . . .'

I think he was looking at himself in a mirror by now, instead of looking at me. 'And then if we got on, don't you know, your mother could have Geoffrey back, couldn't she? You can't really want to be with such an old man, apart from the need to perpetuate the triangular relationship that fits your psychological pattern.'

I am not sure if it was then that I threw the contents of my glass of beer at Jimmy's face and missed. He was with my mother for a number of years, off and on, and many of my memories of him are to do with throwing things at him, or wanting to throw things at him and wanting not to miss.

He called her Pussy, or Pussycat. For a while they lived together in Cambria Lodge and then, after Miss Glazier and her white cat had both gone, he rented the upper part of the house and brought girlfriends home, and would make very noisy love to them right above my mother's head. Sometimes she would bang on the ceiling with the handle of a broom, hard as she was able, *boom, boom, boom!* It was all part of their relationship.

◦ ◦ ◉ ◦ ◦

Not long after that failed first meeting with Jimmy, my mother telephoned me at work and said she wanted to come for tea with me and Geoffrey. Dutiful daughter that I was, I said, 'Oh, how nice!' and asked what day we could expect her.

So there she was at the door. I think Geoffrey let her in. She was very polite and subdued and it was as if she was visiting older relatives.

She sat on the white sofa and I served tea on the glass-topped table and the three of us made meaningless conversation. She looked at the mantelpiece on which stood the little figure I had stolen from her studio, but didn't appear to notice it. Her eyes swept around the small flat, taking in the architect's table, my little cut-out figures pinned to the cork board and the double bed, partially concealed in darkness in the back part of the room. She gave me an early Christmas present: two records of Bessie Smith singing the blues, which is what I had said I would like. On the back of both records she had written *For Julia with love from Rosalie, xxx* and the date.

Just before leaving she said she'd like to go to the lavatory and I showed her where it was. After she had gone, I found that she had done a pee all over the floor, so I mopped it up and even then I kept the lid of my thoughts firmly shut.

◉ ◉ ◉ ◉ ◉

1 April 1999

Rosalie is slipping away. I stayed with her at the hospital, but I felt I was holding her back. I was terribly tired from the merging of the days and the nights. Her friend Simon said he would stay, if I wanted to go home for a rest.

I said to her, 'If you don't mind, I think I'll go home and have a bath with lavender oil. And then a sleep.'

'Oh, how lovely!' she said in her deep whisper. 'You do that. I shall be thinking of you. Sleep well, darling. Goodbye.'

And I kissed her cheek and then her hand.

(From Julia's Notebook)

◦◦◦ 31 ◦◦◦

Thinking Things Over

A whole year had passed and Geoffrey and I went on a second holiday together. Two weeks on the island of Minorca and we walked along a sandy beach and I swam while he rested in the shade and read a book. There was a cave close to the beach and we sat there side by side and watched the sun setting over the sea. I looked at his hands in the falling light and they reminded me of those mummified hands in the museum, but I didn't say so.

We met a retired English couple who lived on the island; they thought Geoffrey was my father and they said how nice of a father to take his daughter on holiday! Neither of us tried to explain we were not related, at least not in that way.

The woman showed me round a beautiful old barn standing in a field near her house. She said I could buy it for just two hundred pounds, if I wanted to. I had inherited some money from my grandfather and I thought, that's what I'll do, I'll buy the barn and replace the missing tiles on the roof and paint the walls white and put a pot of flowers on a table and then I can stay here for as long as I like.

I was filled with enthusiasm and I told Geoffrey my plan. He was horrified. He asked how I could possibly consider leaving him like that, without so much as a backward glance. For my part I was indignant and angry. I said he didn't own me and he had no right to think that he did.

◦ ◦ ◎ ◦ ◦

When we returned from our holiday I started keeping a journal again, something I hadn't done since the move to Camden Town. There are no dates in this journal and very little clear information about what was happening around me, but on the opening pages I made the following declaration:

> The clock on the mantelpiece has always said ten past two ever since I came into this room. I still stand by nothing-in-particular and the earth still gapes with a wide-open grin sometimes. All I want is to burn as many bridges and boats as possible.

Shortly after we got back, Geoffrey learnt that his previous girlfriend, a woman called Ann, had killed herself, and I wrote that he and I had our first quarrel, *because of her death*. He wouldn't talk about it and he made no display of grief or remorse and it was that coldness that frightened me. His second wife, the mother of his two young children, had previously attempted suicide and now this other woman whom I had never met had tried and succeeded. In my journal I accused him of being *like Bluebeard, with dead women hanging from hooks in a room I have never been allowed to enter*, but I don't know if I said anything as sharp as this to his face.

After our quarrel, Geoffrey announced that he wanted to be on his own for a while. He went to the cottage 'to think' and to write his book about the meaning of design, while I stayed in London and went to work every day, with Tart in her straw basket for company. I looked forward to Geoffrey's return, but then when he did return I was filled with desolation.

He announced that during those solitary days he had considered taking his own life. He said he had worked it all out, he'd even arranged to cancel the milk and hide his car so nobody would become suspicious.

'What about me?' I asked him. 'What about your children, the little ones and the older ones? How do you expect us to go on living with the knowledge of your death?'

It seemed that such considerations had never crossed his mind. He looked puzzled and confused, and when he saw me crying he apologized and said he hadn't realized the idea would cause me so much pain. I asked him to make a solemn promise that he would never think of doing such a thing again and he made the promise and held my hand to clinch it.

But now the world no longer felt so safe. One night I was determined to talk to him about the implications of what he had almost done, but he only wanted to explain more about his theory on the meaning of design. I started to scream and in my journal I wrote that the sensation of screaming *was like gutting and disembowelling myself through the mouth.*

It was February 1969. By now Geoffrey had abandoned sleep altogether. He would stay up at his desk for hours, writing and rewriting the same sentences in his clear, elegant script, and when he finally came to bed he would sit propped up with pillows, chain-smoking and staring all through the night and no talk possible.

He said it was because he had almost reached the age of fifty. He realized he was suffering from a 'mid-life crisis', so he went to see a doctor who was also a personal friend.

I had seen this same doctor once when I had a bladder infection. Having asked for a pee sample, he told me to take my knickers off and lie on the table so that he could 'examine the problem'. He fiddled about with his fingers inside me for a while and when he was done he washed his hands and announced, 'Nothing wrong with you, my dear. It feels lovely in there. Geoffrey *is* a lucky man!'

Now the doctor wrote out a prescription for the latest antidepressant pills. They did nothing for the depression, but they seemed to push Geoffrey further and further away from the shore. He had a curious fixed expression on his face, apologetic and hopeful at the same time, and the talk on the meaning of design continued, obliterating all other conversations.

One evening when I was wandering aimlessly down the Charing Cross Road after work, I bumped into Geoffrey's first wife, whom I'd met a couple of times before. We walked side by side for a while and I told her how worried I was about Geoffrey and asked her what I should do. She said there was no need to worry, he had always been a bit moody, even when she was living with him during the war he'd been like that at times. 'It's all an act,' she said, 'a way of getting attention. Take no notice and it will pass.' And with that she bustled off, impatient to get away. I watched her as she disappeared among the crowd on the pavement. She reminded me of my mother, the same heavy body, the same unspoken anger.

I telephoned Herman and said I needed to talk to him. I went to his house near Brick Lane and sat on the edge of a chair in front of the little metal-topped table in his kitchen and no words would come out, so I remained silent. Herman didn't seem to mind and he didn't question me about why I had come.

His black-and-white cat was heavily pregnant. I picked her up and stroked her and she began to purr like a little engine. I could feel the bodies of her kittens twitching and pressing against her stretched sides. Herman pottered about, busy with whatever he was doing, and I remained with the cat. I said I didn't want to leave until the kittens were born in case there were any complications and she needed my help.

In the early hours of that morning four damp parcels of new life finally arrived. As soon as I had made sure that they were safe, Herman and I got into bed together. Lying beside him I felt happy for the first time in ages. It was as if I had come home after a long absence.

◦ ◦ ◉ ◦ ◦

I was back in Camden Town on the following day. I told Geoffrey where I had been and what had happened. He was quite calm. He said he had always known I would leave him. I was too young. He had nothing to offer me.

But before we made any final decision about what to do with our relationship, he again suggested we have a few weeks apart, to think things over. And so, on 29 March and with Herman's help, I rented a little house just off Brick Lane in a narrow cul-de-sac called Black Lion Yard and moved in.

All the houses in Black Lion Yard had been built in the eighteenth century and they had wooden panelled walls and wooden ceilings, which provided an ideal stamping ground for rats. These rats ran like heavy rabbits across the ceilings and sometimes they tumbled down the cavity of the walls, screeching with what sounded like hysterical laughter. I had brought Tart with me and she seemed to enjoy listening to the sound, but made no attempt to catch the rats.

One side of Black Lion Yard was occupied by recently arrived Bangladeshis, who had established food emporiums in which they sold all sorts of mysterious ingredients and cooked sweetmeats in big open saucepans, and chattered together like happy songbirds. The other side was

still the property of the earlier inhabitants, Jewish jewellers who bolted themselves into their little shops and occasionally emerged blinking into the
daylight with a great rattling of chains and banging of metal bars. My house
belonged to Leon Elgrod. He also owned the house next door, which had a
faded blue wooden gate leading into the remains of an old stable in the yard
at the back. You could still just read the words 'Keeper of Cows' on the gate.

Every evening a one-legged beggar used to swing down the street,
supported by a wooden crutch. And then he'd prop himself into the corner
of a doorway opposite my house and he'd look up towards my window. I
wondered if he had once lived here and I invented stories about how he had
lost first his money, then his leg and, finally, his mind.

Geoffrey set off for the cottage on 3 April, the day before Good Friday.
He told me he'd let me know when he had arrived and we would see each
other in six weeks' time. 'Don't worry about me, I'll be fine, I promise,' he
said, with the new and cheerful grin that seemed to be a side effect of the pills
he was taking.

○ ○ ◉ ○ ○

2 April 1999

*I woke up on the morning of Good Friday at seven o'clock. I telephoned the
hospital and the nurse in charge said that Rosalie's breathing had changed and
it wouldn't be long now. I made myself a hot-water bottle and a cup of tea and
went back to bed, the warmth on my belly and in my mouth. Then the nurse
phoned and said that Rosalie had passed away.*

(From Julia's Notebook)

⤞ 32 ⤝

One Spring Morning

It was Easter Monday and in the morning I thought I might visit a friend of Geoffrey's. During the last few months she had let me use a spare room in her house and I had a table and a chair and an Olivetti portable typewriter all to myself, and I'd go there sometimes for a few hours, to try to write and maybe gather my thoughts a bit in the process. I'd written a story without any plot or progression and called it 'Two People and Perhaps an Owl', and one about a man who was dead but didn't realize it, and a simple fairy tale in which a princess goes in search of the husband she has lost and a black dog gives her three of his hairs. Every time she needs help she must throw one of the hairs into the air and cry,

> Black dog, black dog,
> The world seems dark,
> Will it ever be light again?

I telephoned the friend, but there was no reply. I wondered about going to see Geoffrey at the cottage, just for the day, but then Herman arrived and said he was on his way to the funfair, so I went with him and we had a wonderful time on the dodgem cars.

By the following weekend, I still hadn't heard from Geoffrey and I was beginning to feel really anxious. He had no telephone at the cottage, but there was a public phone at the pub and several of his friends lived quite close by.

Then I did an odd thing. I could have gone to Herman's flat and made a few enquiries from there, but instead I went to Cambria Lodge. I don't know if I warned my mother that I was coming, or whether I just arrived unannounced.

Anyway, I opened the door with my key and walked in, and there she was. I wonder if we kissed each other on the cheek and what kind of a conversation we had. I must have told her that I was worried. I knew she had the telephone numbers of some of Geoffrey's friends in the area and I asked if I could go through the names in her address book.

I can remember being in her studio on my own. I sat at her writing desk by the big sash window, the address book open in front of me, and I began to make the phone calls.

Finally I got through to a man who lived in the next village. I had only met him once, but he knew my mother quite well. He was very reassuring. He said not to worry, he'd pop over immediately. He phoned back half an hour later to report that everything looked fine, the car was not in its parking place, so Geoffrey must have gone out, after all it was a lovely spring day. 'I'll try again tomorrow,' he said, 'early in the morning, bound to catch him then.'

I returned to Black Lion Yard and on the following morning, while I was having breakfast, I heard a loud hammering on the door. I went down to the street and there was my mother. 'He's dead!' she said, standing forlorn in the street. I never thought of asking her to come inside.

'I don't have the right to be as sad as you!' she said, holding back the tears.

'What do you want to do?' she said. 'You can come home with me if you like.'

⊙ ⊙ ◉ ⊙ ⊙

I asked her to take me to Herman's flat. He threw the key down when I shouted up at his window and I walked very slowly up the three flights of uncovered wooden stairs, my mother trailing behind me.

Herman realized that something had happened the moment he saw my face.

'You can go now!' I said to my mother, dismissing her as if she were a taxi driver who had already been paid.

I was suddenly so exhausted I could hardly stand on my feet. I went to lie down and Herman put on a Billie Holiday record: Volume One of *The Golden Years*, with a black-and-white photograph of Billie on the cover. She was about my age and she looked brave and sad at the same time. The first song on the record was called 'Travellin' Light.'

> Who will see and who will care,
> 'Bout this load that I must bear?
> Travellin', travellin', all alone.

Later in the day I asked Herman to make love to me. I remember looking beyond his shoulders at the white curtains flapping in the open window and the yellow daylight pouring through them, while Billie went on singing her songs of love and heartbreak.

⊙ ⊙ ◉ ⊙ ⊙

I was back at work within three days. It seemed like the best thing to do. I must have looked strange because several people asked me what was the matter, and then I was told that the woman who ran the company wanted to see me.

I was ushered in like a schoolgirl and stood there with my hands behind my back, as if waiting to be reprimanded for some minor misdemeanour. She sat behind her big desk and asked me a few questions and the whole story came out. She looked at me very steadily and said, 'How old are you?'

'Twenty.'

'Poor child, you are much too young for something like this.'

I thanked her for her kindness and apologized for the inconvenience. She advised me to take a few more days off, but I said I'd rather not. When I walked back to my office through the design department, I was aware of everyone looking at me and then looking away. I felt they could see blood on my hands. I felt like Cain with the horn growing out of his forehead to let the world know he had murdered his brother.

⊙ ⊙ ◉ ⊙ ⊙

My father contacted me and suggested that we should meet. So there we were, back in the Fitzroy Tavern. I hoped he would be as sympathetic as he had been the last time, when he wrote the poem called 'Mercy'.

The skin of his face had a waxy gleam and his hands shook when he lifted a glass of beer to his lips. I gathered that his home life was not going too well. 'Ted Hughes is just like you,' he said, hardly bothering with the niceties of a greeting, 'attracted to suicides. There was another one after Sylvia Plath, you know, but she rarely gets a mention because she wasn't a poet. I do think the Plath poems are marvellous, although Hughes is over-rated. He copies her style, but hasn't got her gift.'

I said nothing, drank a double whisky and thanked him for coming. After a while he set off back to Putney and I returned to the East End.

⊙ ⊙ ◉ ⊙ ⊙

I couldn't talk to my new friends about Geoffrey's death and none of the members of his family who had known the two of us together got hold of my address to find out how I was managing. It was as if everything that had happened in the last eighteen months had been a figment of my imagination, a child's game of let's pretend.

I avoided being on my own, especially at night. Sometimes I stayed with Herman and sometimes I'd ask him to come to Black Lion Yard. When I was on the edge of falling asleep, I'd hold tight on to my own hand and that gave me a sense of companionship.

I began to dream about Geoffrey and in my dreams he was very friendly with no trace of the old despair. We'd talk and wander through streets and empty houses, while he explained in a calm and matter-of-fact way that there had been a mistake and he wasn't dead at all. This meant that when I surfaced from sleep there was always a moment of sliding transition, when the dream seemed so much more tangible and convincing than the waking state.

◦ ◦ ◉ ◦ ◦

If it weren't for my mother's little diary for 1969, I would have been convinced that I hardly saw her during this time, but apparently that's not the case. In between the little stars to mark the number of times she made love with Jimmy and the little comments about their relationship and its difficulties when they had a quarrel or he was sleeping with other women, she made a note of all our various meetings.

On 20 April she wrote, *Geoffrey dead. To see Julia. Take her to Herman. Grief.* And then on the following day, *Julia comes over 11 a.m. Walk Richmond Park.* After which she apparently met up with Jimmy and Geoffrey's friend Anthony and one of Geoffrey's older children. Next to these names she wrote the word *scene*, so there must have been some emotional outburst.

It's strange for me to realize that throughout the time I lived with Geoffrey, my mother had kept in touch with his second wife and with other members of his complicated family, and she was much closer to them than I had ever been. So now she talked to them and they shared the shock and sadness with her and kept her informed about what was happening.

It was my mother who let me know the date on which Geoffrey's body would be cremated, immediately after the inquest. When she told me, she said she didn't think she wanted to go and suggested I might like to come for lunch with her on that day instead. She wrote a question mark next to my name and then she crossed it out in a different coloured biro, so I must have cancelled at the last minute.

I had never been to a funeral in my life and I did think vaguely that I should attend this one. It was to be in Bath, not in London, and because I couldn't face going on my own by train, I telephoned Geoffrey's first wife and asked if I could accompany her.

I heard the shock in her voice when she realized whom she was speaking to. She paused for a moment and I imagined her covering the receiver with her hand and saying to her husband, 'It's *her*! What a cheek!'

She told me she was very sorry, there was no room in her car and she muttered something about how anyway she would rather not see me 'in the circumstances'. Then she put the phone down in a hurry.

So I didn't go. I heard much later that it was quite a large gathering of all the family and a number of old friends, and drinks and food were served at the cottage afterwards. Geoffrey's second wife was suddenly transformed into the grieving widow and she gave an interview to the local paper in which she spoke of the 'shocking and inexplicable death of a "brilliant" man'. When

I read the article much later, I was surprised that the word 'brilliant' was put in inverted commas, which somehow seemed to invalidate it.

⊙ ⊙ ◉ ⊙ ⊙

Once again, my few possessions had been scattered. I thought it was Herman who took me to the flat in Camden Town to collect some things I had left behind, but according to my mother's diary she was the one who did it. Even now with the evidence in front of me, I find it hard to put her in the picture. I do remember Geoffrey's eldest son being there when I arrived and he was very cold and formal, and perhaps I have a dim recollection of him embracing my mother and the two of them sitting and talking together while I went about my business.

I hardly dared to claim anything that was mine, but I took some clothes and shoes and the figure of a naked woman that had belonged to my father and which stood on the marble mantelpiece next to the clock with its hands stuck at ten past two. I took the bedspread that I had stolen from my old room at Cambria Lodge and the three little cut-out figures I had made, but I abandoned letters and books and photographs and drawings and the picture of the inside of a slave ship that Geoffrey had given me and a very old map of London, which I had bought just recently. It was painted on a sheet of canvas as big as a bed and it showed the blue sweep of the River Thames and all the little houses standing to attention in their streets. It had been made in a time when there were still houses on London Bridge.

All my records were still at the cottage and Herman said he would drive me there. I sang Billie Holiday songs throughout the journey there and back again, one song running straight into the next so as not to allow any space for thought.

Herman stayed in the car and I went inside. Geoffrey's second wife and the two young children were in the upstairs room and all three of them froze when I walked in. The little boy charged at me and pummelled my legs and belly with his clenched fists. 'Why didn't you do something, Julia?' he shouted at me in a thin high voice. '*You* could have saved our daddy!'

2 April 1999

Her face was cold and the lines of age had begun to drop away so that she looked relaxed and much younger. Her hands were still warm. She was there and yet she was gone, presence and absence combined. I had never seen a dead person before and yet this meeting with death felt very familiar and unfrightening. I kissed the cold face and held the still warm hand in my own.

(From Julia's Notebook)

❧ 33 ❧

Putting It in Writing

When I was on my own I played Billie Holiday very loud, singing along with her from one verse to the next and I could even do the *plinkety plink* of Teddy Wilson's piano playing on songs such as 'I Cried for You' and 'Pennies from Heaven'.

If I couldn't get to sleep at night, I read *Winnie the Pooh* and my old Beatrix Potter books. I avoided the *Tales* of the Brothers Grimm because there was too much trouble in them and, come to think of it, I also avoided *The Tale of Samuel Whiskers* and *The Tale of Jemima Puddleduck* for the same reason.

I still had a journal, but instead of writing anything, I filled the blank pages with little drawings and paintings. I drew whatever came into my head: a nun screaming, a girl in a thick forest carrying a heavy sack on her back, that sort of thing. I wrote the word 'dead' quite often, to try it out.

○ ○ ◉ ○ ○

A few weeks after Geoffrey's death I received notice from a solicitor's office that they had a letter in their possession that was addressed to me by 'the deceased'. They went on to explain in extremely formal language that I could only become the recipient of this letter once certain legal matters had been dealt with. I wrote a typewritten reply in my most grown-up style, thanking them for their information and asking how long a delay I was to expect. 'We should have the matter dealt with in about six months,' came their reply.

I went on working at the publishing company and living in Black Lion Yard and seeing Herman and, although I have forgotten it, I also saw my mother quite regularly. *Julia for lunch* on 11 May, *Jules phones in distress* on 27 May, *Jules and Herman supper* on 24 June, and then, on the twenty-ninth, she and I went to see Geoffrey's kids and their mother and had a family picnic in the garden.

Geoffrey's second wife was quite friendly towards me and I had her children to stay from time to time. In August I went with them and a girlfriend for a week's holiday in Norfolk. The house we stayed in belonged to old friends of his and it was called Paperhouse, which sounded like something in a fairy tale. It stood on its own, far from any village, and it had a thatched roof and hollyhocks round the door, and low-ceilinged rooms that were permeated with a soft light and the sweet smell of wood smoke. It had no telephone or electricity, so you had to go through the evening ritual of lighting gas lamps, which made a strange hissing noise and produced a ghostly illumination.

The children were nervous and restless and affectionate. They clung to my hands when we went out walking and clambered over my body whenever I sat down. I read them the same stories I had always read to them, the one about the cat and the rat and one about a brave little boy from Finland called *The Terrible Olly* who stole all the treasure from a wicked troll and brought the spoils back to his mother. We sang 'I wonder why nobody don't like me' very loud with lots of ooh and aah noises, and we sat at a low table and made drawings of Geoffrey because that is what they said they wanted to do. I still have one of those drawings which shows him naked with his hands together and tears running down his face and I remember how startled I was when the little boy drew an erect penis on the body of his father. They wanted to write *Dead Now* as the title of the drawing and I helped them with the spelling. They asked me if I thought Geoffrey had died because he was so tall, because they knew that the older you are the taller you become and he was the tallest person they had ever seen.

⊙ ⊙ ◉ ⊙ ⊙

Just as I was surprised by how often I saw my mother during those months, I was also surprised by how regularly I wrote to her whenever I was away. I had started to call her Rosalie, instead of Mummy, but in spite of this statement of separateness I was clearly asking for her love and trying to be a good daughter. From Paperhouse I wrote to tell her that over the recent months I felt I had turned into a poltergeist: banging doors, picking up books, dropping cups and yet nobody seemed to see me.

My mother would reply, telling me about her difficulties with Jimmy and what she had done, whom she had seen, where she was going next, and at the end of this chattering catalogue of events she would close with *lots of love, Rosalie*. What neither of us ever mentioned, in any of these exchanges that continued in the same tone from one year to the next, was the enormous presence of the dead man who now lay between us.

'The only way you can ever escape from your mother', Geoffrey had said, 'is by living with me.' But with his death he had bound the two of us together all the more tightly.

◦ ◦ ◉ ◦ ◦

On 7 October 1969, and again according to my mother's diary because I would never have known the date otherwise, I went back to York University to start the second year of my degree. I was still renting Black Lion Yard and I never spent more than a week or two in York. Whenever possible I wrote my essays while I was in London and posted them to my tutors, who didn't seem to mind. They also didn't seem to mind the eccentricity of my thought processes. I still have a copy of the essay I wrote about Strindberg's play *Miss Julie*. I called it 'Miss Julie and the Razor' and the first paragraph goes like this:

> Miss Julie is Miss Julie. This is her problem. She would like to be someone else, perhaps a servant. If she cannot be someone else she would like to have a tragic end.

In November 1969 I received another communication from the solicitor's office and they enclosed a white envelope with an unused first-class stamp in the right-hand corner and my Black Lion Yard address written in black felt tip in Geoffrey's elegant handwriting.

The letter inside covered two thin sheets of onionskin paper. *Dearest Julia my darling*, it began, and I found that a relief; at least it sounded friendly.

I kept the letter for all these years and I even treasured it in a way because it did tell me that I was not to blame for what had happened. But I never really tried to understand what it said.

At the time I found Geoffrey's words strangely poetic. On Easter Sunday, two days after arriving at the cottage, he wrote that he realized *the bottle was empty*, but rather than taking his life on that night, he went to bed and slept, *to be sure that what seemed so eminently reasonable at 8 p.m. would still hold at 8 a.m. and 12 noon.*

> So I slept, fitfully, and the dawn was one of the most lovely I have ever known, I could not wish for a better day to die on . . .
>
> I cannot face the gradual decline into melancholia – you gave me two years of happiness . . . if the clock had stopped for us two years ago, I'd be free from that terrible load of guilt of these last eight months, a little sad perhaps but joyous, so that even the movement of your wrists seemed somehow more meaningful – oh my love I cannot think of you except joyfully.
>
> When you left, I had hoped to turn, to return, to writing – but the enemy is no longer there and I cannot set him up afresh . . . My ideas cannot be articulated and will not be now.
>
> Perhaps one day – if that is what you want – you will be great. Never forget that just by *being* you, you brought great joy to someone you loved and will again to others. Perhaps with someone nearer your own age you will not be so transparent, so vulnerable. I couldn't help you – for me it was the last drink from the bottle and the days of emptiness ahead and I was peevish, petulant, irritable.
>
> So at the moment – this long drawn-out day of spring sunshine – when I have neither failed nor succeeded, when the past is in an equipoise of meanings – I can leave peacefully. Life has been generous to me these last 35 years. I have incurred a debt I cannot repay. Better to leave it like that.

And then the familiar signature.

I suppose if I had been able to read the letter more carefully all those years ago, I would have realized that there was a lot I didn't understand about what was being said, or about the man who was saying it to me from beyond the grave. And I would have had to face up to the fact that in spite of everything, he still didn't pause to think about the people he was leaving behind, to ask how I would manage with the guilt, with my mother, with my life. And what about his children, the two big ones and the two little ones?

⊙ ⊙ ◉ ⊙ ⊙

Not long before we parted, Geoffrey bought himself a brand-new pale-blue pick-up truck and he drove to the cottage in it; speeding along the motorway in the middle of the night, while I sat in the open back with his two children, the wind whipping at our faces and trying to snatch away the blankets we had wrapped round our bodies.

It was very exciting and we sang and screamed with delight hugging each other to keep warm, as we looked up at the dark sky and the stars. But if he had needed to stop suddenly, then the three of us and our blankets would have hurtled over the side of the truck and that would most probably have been the end of our little lives.

And then there was another time in another car. We were going down the one really steep hill that led to the cottage when Geoffrey announced almost proudly, 'The brakes have gone! They're not working at all!'

We went faster and faster and at a certain point we shot over the stop sign at a crossroads, before going up the other side and slowly grinding to a halt.

'We could've died!' I said to him.

'Yes! We could!' he said and when I turned towards him, I saw that he looked really happy and was smiling for the first time in ages.

⊙ ⊙ ◉ ⊙ ⊙

3 April 1999

Rosalie's coffin was delivered this morning and it's standing on wooden trestles in the garage. I have been painting it cerulean blue, the colour that Heaven must have if there is a Heaven.

So I don't need to cancel my flight to Italy after all. I'll leave in two days' time and be back here for the funeral on the tenth.

(Fax to Herman)

The Scent of Adrenaline
in the Air

So here we are and the curtain rises.

Geoffrey's dead body lies across the front of the stage and the theatre spotlight shines on him in such a way that the audience can see his outline in silhouette, like a mountain range.

His grey hair is swept back to reveal the wide sweep of his forehead. His nose in profile is arched and elegant. His mouth is closed. His hands are folded across his chest as if he were a saint, carved on the lid of his own stone sepulchre. He is wearing a dark-green shirt with a nice gleam to it, a narrow tie of woven silk and a pair of dark trousers that fit his long legs perfectly. His shoes are brown and well-polished and they, along with the feet they contain, point up towards the ceiling.

My mother enters stage left, or it might be stage right. She's in her early fifties by now, but she could easily be several years younger; she vibrates with such a wild energy and everything about her is strong. She has strong shoulders leading into strong arms and she stands firm on strong legs. Her teeth are good for chewing meat and biting into apples, her cheekbones are high, her mouth is firm and her eyes are as green as ever. She looks ready for a fight, ready to take on ten fierce men and a dog without a moment's hesitation; or even ten women.

She holds her head high as she strides purposefully towards the dead man. She places herself close to his feet, then turns to face the audience. 'This,' she says, her voice reaching into all four corners of the auditorium, 'this is the only man I ever really loved. My daughter seduced him and stole him from me and then . . . she killed him.'

The audience sucks in its collective breath with shock and horror. And within the reassurance of that sound, my mother begins to cry. She stands there with the spotlight warm on her face and great heavy tears run down her cheeks.

This is my cue and now I walk out on to the stage. I look at the two figures who are – as it were – waiting for me, and after a bit of hesitation I go and take my position quite close to Geoffrey's head. I am also strong and I am also ready for a fight. All the muscles in my body are tense with anticipation. My neck is tight, my jaw is tight and my fists are clenched.

I do not look at my mother, or at the dead man, or at the audience; instead I look down at the wooden boards beneath my feet. 'It was not my fault,' I say, and you can hear the sharp anger in my voice. 'And anyway, he had already left her and he would never, never have gone back to her! He hated her, he told me so himself.'

'That's a lie!' cries my mother, addressing the audience from her end of the dead body. 'He swore that he loved me and that he would never leave me! He would have grown tired of my daughter soon enough and then he would have come back to me. He and I would have been happy together for the rest of our lives, but she spoilt it all!'

'It was not my fault!' I say again, through clenched teeth.

'Then let's have a vote on it!' says my mother. 'Those of you here today who think my daughter killed him and must bear the blame, put up your hands so I can count you.'

I hear a rustling of movement as the hands decide whether to lift into the air, or stay still. I close my eyes. I do not want to see the result. The curtain comes down.

And this is the scene that was enacted in all its possible variations, between me and my mother for more years than I care to remember. Sometimes we kept quiet for a while, either through not seeing each other or through maintaining a formality of friendliness and politeness, but every time again when the lid was lifted, there we were on the stage and there was the evidence of Geoffrey's cold corpse, lying on the wooden floor between us.

⊙ ⊙ ⊙ ⊙ ⊙

My mother was very good at telling the story of how I had betrayed her and killed the man she loved, and she told it to many of her friends and to some of my friends too when I wasn't there to interrupt. Quite often I would suddenly be aware that I was talking to someone who *knew what I had done* and they would look at me in a funny way as if they could see blood on my hands, or the horn of Cain pushing out like a little bud between the hair on my head.

I remember answering the telephone one day at my mother's house in Suffolk – this must have been in 1990 or thereabouts. It was Barbara, who had once been my father's student in Leeds and who had sometimes babysat for me when my parents went out in the evening. She had later married our first lodger Bob, he of the perfume bottle and the comic book about dogs. I had always liked her.

'Rosalie? Is that you?' said Barbara – it was true that my mother's voice and mine were very similar.

'No, it's me, Julia. How nice to hear you. Haven't seen you for ages.'

There was a pause and then very slowly and deliberately Barbara said, 'I'm sorry to have to say this, but I couldn't bear to meet you ever again; knowing what you have done to your poor mother, the pain you have caused her.' And with that she put the phone down.

'Who was it, darling?' said my mother, walking into the room and smiling; we were going through a benevolent phase.

'Wrong number,' I replied.

⊙ ⊙ ◉ ⊙ ⊙

But never mind, as my mother said, right at the end of her life, with only a few more days left. 'Never mind, it's all water under the bridge now.'

∽ 35 ∽

My Stumbling Father

After the one conversation with my father in the pub, about people who chose to live with people who kill themselves, he and I never again alluded to Geoffrey's life or his death. He kept silent in his notebooks as well, so I suppose that for him the subject really was closed.

If he was in a good mood when we met and not too swamped by pills or alcohol, then we would return to our old pattern and discuss the books we had read and the poems he had written. If things were not going well, then he would thrash about in a net of remorse and despair and irritation, but I didn't feel burdened by the drama of his troubles, simply because he didn't blame me for them.

I sometimes tried to tell him about my mother. I said I was frightened of her and couldn't talk to her and didn't know what to do. He would listen rather abstractedly and mutter things about it not being her fault, her childhood had been difficult, so had her marriage with him. Reading through his notebooks now, I realize he was more concerned than I would have thought and very aware of the dangerous battle going on between his daughter and his ex-wife.

He describes an occasion when my mother contacted him and said she needed to come and talk about me. Apparently I had written her an *angry and dismissive letter* and she was very upset.

So there they were, the two of them together, facing each other across the Formica table in the kitchen perhaps, each with a cup of hideously strong tea in one of those blue and white striped china mugs, like the one in the photograph. Or they were in the room next door, sitting side by side on the sofa, its green stretch nylon cover pock-marked with brown holes where the tips of so many lighted cigarettes had burnt through.

My father wanted to be benign and helpful; after all, as he told himself in his notebook, they had spent sixteen years together and had once been happy and now they had a daughter in common, if nothing else.

I have no idea what my mother said to him, but he was clearly very shocked by the violence of her condemnation of me and when he tried to balance out her version of events, she burst into tears and exploded with anger, not just against me, but against him as well. They looked at each other through what he called *enraged myopic eyes* and she told him he was a bastard, he'd always been a bastard and she hated him, while he ground his teeth and doubled over his bottom lip and shouted that she was *scarcely human*. It was just like old times.

After my mother had stormed out of the house, banging the door behind her, my father wrote the first draft of a poem, complete with awkward rhymes:

> It's obvious to me that I am not a nice man,
> But admit my shadow-side I think I can.
> She tries to think she casts no shadows
> And meets with shades where'er she goes . . .
> She wishes to be loved and yet she cannot see,
> They are not lovable that lack charity.

He then wrote the heading WORDS FOR JULIA in capital letters, starting with,

> You think she is impossible.
>   Why then for you, she is impossible . . . It is not stupidity, but a disabil-
> ity. But you are supposed to go further, than myself who is your father and
> if you cannot love her, then understand *why* you cannot.

He never discussed any of this with me, although from time to time he would say, 'Try to love her, darling. It would be better in the long run, don't you think?'

◦ ◦ ◉ ◦ ◦

But however much wisdom my father might have had in relation to me, he was still tangled into a terrible rage about how he had been treated by his father and damaged by the treatment. I remember being with him in a pub with his younger brother John, when suddenly he began to thump on the table, crying out, 'I hate him! I hate the bastard!'

'But he's been dead for three years now!' said John, who always tried to keep things in balance.

'I don't care how long he has been dead. I still hate him! I wish I'd strangled him with my bare hands!' and he collapsed among the glasses of beer and began to sob.

⊙ ⊙ ⊚ ⊙ ⊙

But that was later. In 1971 my grandfather, the object of my father's undiluted hate, was living out his last days in an old people's home in Putney. I went to see him there and I remember it as a stuffy building, its windows covered by half-drawn curtains, its little front garden like a plot in a modern cemetery.

'I've come to see Canon Blackburn,' I said to the uniformed nurse who opened the door, a smell of old age and disinfectant blowing towards me from behind her back.

She led me into a room crowded with armchairs and there among other abandoned geriatrics was my grandfather. He was in his usual grey suit, complete with waistcoat, but his gleaming dog collar was partially concealed by the bib tied round his neck. He was fast asleep with his chin on his chest and he was drooling.

The nurse bent over him and slapped him sharply on both of his soft red cheeks. She didn't seem to like him much. 'Wake up, Canon!' she said. 'We've got a visitor!'

He spluttered into a sort of wakefulness, looking shocked and frightened. I don't think he recognized me, although he took my hand and held it in a tight squeeze. I sat beside him and in his cold grip I could feel the electric tremors of Parkinson's disease pulsating through his body. After a few unsuccessful attempts at conversation, I extricated myself and said goodbye, and went to have tea with my father and Peggy; they were only a few minutes' walk away.

My father said he sincerely hoped the Old B would soon be dead. 'He's going to roast in Hell and a good thing too!' he said confidently.

He told me there had been a lot of trouble at the nursing home because of the Old B's obsession with skin colour and with sex. My grandfather was convinced that all the nurses, especially what he called 'the foreign ones', wanted to commit what he called 'carnal acts' with him. He said that when they washed him they tried to lower their faces as close as possible to his genitals, so that they could breathe in the smell of him.

'The leopard is finally showing his true spots and very unsavoury spots they are too!' said my father.

⊙ ⊙ ◉ ⊙ ⊙

I never saw my grandfather again and he must have died during the summer of that year. Herman and I were on holiday in Corfu and on our way back we were going to meet my father and Peggy, close to where they were staying in northern Italy.

We met them in Venice. It was a bright clear day in late August and there they were sitting in the sunshine at a white plastic table, among a cluster of other café tables set out in Saint Mark's Square.

As I approached my father I could hardly recognize him. He looked very old and decrepit, and he seemed to have metamorphosed into a caricature of his own father. He stood up and took a few shuffling steps towards me, walking in little trembling jerks. His head was bent forward and he was mumbling to himself making his bottom lip move and twitch. His face was pale and uninhabited.

'Hello, Daddy!'

'Hello, darling. Crisis . . .' and he fumbled his way back to his seat.

His hands were shaking so much that he spilt half his drink down the front of his shirt. I noticed he was drinking brandy even though it was not yet eleven o'clock. He swallowed what was left in his glass and gazed blankly across the sunlit square.

'Isn't it beautiful!' I suggested, but he didn't answer.

'He's been like this ever since we arrived,' said Peggy apologetically, standing next to him and dusting the back of his jacket with her hand, as if that might help. 'Sometimes he doesn't speak for days. But he was looking forward to seeing you. Let's hope you can cheer him up a bit.'

'You are pleased to see Julia and Herman, aren't you, Thomas? Don't they look well!' she said, speaking slowly and at full volume, as if he were deaf as well as mentally absent.

'Menopause, it's all very dark,' was his reply.

◦ ◦ ◉ ◦ ◦

We went for a walk, across the square and over the miraculous Bridge of Sighs. My father led the way, stumbling forward at an angle as if he were battling against a strong wind, head down, stiff arms flapping. He didn't look left or right and he was still muttering to himself.

We reached a church, I have forgotten its name. He walked up the wide steps, pushed his weight against the heavy wooden door and almost fell headlong into the darkness on the other side. I followed close behind him, watching as he propelled himself towards the altar at an alarming speed so that people had to move away to let him pass. And there, before some ornate image of the crucified Christ surrounded by angels and the luminous clouds of Heaven, my father let out a little cry and threw himself face down on to the cold marble floor.

He lay there groaning and then he began to chant quite loudly, '*De profundis, Domine*, Out of the shadows, oh Lord, I cry to Thee.'

I hoped that everyone in his vicinity would be impressed by such a display of religious devotion and wouldn't call a guard to expel him.

'Come along, Thomas, get up, do,' said Peggy, bustling around the enormous bulk of this supine body and then going down on her knees beside him to stroke his hair and encourage some sort of action.

'It's getting worse,' she said, apologetically. 'I'm at my wits' end.'

And putting her mouth close to my father's ear, she added, 'I said I'm at my wits' end, Thomas. They'll be calling an ambulance to carry you away in a minute and look, here comes a nice priest.'

My father rose to his knees – priests made him more nervous than policemen, he called them 'the gangsters of Eternity'. He opened his eyes and looked around the church in a daze as if wondering what sort of a place he was in. He caught sight of the image of Christ on the Cross and he began to intone, 'Eloim! Eloim! Father, Father, why hast Thou forsaken me?'

'Oh, do shut up, Thomas!' said Peggy as the priest drew closer.

By now my father was back on his feet and heading for the church door and the bright sunlight outside.

We entered the next church and the next, and each time he went through the same ritual; sometimes he even prostrated himself on the floor with his arms stretched out in the shape of the cross.

⊙ ⊙ ◉ ⊙ ⊙

Two days later Herman and I went with my father on a long walk in the Dolomites. I must have hoped his mood would shift in the mountains, just as it used to do when I was a child. We set off with the first light of dawn. He was carrying the familiar bundle of nylon climbing rope on his shoulders and before we started the ascent he said we had better rope-up, for safety's sake. And that was also like childhood: being connected by this strange umbilical cord, although now Herman and not my mother was at the other end of the rope.

My father knew the route because he had done it before and so he led the way. He moved with the haphazard determination of a wind-up toy and with a new-found awkwardness, as if he was carrying an ungainly weight on his shoulders.

This was a *Via Ferrata*, which had been constructed during the First World War, and it made it possible to climb the almost vertical slabs of rock with the help of metal rungs and threaded metal cords. It was like ascending a huge staircase that led through the clouds and into the space beyond.

We had just completed one of these steep ascents and were making our way along a narrow stony path, when my father tripped and fell. He went down sideways and rolled over on to his back, close to the very edge of the path and within inches of the steep drop beyond it. He lay there helpless and gasping like a huge fish that had been pulled out of the water. The whole process of his fall seemed to have been enacted at the wrong speed – it was like watching a slow-motion film sequence – and I realized that my father had no reflexes with which to steady himself, no instinct to stretch out a protective hand.

Herman and I heaved him back on to his feet, struggling with his huge and almost inert bulk. It was clearly too risky being tied to him because if he fell he would pull us both with him, like souls cast into Hell.

We told him we didn't want to use the ropes any more. My father was very shocked and said we were irresponsible and what he called 'foolhardy', but we untied ourselves anyway. He didn't have another fall that day, but every so often I saw him teetering on the edge of losing balance and there was always an odd little grin on his face, as if he quite enjoyed the idea of taking leave of life so abruptly.

◎ ◎ ◉ ◎ ◎

He began to close in on himself as we made the descent and when we were coming in sight of the road from which we had started, it was as if I could see the Old B complete with grey suit and gleaming dog collar, climbing back on to the shoulders of his son and perching there, holding on tight with shaking legs.

It was the last big mountain expedition my father was to make. When he had returned to London he tripped in the street and broke a rib, and that meant he could hardly walk at all for a while. And he began drinking more and more and taking more and more of his pills, the blackness of his despair gathering around him in almost visible clouds.

◎ ◎ ◉ ◎ ◎

6 April 1999

Here in Italy. The sweetness of the house smelling of cedar wood, the folds of the mountain valley, the owl at night. The fragment of a dream in which Rosalie was as helpless as a mermaid and I was trying to lift her up in my arms.

Yesterday Herman and I went for a walk. We followed a steep path through the forest of chestnut trees and emerged into the open landscape of the high mountain ridge. We saw a floating pair of eagles and a chamois in the distance, but no people. The pale grass was scattered with tiny anemones, hellebores, yellow crocus and deep-blue gentians.

(From Julia's Notebook)

36

Dear Rosalie, Dear Tommy

In October 1972 Herman and I went to Deia for a short holiday and decided to stay there. We met people I had known years before and rented a house in a street called Es Clot. We had a roof terrace and Herman had a studio, and I had what I called a writing room with a window that looked out across biscuit-coloured roof tiles and into the orchards and olive groves that surrounded us.

On 1 November I sent my mother a letter, wishing her a very happy birthday and saying how sorry I was that *it can't be wished face to face*. I told her the village was even more beautiful than I remembered it, *but possibly I was then too caught up in an adolescent whirl to notice*, and the sun was warm and the oranges were orange and we had a spare room and *if you feel like coming over at Christmas that would be lovely*. I asked her to tell my father and Peggy that I would be in touch soon and to *send them love in advance*.

I wrote to my father and asked after his health and told him that the weather in Majorca was perfect for long walks in the mountains and we had seen *the great white god Robert Graves striding along the road with his wife and he was wrapped up in a purple scarf and a red something, with a great black woollen cap pulled over his ears.* I ended the letter with the hope that *writing and life goes well.*

In his reply my father instructed me to *Tell Graves I think* Counting the Beats *is one of the finest works of the century, if that sort of remark means anything to him.*

And my mother wrote to say she would come for Christmas. She asked if she could bring Jimmy with her, otherwise she felt the *male-female balance wouldn't be right.*

'Oh, do bring him,' I said, blocking out my dislike of Jimmy and the memory of that meeting with him in the pub. 'It would be lovely to see him again.'

I wrote again to my father and I invited him and Peggy for Christmas and never mind that my mother and Jimmy were planning coming too, I was sure we'd all manage somehow. The style of my letter is curiously formal:

> It would give me great pleasure to be able to provide you with a place and hospitality for once in my sweet and muddled life . . . I have my own workroom and the house already has a strong home feeling about it . . . The sun is shining on my back through the front door. Love and kisses.

My father replied in very shaky handwriting that he wasn't able to go anywhere at the moment, because he was still deep in what he called his Menopause. He said he spent all day and all night sitting in a chair and wanting to die, and he couldn't keep the sadness at bay; he felt he had caused too much pain to others and Peggy blamed him for lots of things and perhaps she was right. On top of that the poetry had dried up again. He was holding on to his teaching job by the skin of his teeth, but the college was about to move to Plymouth and he hated the prospect of leaving London or of applying for a different job where the staff and the students would be strangers to him and his somewhat eccentric habits.

I responded in full parental role, telling him,

> Neither you nor your life is nearly as bad as you want to think.
>
> You are full of guilt, self-hatred and a kind of rage that seems to be devouring you . . . But you cannot for instance have any guilt about your role as a father, because I feel no resentment or blame . . .

My father didn't answer for some time, because by then he was too busy drinking and crunching his pills to put pen to paper. My mother wrote to say she'd had another quarrel with Jimmy and so they weren't on speaking terms, but she'd decided to come and stay with us anyway, because she didn't want to be on her own for Christmas and never mind the male-female unbalance.

We collected her from the airport and she and I went through the ritual of kisses and smiles, and all the time I felt her assessing me and I never once dared to look her in the eye.

On Christmas Day the sun was warm and the sky was blue, and my mother and I swam from the jagged rocks further along the coast and Herman took a photograph of us standing side by side in the cold sea. And then the three of us sat on the rocks in the sunshine and drank a bottle of champagne and wished each other well.

The superficial chatter continued. I don't think we mentioned my father and his galloping despair and we certainly didn't mention Geoffrey. My mother said Jimmy was a fool and she only tolerated him because he was so good in bed and we all laughed at that because it seemed like a cue for laughter. After the week was up we returned her to the airport and she sent a nice thank-you-for-having-me letter and said what fun it all had been.

○ ○ ◉ ○ ○

In February I heard from Peggy that my father was getting worse. He had begun to *drink in earnest*, which I gathered meant gin mixed with strong cider. He wrote about the experience later, in the first draft of the opening chapter for a second volume of his autobiography, which he planned to call *The Last Farthing*.

> Shaking and almost speechless after a night in my clothes in my study chair
> and the consumption of maybe two and a half bottles of Gordon's I would
> teeter to the off licence which opened at eight thirty with a package to hold

the bottles and buy two or three more. As soon as I was out of the shop, I would gulp half a bottle down . . . swigging it into my empty stomach with a sense of sizzling, like a fried egg on a piece of red-hot metal . . .

◎ ◎ ◉ ◎ ◎

In March 1973 Herman and I decided to separate. We felt this was the right thing to do even though neither of us was quite sure why, and we reassured each other that we would be back together very soon. We had a separation party and invited our friends to come and celebrate the end of something and the uncertain beginning of something else. We served stewed rabbit with black olives and everyone drank a lot of wine and wished us well. I went back to England, then to stay with Caroline, an old school friend who lived in a cottage in Wales. I was just in time to witness my father's complete breakdown.

The climax came after the fourth week of my excesses. I was returning at 8.45 with a replenished supply after a long night of intoxication. I tripped against the kerb on our street, fell on my back and remember only the sound of breathing and a great blackness. My wife found me and with the aid of a neighbour, got me into bed and called the doctor. I entered a nursing home called The Priory.

I took a train down to London to visit him at The Priory. I went there with my stepmother. The two of us were afraid of what we might find, but as it turned out we never got further than the office of the man in charge of the ward. He explained that we couldn't see my father right now because he was going through the first stage of the detoxification treatment, which involved something called Deep Sleep. 'We have a special room,' he said, looking up from his paperwork and smiling as if with pleasure at the thought. 'We keep them sedated for ten days and that cleans the system out and then we are ready to begin.'

After this visit I returned to Caroline's cottage in Wales. We made marmalade and planted lettuce seeds and mended a stone wall, and in the evening we sang songs together by candlelight because there was no electricity.

⊙ ⊙ ◉ ⊙ ⊙

Meanwhile, after three weeks at The Priory, my father was back home. He wrote to tell me he was *off the booze*, but it didn't last and in July he was admitted to the alcoholic ward at the new Charing Cross Hospital where they planned to give him Aversion Therapy and ECT.

Whenever he was in hospital, my father kept me informed about what was happening and his letters were so vivid that I felt as if I were sitting beside him, watching over him as he went through the various treatments that were supposed to help. In Charing Cross Hospital he had offered himself as a guinea pig for some experiments with LSD, but they must have been disconcerted by his enthusiasm and didn't take him on. He was, however, considered a good candidate for ECT, which he called 'that modern brand of magic'; but although he enjoyed the ritual of being strapped to a table and wired up with electrodes, the passing of volts of electricity through his brain had no apparent effect and didn't even make him lose his memory. But he was pleased to announce that the Aversion Therapy seemed to be going very well, even though it was hard work. In another chapter from his unfinished autobiography he described the experience in detail:

> It took place in a small basement room and when I entered I saw a white table covered with assorted bottles, a syringe, two towels and a large basin. Nurse Waters got me to roll up my sleeve, injected my right arm with a substance allergic to alcohol, which when combined with drink produces an overwhelming desire to vomit. I waited while he poured a queue of drinks, six in all, half glasses of gin and brimming tumblers of beer.
>
> Then he said, 'Right, Mr Blackburn. Now you're for it!'
>
> He pushed a glass of neat gin before me and I swilled down the nauseous liquid. My eyes went black for a moment and my head swam and I felt my stomach heaving . . .
>
> 'Now the gin! Keep it down!' Waters's eyes were shining with amusement – this would teach these intellectual frauds. 'Now the beer!'
>
> Three sessions, each one entailing twelve glasses of spirits – wine for some reason was not included – ending with my sinking on to the pillowed bed. Nurse Waters threw a couple of blankets over me and left me to simmer down.

After three weeks in Charing Cross Hospital he managed to leave the building dressed in only his striped pyjamas and was seen walking unconcernedly down the middle of the Fulham Palace Road, with cars hooting at him from both directions. He made his way to an off-licence and there he bought himself two bottles of gin on tick. He took the gin back to the hospital and shared it with the other recovering alcoholics. As a result he was thrown out in disgrace and told he could never come back.

⊙ ⊙ ⊚ ⊙ ⊙

I continued to live with Caroline in Wales and continued to write to my father, encouraging him in whatever way I could. I became much closer to Peggy, the two of us discussing 'poor Thomas' as she now called him and how to avert disaster. Peggy was so busy trying to maintain contact with various doctors and their plans and prognoses that she had given up lipstick and drink.

I must have had some kind of meeting with my mother, because among the bundles of my letters that she kept there is one from this time in which I *apologize for all those scenes*. I have a vague memory of her coming to the cottage for my birthday and she gave me a field guide on birds, which I still have, and then we had a fierce quarrel about Geoffrey and the past, with neither Geoffrey nor the past being mentioned, and she left in a huff.

Back in Putney, my father was on what was called 'sick leave' and he continued to rumble through the disordered chaos of the days, with Peggy doing her best to keep him and the house under control. In the first week of January 1974 she arranged for him to be sent to a hospital in Epsom. He wrote to tell me that he was sharing a room with a man who cried all through the night because he wanted to be turned into a woman.

The doctor in charge was a specialist in sex changes. He was also a keen advocate of all sorts of new drugs and he tried my father out on several anti-psychotic, anti-schizophrenic and antidepressant drugs, and finally came up with something called Parstelin, a recently formulated anti-psychotic and antidepressant, which could be used as a short-term treatment for severe anxiety. Its side effects included movement disturbance, muscle tremor and muscle rigidity, as well as hyperactivity and insomnia, especially if taken in the evening. But never mind, my father was delighted with it:

Dear Julia,

Two weeks in this dump and the deep depression has lifted, I just have my normal angst and moods of sadness and for the first time in my life I have no desire to drink at all and please god it is the end of all my boozing . . .

We pass our time in the strangest ways the strangest ways [sic]. In the morning we get up at seven, we have a meeting from nine to twelve. The first part is devoted to such interesting topics as the absence of a toilet roll in one of the lavatories, the fact that we were one rasher of bacon short for breakfast. Then one of the patients mumbles out his or her depressing life story, police courts, hospitals, broken marriage, which is then discussed by the omnipotent group.

In the afternoon we all trail off to the geriatrix or psychotic and schizo-phrenic ward where we play Bingo with speechless and often rather savage patients. My job is usually to help them to put the counter on the correct number and then shout out 'Bingo!' when someone has achieved the requisite sequence. I also have to hand out chocolates and sweets . . .

It would be my delight if you came back to London and stayed a bit with Peggy and me. I am reasonably certain that if you do come and stay with us, the blackness will be lifted and I dry. . . .

I never considered going to stay with him and Peggy, dry or not dry, and anyway by now I had returned to Deia. I rented a house with a very dark kitchen that smelt of mould and a very light bedroom with the tendrils of a grapevine creeping in through the open window. I got a job helping a rather pompous painter writing a book about another painter who reminded him of himself and another job, helping Beryl Graves to sort out the vast correspondence that her husband had accumulated over the years. We read the funny bits of letters aloud to each other and I sometimes sat with Robert and he would hold forth about love, as if he were in the first bloom of youth and not an old man with grey curls, teetering on the edge of dementia. Something about his tenacity reminded me of my father, even though the two men couldn't have been more different.

◦ ◦ ◉ ◦ ◦

10 April 1999

The day of the funeral.

The children and I covered the blue coffin with orange and red wallflowers.

The church was full of friends and neighbours and my daughter read a poem and my son gave a little impromptu speech about how much he had loved his grandmother. I gave a little speech too, starting with an account of Rosalie's bravery on the mountains when she first met my father and ending with her bravery and jollity during the final month of her life.

Geoffrey's daughter arrived late and in tears, having been stuck in a traffic jam. His son is still in America but coming to England soon.

(Fax to Herman)

⤚ 37 ⤛

Seeing God

In London my father was enjoying his Parstelin. He had been warned not to eat cheese or Marmite while he was using the drug, but I don't think he was aware of its other possible consequences, or if he was, he didn't care. He was supposed to take six pills a day, but he often used more than that and once the Aversion Therapy had worn off, he combined the medication with lots of alcohol. The known side effects of hyperactivity and insomnia kicked in almost immediately, and this often led him to crunch his way through a second batch of six pills as he worked through the night. Or more, if he could get them.

⊙ ⊙ ◉ ⊙ ⊚

I wrote to tell him that Herman and I had separated and about my new job working for Beryl Graves, and a study of the Genesis Myth I had been working on, which I would like to discuss with him, especially some interesting material on Dualism and the early Gnostics. He replied in a new and unfamiliar tone of voice. He clearly wasn't interested in discussing Dualism, but he sounded very chirpy and confident, *after the rather miraculous change that has taken place.*

He told me he would love to see me soon, but there was no hurry because *unlike Peggy and perhaps Rosalie, I am not the least dependent on physical presence.* He told me that he found sleep *a superfluous bore.* He usually composed his letters to me in the early hours of the morning.

14.3.74

Dearest Julia,

5.30 a.m. . . . Peggy worries about my all night writing sessions when I start at 12 and go on till breakfast and then off to lecture, but I sleep for two hours when I come back at four-ish and that seems to do the trick. . . .

Six thirty now and I am sipping coffee and listening to the birds beginning to chirrup and the light seeping over suburbia. Then it will be off to lecture on the Supernatural in *Macbeth*, which is a piece of cake.

8 April 1974

. . . I wake at 3 a.m. and then write poems 'til breakfast time . . . it's as if a cistern filled up in all those terrible months and now is overflowing . . .

What was Christ up to in the twenty years between his appearance in the temple and the start of his mission? . . . No doubt Mary Magdalene, the first person to see his risen body, could tell us a thing or two. But he must have had magical powers, the cataclysmic effect of the New Testament is too great . . . We must in our age able ourselves to fit the miraculous into the fabric of Science or we will die of boredom . . .

So very glad all goes well.

See you soon, lots and lots of love, Thomas

He kept saying he and Peggy would come to Deia now that he was happy, but he never managed it. However, my mother again arrived for Christmas. She gave me a pair of socks and as she watched me put them on she said, 'That's odd, they were much shorter on me. You must have stretched them when you pulled them up!' And when we were walking side by side down the little road that led towards the sea, she stopped and demanded angrily, 'Why are you taller than me? Are you standing on something or wearing high heels?' And then she stared at me with that complex wounded expression, which made her face blank and impenetrable.

After a year in Deia I decided it was time to leave and I felt it didn't matter where I was, so long as I was not in England. So I settled in Amsterdam

and there I met the man who would be my first husband. Hein was four years younger than me and he had a large family who welcomed me into their nest. I said very little about my parents or the life I had lived so far and the past seemed to drop away from me, like layers of old skin.

My mother arrived unexpectedly in Amsterdam. 'Jimmy's coming to join me here,' she said. 'We're going to Turkey on his motorbike. It's a Harley Davidson and he says it's very comfortable. Not bad for a fifty-six-year-old, eh! I'll bring you back some dried apricots if I can remember.'

○ ○ ◎ ○ ○

I introduced her to Hein and to Hein's mother and his father and his three brothers and she thought they were wonderful, and they were all very impressed by her enthusiasm and her friendly smile. We hardly exchanged any talk, but she helped Hein and me to paint a bathroom.

○ ○ ◎ ○ ○

In 1974 Hein and I moved to England and we rented a big, empty space in one of the semi-derelict warehouse buildings next to Tower Bridge. My mother came to visit us there as well. She still looked well and happy and

there was no time for talk and once again she rolled up her sleeves and put on an old apron and helped us to cover a great expanse of red-brick wall with white emulsion paint.

My father also came to the warehouse. He was still in the same mood of strange elation, but on this occasion he wasn't very nice to be with. I remember the sound of him clanging up the metal fire escape that led into our warehouse and then there he was, distracted and overweight and exceedingly pleased with himself.

He was wearing his favourite white linen suit and he was carrying a black leather briefcase. I thought the briefcase might contain books or sheaves of poetry he wanted to read to me and talk about, but instead it was filled with cans of Long Life beer. He tipped them out on to a table and I fetched three glasses. 'No need for that,' he said, 'there's none for you, only just enough for me!' He proceeded to open all the cans one after the other, and then in almost complete silence he gulped them down in quick succession and left when he had finished the lot.

'Goodbye, darling, goodbye, Heinz! Lovely to see you!'

Clang, clang, clang on the steps and then the louder clang of the metal warehouse door that led out into the street.

He was equally remote and odd when we went to visit him in Putney. He said later that it was his fear of death that was troubling him; by which I think he meant he was afraid of meeting his father on the other side.

⊙ ⊙ ◉ ⊙ ⊙

In the summer of that year he and Peggy were at their cottage in Wales. One Sunday morning he realized that his supply of Parstelin had run out and there was no chance of getting any more until the next day. The effect of such deprivation was devastating and having rummaged through every cupboard and kitchen drawer searching for something that would alleviate his suffering, he finally came across a bottle of antihistamine tablets and swallowed the lot, twenty-five in total.

After ten minutes he collapsed on the bed and lay there writhing and moaning. Peggy thought he must have had a stroke and he was carted off to the local hospital in an ambulance. Once he had emerged from his stupor, he was given a new supply of Parstelin and within three days he was back at the cottage.

On the first night of his return he had an experience which *started as a dream of Heaven and then went on awake like a cinema.* He found himself standing on a floating carpet of shimmering gold light, surrounded by intense colours, especially blues and reds. He then walked through a street *under a plethora of glittering trees.* He knew he was dead but would return to life and must preserve every moment of this visitation, which would remove for ever the terror of dying.

He was delighted with the experience, although Peggy was less convinced.

'I'm furious with him,' she said. 'I'll give him Cinema Heaven! You know he also got hold of our neighbour's contraceptive pills and ate them too! He'd eat rat poison if he found it lying about!'

◦ ◦ ◉ ◦ ◦

I saw him from time to time. Thanks to the Parstelin, his body had gone through another change: he was heavier than he had ever been, his face was puffy, his hands were red and swollen, and his movements and re-flexes were erratic as well as unnaturally slow. The nails and the skin on two fingers on his right hand and the thumb and index finger on his left hand were burnt a shiny orangey brown from his fumbling attempts to light cigarettes.

One day Peggy phoned. 'He set light to himself in bed. I saw smoke coming out from under the door and when I went in I found him sitting on the smouldering blanket and he was laughing. I threw a bucket of water over him. Oh Julia, I'd like to leave him, but I don't think he'd last a week on his own!'

By now his sick leave had come to an end and he was teaching again, but having a lot of trouble at the new college. Some of the students had made complaints about his strange behaviour and his obvious drunkenness, and all the members of staff were keen to persuade him to take early retirement.

He hated the idea of being without the structure of daily work. In one of his notebooks I found two unfinished letters to the college principal. The first is full of humble apologies, asking to be allowed to keep his job and promising that from now on *this ancient canine will try to keep up a full head of steam and not go shunting down byways.* The second letter was written after his dismissal had been confirmed; the tone had changed dramatically:

> Perhaps it is unnecessary for me to write to you, because what I have to say, duly vetted for libel, will all come out in my next book.
>
> I feel I have been made a convenient scapegoat for the appalling inefficiency and utter aridity of the English Department of your College . . . and I have been dismissed wrongfully . . . by your nebulous self.

But anyway, there he was, without a job and without much money either, because his pension was much less than he thought he was due. When he tried to economize on house expenses by repairing a gutter, he fell from the ladder he was climbing and damaged his back. After that he had to wear what he called a 'steel corset' to control the pain and it meant he couldn't even go for short walks.

I was very afraid he was getting ready to roll over and die in a gutter, to be found by strangers who would rifle through his pockets in search of his name and address. But then on the day of his sixty-first birthday, 10 February 1977, he made contact with a Jungian psychiatrist called Neil Micklem.

The two of them liked each other immediately. They could talk about music and William Blake and the archetypes of the collective unconscious, and Micklem had read some of my father's poetry and was able to discuss that as well. My father was overjoyed and convinced that he had at last found *an admirable curer of souls.* There was no money to pay for regular visits, but the Royal Society of Literature gave him a grant, which would cover the cost for a number of months.

Micklem was horrified by my father's use of Parstelin, but since it was clearly an addiction that couldn't be easily broken, he arranged for him to collect daily doses from his local doctor, which at least stopped him from guzzling a week's supply in one short night. Perhaps most crucially, Micklem told my father that he must learn to live with his depression, *naked and without panacea*, and he presented him with a new approach to the miseries of his childhood that had haunted him for so long. 'We chose our parents,' said Micklem, and through the process of coming to terms with them, we become our own selves.

My father was delighted with the logic of this theory. Suddenly the dead old man who had been clinging to his back for so long was turned into part of a mythic process. *Abracadabra!* and almost overnight, the Old B had released his hold and had gone back to wherever he came from. My father was quick to share this revelation with me and he wrote me a letter in which he explained:

> . . . you can't live without traumatic experience and before your birth you chose Rosalie and myself for your destiny and growing, just as I chose my parents.
>
> Does this sound too fanciful to you? I can only say that from dreams, waking visions and my Jungian experience, it is as much my conviction as our continuance after death . . . And because we chose our parents we must forgive them, if we are to forgive ourselves and be free of tension.

⊚ ⊙ ◉ ⊙ ⊚

25 April 1999

I've spent the day in Rosalie's house, getting to know her in a way I never did, not even during the last month. I met her loneliness, her battle with the world, her physical difficulties in old age.

I was going through her leather briefcase: there are lots of tight little pockets in the inside lid and they seem to be full of clues about the things that happened in her life, the things that mattered. There's the cut-out photos of herself with nothing on and a tiny picture of a man with a moustache who was her first lover and the newspaper announcement of the death of her sister and then I found two pages torn quite roughly from a 1951 diary. The entries were in her mother's handwriting: 'picked apples . . . spoke to Dr Martin . . . Tea

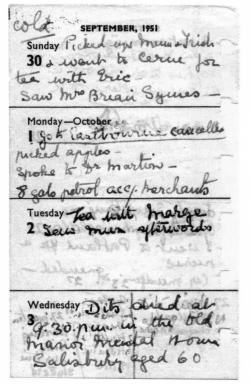

with Marge . . . 8 gals petrol' and then, for Wednesday, 3 October: 'Dits died (Dits was the name the family gave to Rosalie's father) 9.30 p.m. in the Old Manor Mental Home, Salisbury, aged 60.'

I once asked Rosalie about her father's death and she told me that he was in a mental hospital at the end, because her mother was sure he was losing his mind and might become violent. Neither of them went to see him there. And afterwards her mother made a bonfire in the garden, setting fire to all his clothes and personal possessions and the portraits of his ancestors.

I made some comment about how I thought he looked quite friendly in one of the photographs and Rosalie's response was very sharp and immediate.

'Don't ever say that!' she said. 'I've hated him all my life. I can't change it now!'

(Fax to Herman)

38

Jubilate

On 8 August 1977 I had arranged to meet my father at Waterloo Station and go on to have lunch with him in a restaurant near the National Film Theatre.

My father was early for our meeting and I saw him waiting for me by the station bookshop. He was wearing his favourite pale linen suit and I noticed for the first time that his hair was white; it had slipped from grey to white quite suddenly. His face was terribly pale and gleaming like a wax effigy.

As I walked towards him, I was watching him as if he were a complete stranger, but if he had been a stranger I would not have dared to stare at him so closely because he looked quite mad; he also looked as if he might be dangerous. But I was accustomed to his oddness, so I wasn't frightened of him.

He didn't notice me drawing closer to him, even though he was gazing in my direction, swaying and smiling with his chin on his chest and his eyes raised. When I stood in front of him and said hello, I seemed to be waking him from a trance.

He kissed me on the cheek so that I felt the cold dampness of the sweat glistening on his skin. He told me how glad, how very glad he was to see me. He said he had been working all through the night and the night before; there was so much energy in him and he had no need of sleep, not any more. He rubbed his hands together as if he was washing them under a tap and said how happy he was, he had never been so happy in all his life. 'I am really looking forward to dying!' he said in a loud voice, announcing this simple fact to the milling crowd around him.

'Let's go!' I said, suddenly embarrassed by the spectacle he was making of himself, and I took his arm.

We reached the restaurant where we planned to have lunch and managed to buy a plate of something and a glass of something, and then we sat down facing each other in the bright sunlit dazzle that came in at us through big windows. We talked about this and that, and he produced a new poem on a crumpled bit of paper and read it to me, his voice rising loudly above the other voices and above the clattering of knives and forks and spoons on the metal-topped table and on thick white crockery.

In a corner several tables away from us an academic-looking grey-haired man was talking with a woman of the same sort of age. My father stared across at them and his face lit up with sudden pleasure. 'Look at that man!' he said in a loud voice, lifting a heavy arm and pointing a swollen finger in the direction of the academic. 'It's the poet, my old friend D.J. Enright! Not seen him for years! He's changed a bit, but we all have, haven't we? How nice! How nice! I always liked him so much! I'll introduce you.'

He grinned happily at the academic and when there was no answering grin of recognition he got up and lumbered towards the other table. 'Dennis, hello, Dennis. It's me, Tom, Tom Blackburn. Put on a bit of weight, but it's me all right. How are you doing? Lovely to see you again!'

The man looked worried, as if the greeting was an accusation, but he quickly regained his self-composure and leaning towards my father said in a soft but distinct voice, 'You must have made a mistake. I am not anyone you know or have known. I am sorry, but there you are.'

My father returned to his seat slightly crestfallen. 'I'm sure it's him, but he doesn't want to acknowledge me. We had a bit of a scuffle some years back,' he said in a loud whisper, looking towards his lost friend.

But then he cheered up and we talked of other things. There was the business about looking forward to dying and then out of the blue he said he was also looking forward to his first grandchild, which was odd because Hein and I had no plans in that direction. He kept telling me he was 'off the booze' and as if to prove it he drank five cups of black coffee in quick succession, making loud slurping noises. 'No time to sleep,' he said. 'Too much to do!'

As we were walking back to the station, my father sailed at quite a speed towards the steps that led down from one concrete level to the next and in the moment before he might have toppled forward headlong, he lurched

Where does it come from
This stranger that joy is

From where is it from
This stranger that joy is
All I know it has come
Where melancholy
Had sovereignty
An idea of the body
Held sway for decades
Rinsing sustaining two
Like the clashing sword-blade
Unlooked for undrawing
That from such experience
Of the soul's dark night
Come novel joy and seize
Shake me with light.

sideways and sat down abruptly on the pavement, like a toddler who is learning the first rules of walking without getting hurt. I wonder if I tightened my hold on his arm, or called out a warning to him, but I can't remember.

◦ ◦ ◉ ◦ ◦

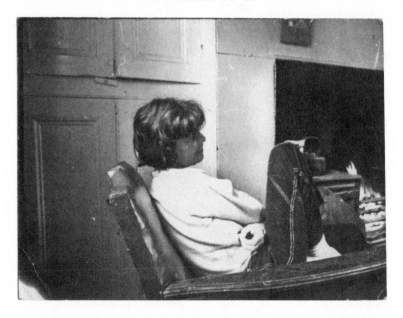

My father and Peggy set off for north Wales on the day after that meeting at Waterloo Station. Peggy's brother had agreed to drive them there because my father had lost his driving licence, ever since what he referred to as 'a little incident' when he had driven into a lamp-post and up the first two steps of the local police station.

Their rented cottage was one of a row of four mean little houses that seemed to have been snatched from the depths of an industrial town and dumped at the end of a narrow road, far from all other human habitation. The front garden was a grubby patch of grass and the fence that divided it from its close neighbours was made out of slabs of slate that stood at crooked angles, like a queue of tombstones waiting for their inscriptions.

Peggy had recently bought a bright-red strip of carpet, which covered the bare wooden treads leading to the upstairs bedrooms with an incongruous glamour and made it look as if you could expect to enter a cinema when you reached the top. My father refused to let her work the same magic in the main room because he liked to maintain its shabby gloom in all seasons, which he said reminded him of a climbers' club. The grey slate floors were cold and damp underfoot, and a crystalline fungus kept blistering through successive layers of gloss paint on the walls in the kitchen and even more so on the walls of the outside privy.

But none of that mattered if you looked out from the sitting-room window, or better still from the largest of the three upstairs bedrooms, because then you were confronted by the wonderful sweep of a green valley rushing into the distance, with the sharp outline of the mountain called Cnicht on one side and the rounded contour of another mountain called Moelwyn Mawr on the other.

Once my father had settled himself in the cottage, he continued to feel very happy, telling anyone who wanted to listen how much he was looking forward to dying. For several days he only slept when he dozed for an hour or so in one of the huge collapsing armchairs in the sitting room. He still wasn't drinking any alcohol, but he had managed to persuade the local chemist to give him a whole week's supply of Parstelin, instead of his regulated daily dose, and he was using them up much too fast.

He kept on writing, urgently, feverishly. He wrote letters and poems and random thoughts in a little red cash book, a big blue hardback one and another blue notebook, the words swarming over the pages, now bold with loops and curves, now huddled together in a tangled knot.

Wanting to be loved, he wrote in the final entry in the cash book. *Just to be. To accept consequences. Julia will still love.*

He sat in the armchair and described each new dawn as it broke across the valley. He wrote about his love for the mountains, about the magpies he could see hopping in the field just outside the window – *one for sorrow, two for joy* – and he kept finding new ways of saying how he knew now at last that he had chosen the parents he wished to be born to and he no longer blamed or hated them, because through them he had been able to follow his own particular and difficult destiny.

Peggy and her brother had no way of communicating with him, they could only watch and wait. They were woken each morning by the smell of cooking as he prepared one of his terrible breakfasts of sweet, black, instant coffee and eggs and bacon fried in a wobbly pan until the clouds of blue smoke in the little kitchen began to permeate the whole house.

Wanting to be loved
Just to be

To accept consequences
Julia will still love

Ten o'clock and though I have worked through three quarters of the night I feel no tiredness . . . Ten o'clock, no ten thirty and my brother-in-law is sitting in front of me biting his nails and wanting to be off to town and wanting the breakfast I must make for him.

He has just taken the hint and can make it himself.

Friday, 12 August was my birthday. My father wrote me a cheque and put it in an envelope with a short letter in which he said he was sure this would be a good year for me. That evening he walked down to the village to post it. When he got back he read Peggy a new poem called 'Morituri'; it was the second time that he had read it to her, but he seemed to have forgotten she had heard it already. He told her he planned to work through the night again, but she was not to worry.

He began a letter to the poet Kathleen Raine.

I can't sleep and I want to talk to you . . .

I have been brooding over the mountain fell-side behind our cottage and they have been talking back to me, as if they were metaphors for our immortality.

I have been thinking how strange and unnatural breathing is, I mean having to draw air in and out from cradle to grave. Then, if you have a cold, having to do it through the mouth. It will be good, post-mortem, to dispense with the process, which interferes with thought and feeling.

He then went on with a long letter he had been writing to his brother and his brother's wife, continuing with it for page after page, the handwriting by now so tangled and strange that it's sometimes impossible to decipher, while the thoughts themselves spin and turn with their own private imagery.

So, said a voice, you have indeed come through . . . Now you will grow here where the eternals are, to further dyings and further births . . .

> Thou hast delivered my soul from death
> My darling from the power of the dog
> Pace, finite, natale, pace, natale, finit.

24 hou   Micklen delig in
        a   new my poor prayer bt

        boante be   more Kind to the
Secday   when   I hae & time half

murdered

Y. But the shaper   "how writing the mystery
   of him sel in fuerture" took oer
        and I have Relived" on the page the
   frightening & complete blackness ledmy to
whatnot after .   leading supported by
what   through. the hairy the hairy thrgh
ser by anes vergillion   guide
wan the   hairy   scrotum of the
   King of Oarknes   to rock,
wran light, sow light, gloria

        well   my dears   aften twelve
   hoiurs of strange travel from dawn
   to thedawn.
thagh still the mind bued leqst they sit thay
least the fee He in & horisonias ans least
All positied easyfee   tang anel piane and
rosth least   bid he   deep.
out breathe   breathe brongand

With the night almost ended, he felt he had said everything he wanted to say.

> Down to earth after just meaning to write a short letter of love and the wish
> to pardon and be pardoned . . . Well, my dears, after hours of strange travel
> from dawn to dawn, though the mind burns, I must lie in a horizontal posi-
> tion and breathe long and deep.
>
> To you both, loving or not loving, I still love . . . Thomas

He left the notebook on the armchair and slowly made his way up the red-carpeted stairs and into his bedroom with its fine view out over the sweep of the valley. Just as he was getting into bed he was knocked to the ground with a violent cerebral haemorrhage.

Peggy heard him cry out. Her first thought was that he had lost his mind, and for a while she stood by the door, too afraid to enter. Then there was another sound, 'like something being torn apart', she said. She went in and could see by the early-morning light that he was dead. She lit a candle and covered his body with an old Indian rug with soft colours and she sat with him for some time, not wanting to disturb the neighbours before they were awake.

⊙ ⊙ ⊚ ⊙ ⊙

5 November 1999

Today is Rosalie's birthday – she would have been eighty-three. I went with my son to the churchyard where she lies and we planted a lavender bush and two purple violas on her grave. Rain and a sharp wind. It was strange dipping my hands into the earth above her coffin.

I read somewhere that the cause of things does not lie in what has happened before but in what will happen in the end.

(From Julia's Notebook)

39

A Funeral in Wales

My twenty-ninth birthday was on 12 August 1977. Hein had given me an American filing cabinet from the 1930s as a birthday present. It had thirty wooden drawers, but one of them was missing, so there were twenty-nine: just like me, I thought.

On the morning of the next day I woke up early. The sun was shining through the grimy industrial windows of the warehouse, suffusing that big dusty space with a shimmering grey light. For no particular reason I felt light-headed and incredibly happy. Music was playing and I was busy cleaning the twenty-nine-drawer cabinet with wire wool and paint-stripper when Peggy telephoned and spoke to Hein. She told him that my father had died during the night.

I went up to Wales by train; not reading, not even thinking, just covering the long distance that separated one place from another. Someone had arranged for a taxi to collect me from the station and I arrived at the cottage in the evening.

There was Peggy standing on her own in the bleak front room. She looked very tiny and tired, and when I embraced her it was like putting my arms round a bundle of thin branches. Her voice came from far away and she kept saying, 'I'm sorry, I'm so sorry,' as if my father's death was something she could have forestalled.

A lot of practical things needed to be done. There was no telephone in the cottage, so all communications had to be made from the telephone box in the village. Peggy had acquired a paper bag filled with a supply of pennies for long-distance calls. She wanted to make sure that even the people who had not seen Thomas for many years were informed of his death and had enough time to arrange to come to the funeral if they wished to. She was also busy ordering wine and whisky and making plans for the food she would serve at the wake.

My father's body was in the local morgue. Peggy said the undertaker was in a terrible hurry to get the funeral over and done with as quickly as possible and she had decided to go and talk to him and find out why. Her brother was going to drive her there and I was to stay at the cottage because I might find the whole business too upsetting.

⊙ ⊙ ◉ ⊙ ⊙

So there I was on my own in that familiar space. I sat in one of the armchairs and looked around me and I could seem to hear the lengths of nylon climbing rope and the jumble of heavy climbing boots, whining from out of the darkness of the cupboard in which they lay, like dogs wanting to be let out. I began to read the last entries in my father's notebooks.

Suddenly there was a little knock at the door. When I opened it I was confronted by a tiny man dressed in a black suit and carrying a black briefcase. He had parked his long black car in the sunshine under the ash tree and I could see the name of his family firm and the words 'Funeral Director' written in twirly letters along its shiny side.

Without looking up, he asked if I was the wife of the deceased and when he realized that of course I wasn't, he became terribly embarrassed. He kept saying, 'But we made an appointment,' until it became clear that he had misunderstood Peggy, thinking she wanted to meet him here. He must have passed her and her brother on the road, both parties too preoccupied to notice each other.

I invited the undertaker to come in and he settled himself into one of the two collapsing armchairs and looked exhausted. He was remarkably small and shy. When he wasn't speaking, he gulped and stared into the far distance.

As a way of making conversation, I asked him very politely whether I might be able to view my father, before the funeral. The word 'view' sounded right in the circumstances, I thought. I had a very vivid image of my father lying in his coffin, his face peaceful and quiet. I would lean over and hold his cold hand in my own and kiss his cold forehead, and that would be the correct way of saying goodbye and of being persuaded that he really was dead.

'View him?' said the undertaker in a shocked voice, holding tightly on to the armchair and staring wide-eyed at nothing at all. 'You could not! You certainly could not! And you wouldn't *want* to view him even if you could. Your father was a city-man,' he continued, turning the word into an adjective, 'and we are having a lot of trouble with him because the weather is very warm. We have never had a corpse like this before here in the valley, a city-man's corpse. It's all the things in his body you see, they are *reacting* and our freezer is not powerful enough to deal with it, particularly in this warm weather. We need to get him buried as quickly as possible, that is what I wanted to explain. As quickly as possible.'

It was so unexpected, this burst of information, and the image in my mind's eye did a somersault as it were. 'Oh I see,' I said, still keeping the formality of tone that I felt was important.

After much head-shaking and sighing, the undertaker agreed to hold the body of my father in cold storage for two more days. 'But that's my limit,' he said, looking anxious at the prospect of what he might have let himself in for.

I thanked him and he left in a hurry. His black car passed Peggy and her brother as they made their way back to the cottage, but again the two parties didn't notice each other.

People began to arrive and offer their condolences: friends from the valley and others from London who had arranged for a place to stay – and here was my father's older sister, coming all the way from Brighton. I hadn't seen her for many years, not since the Christmases with the Old Bs.

I had used up most of the pennies in the paper bag, trying to persuade my father's younger brother John to come as well. I even took the blue notebook with me to the village and read out the most loving bits from my father's letter down the telephone as bait, but still he wouldn't make the journey. The quarrels between the two of them over the last few years had hurt him too much. 'I just can't do it,' he said and his voice broke as he put the phone down.

On the morning of the funeral my mother arrived. I had somehow never expected her to come and I didn't even know she had been informed. I was horrified to see her. I felt she had no right to be here. No right to enter the cottage. No right to say how sorry she was. I was cold and formal towards her and I kept my distance and didn't allow her to embrace me.

We all set off in various cars, past the high banks of rhododendrons, past the silhouette of a ruined castle that had been built as a folly just after the last war and past the café painted blue and white where the girl who served tea had a cleft palate, which made it hard to understand anything she said. I sat with Peggy and her brother. I don't know whom my mother travelled with.

And then first right and up a little track that led to the cemetery gates. The sun was shining and the air was clear and bright, so that a seemingly endless succession of mountains and hills were exposed to view and far away down the valley and across the plain there was the misty sea, almost indistinguishable from the sky.

The cemetery was set on a steep hill with all the gravestones planted in tiers like the seats in a theatre. The funeral car was waiting for us by the entrance. Three gentlemen wearing black top hats and black uniform heaved the coffin out and you could see at once that it was very heavy with its city-man weight.

The Marxist historian Eric Hobsbawm, who rented the next-door cottage, and a shepherd called Len, who had wonderful stories about the wisdom of sheep and had taught me the earliest Welsh poem, and a painter called Tom Kinsey, who was having trouble with his wife, and Hein who would soon be my husband, each took hold of a handle of thick red rope. They moved slowly up the hillside and several times it looked as though they would have to stop and put their heavy burden down. I silently begged them not to drop it, or else who knows what final drama might have been enacted.

The grave was in a far corner next to a line of trees. The freshly broken earth was a reddish colour; it looked almost Mediterranean. I thought the hole was much too shallow and wondered if that was because the ground had been hard to dig after such a long dry summer. I hoped no night-time animal would try to reach my father, lying there so close to the surface.

The poet R.S. Thomas had come to officiate at the ceremony. He stood in his priest's robes on the steep grass slope and read the passage from the Book of Common Prayer, *Man that is born of woman hath but a short time to live*, and his voice was beautiful in the sunshine. Then he read a poem called 'The Climber', which he had written for my father. The ceremony was over.

Peggy was the first to make a move. She stepped forward to the edge of the grave and stood there, as frail as a little bird. 'Goodbye, Thomas darling,' she said, quite matter-of-fact as if he were just going to be gone for the week-end. She was clasping a white handkerchief and it fluttered down on to the coffin alongside a tiny handful of red earth.

I was facing my mother across the grave. I saw her hesitating, wondering whether it was her turn to step forward now, to say farewell to the man she had once loved, but then our eyes met and she paused, nodding her head to indicate that I should go before her.

⊚ ⊚ ◉ ⊚ ⊚

My first child was conceived in November and, according to the doctor's estimation, was due to be born on 13 August, the anniversary of my father's death, but she held on and was four days late.

My mother came to see me at the hospital. She burst into the crowded ward wearing a cotton dress covered in exploding patterns of red and yellow and carrying an enormous bunch of sunflowers. I felt embarrassed and over-whelmed by rage. I let her look at the sleeping baby and I thanked her very formally for the flowers and said they were too big, too messy, there were no vases in the hospital that could hold them, so she had better take them away again. I don't remember if she did, or if she found a nurse who cut the stems and managed to find a suitable container.

But then, when my daughter was a few weeks old, I invited my mother to come and see us at the warehouse. She took the little baby in her arms and I was surprised to see how tenderly she cradled her granddaughter.

◎ ◎ ◉ ◎ ◎

Suffolk, 19 December 1999

Herman and I were married two days ago and now we are staying in this wooden house by the sea. We went walking along the beach in the bright cold sunshine, and then the light went storm-bright and we watched the approach of a rippling curtain of snow, which covered the land and lay in the branches of the trees.

It's still snowing and I've lost my voice.

(From Julia's Notebook)

40

Rosalie

Rosalie lies in her granddaughter's bed in her daughter's house. Her granddaughter has come down from university for the Easter holidays, but she said she didn't need this room and has made a nest for herself and her boyfriend in the studio in the garden. So that's good. Her grandson is upstairs in the room next to Julia's room. The dog is in the kitchen. It's still early in the morning, with the first glimmerings of the dawn.

In the soft light Rosalie can just distinguish the painting of a red amaryllis flower, which she made quite recently. She has always loved these flowers because they are so shamelessly loud and bright. Julia must have put it on the shelf there. It's quite a nice painting although the pot looks a bit flat, as if it's been cut out of cardboard.

And next to it, the painting of two naked women. When on earth did she do that? Must have been during the war. Also quite nice. Two thin young ladies with small breasts and big triangles of pubic hair. They seem to be friends. Sisters perhaps. Maybe she did it shortly after poor Boonie died, as a way of thinking without the effort of thought. Because what can one do with a death like that? Where can one store the knowledge of such a terrible thing? Her own sister, going out into the garden in the early morning on the day after Christmas and shooting herself in the mouth with Daddy's gun! No wonder Daddy didn't want to talk about it.

'You must never mention it to him, promise me that. He can't bear to be upset!' said Mummy, very stern. And she never did. Obedient daughter that she was, or tried to be.

○ ○ ◉ ○ ○

She wonders now if she had loved Boonie. Well, of course she loved her, they were sisters, but apart from that. She was jealous of her because Boonie got all the attention, and all the praise – she even got a horse. And when they were both little and sleeping in the same room, Daddy used to get into bed with her sometimes, the two of them snuggled up together and poor Tuggie all on her own, listening to them having some sort of fun.

'Two little babes in a bed!' that's what he used to say when he got into bed with her sister. She'd forgotten all about it until the other night, when Julia came and lay beside her, close and warm and comforting, and she felt as if she were a child again, but this time *she* was the one getting the attention and that was nice. Two little babes in a bed.

What if Boonie was jealous of *her*? She'd never thought of that until now. Maybe Boonie was jealous because Daddy didn't climb into bed with Tuggie and she would have preferred to be left alone and not cuddled and kissed by her daddy who loved her so much. They never spoke about what happened sometimes at night, but in the morning they would fight those terrible fights, biting and scratching and screaming hatred at each other. And when Daddy heard the noise, he would come rushing into their bedroom to watch what was going on. All smiles. 'Come on, Boonie, you can do it! Hit her, that's right, now hit her again!'

◎ ◎ ◉ ◎ ◎

Rosalie, lying in her granddaughter's bed, thinks about sex. She enjoyed sex from the first time she did it. A Frenchman with a moustache, and she was sunbathing by the sea on her own in France, in that little fishing village near Dieppe. They did it in a cave and then again back at her hotel, careful not to let the proprietor see him creeping in, careful to keep quiet.

Afterwards he sent her a tiny photograph of himself and on the back he had written, *This is the man who would like to marry Rosalie de Meric.* She never wrote to him because she had no desire to marry him, but she kept the photograph in a little pocket in her leather briefcase, next to the two photographs of herself with nothing on, the ones she cut out so carefully with nail scissors.

'Do you want to see Mummy with nothing on?' she'd say to Julia. She did look lovely, not at all fat, just soft and curvy.

She can't remember the name of the man who took the pictures, but she can remember that they made love on the floor as soon as he had taken the last one. Oh, it was always so wonderful to be desired; to be undressed and kissed and made love to and then the spinning delirium of an orgasm, or lots of orgasms, or lots and lots.

But what about love? The first man she had loved was someone called René Buller. French and Jewish blood, so they had that in common. But he was in love with another woman and he even married her later.

'Get rid of her and choose only me!' said Rosalie, lying in his arms, her body wet with sweat, her face wet with tears. 'Love me and don't love her!' she said. But he only smiled and kissed her some more, and then he went back to his other woman; over and over again, he went back to her.

⊙ ⊙ ◉ ⊙ ⊙

There were lots more lovers, but the next Love must have been Tommy. She really had loved him, you can see it in the photographs of the two of them together in the mountains, smiling and happy. Perhaps that was why she hated him so much once the love had gone. And she became afraid of him, as afraid of him as she had been of Daddy. Even after the divorce, the fear stayed. He'd suddenly turn up at Cambria Lodge and the moment she saw him her heart started to race like a rabbit's and her mouth went dry. 'Hello, Tommy dear!' she'd say in a squeaky voice, feeling as helpless as a little girl.

She didn't go to Daddy's funeral, because Mummy said *she* wasn't going and it didn't seem right to go without Mummy, but at least she went to Tommy's funeral in Wales. She had always been curious to see his cottage and it was such lovely weather. Dropping a handful of dry earth on to his coffin and Julia staring at her, her eyes just like Tommy's.

Everyone said how much he had suffered, poor man, but at least he was always loved; lots of women had loved him and Julia had loved him too, even when he behaved atrociously she went on loving him. Rosalie wonders if she will meet him again when she dies, and maybe then she won't be frightened of him any more. Boonie might be there too, that would be nice, they'd have a lot to say to each other.

Sixteen years she and Tommy were together and it seemed like a lifetime then, not just a short chapter in the middle of it all. When she left him she thought, 'I'll show you, you bastard! I'll show you just how happy I can be with someone who really loves me!'

But it didn't work out like that. Tommy moved in with Peggy within days and she was on her own – with Julia – but on her own all the same.

It wasn't easy being a woman. Really she'd have liked to be a man, with the authority of a penis. If she'd been a man, Daddy would have been proud of her and people would have taken her more seriously as a painter, that's for sure. Look at Francis Bacon. And a man can say, 'I want to fuck you, now!' and he doesn't have to go through that nonsense women are supposed to go through, fluttering and wavering and hoping that they're going to get what they want and yet if they say what they want they get nothing. Except Jimmy. He was good like that. He didn't mind being told what was wanted.

She'd often thought she would have liked to have had a son instead of a daughter. Imagine, giving birth to a penis! And if Julia had been a son, then the trouble between them would never have happened. Too late to change that now, it's all water under the bridge, and anyway Tommy might have been very difficult with all his stuff about Oedipus. It was easy for him, though, having a daughter.

⊙ ⊙ ◉ ⊙ ⊙

Funny to have lived close to Julia for the last twenty years, the two of them not more than eight miles apart – ten minutes by car – and yet they were not close at all, until now.

Of course they'd had fun, as well as all the quarrels and the angry letters in which they both blamed each other for what happened. And although she had never ceased to be nervous in Julia's company, she had felt very relaxed with her two grandchildren right from the start; it was a different sort of love from any she had known and sometimes their beauty took her breath away.

It was so nice, sitting with them in the garden with chickens and guinea pigs wandering about in the long grass and Mop-Mop the cat and the dog called Bark because he didn't ever and the children laughing and hugging her and making her feel she belonged, because she was part of their family. And sometimes she and Julia and the children would go for walks with those two pigs they kept on the farm for a while and Julia kept saying the pigs reminded her of Uncle Guy, which was ridiculous. Or they'd fish for roach in the pond and the roach would push and shove each other to get into the net to eat a few crumbs of soggy bread. And then they'd set them free and start again.

Best of all, they'd go swimming in the sea. She had always loved swimming in the sea. Sometimes she wondered if she enjoyed it more than sex.

She last went swimming two years ago. That was when she was almost eighty and her grandson held her by the hand in case she got knocked over by the waves.

The shingle hard under her feet, the waves going in and out like breathing; the water rising up and up over her legs and over her belly and then

woosh! into the cold embrace that took her whole body and held it close. Wonderful to float and move without the sense of the body's weight. In the sea she felt like a porpoise or a seal and it made her want to shout and splash and dive under and rise up laughing and triumphant, and sometimes she did and people, even strangers, would laugh at her delight.

◎ ◎ ◉ ◎ ◎

Now that she was dying she often thought with pleasure of the sea. She wished she could be brought to its edge and then perhaps with a grandchild holding each hand she could get back into the water one more time. It might kill her, but that wouldn't matter, would it?

She didn't mind the fact that she was dying and she was proud of her lack of fear. Of course it was made a lot easier because of that little talk with Julia in the hospital. They hadn't said much, but it made her realize that they really had loved each other after all and that was what mattered. And now it was all such fun. Like a party and she was there, right in the middle of it all, the centre of attention. 'Was I ever so happy before?' she wondered, but didn't wait for an answer.

◎ ◎ ◉ ◎ ◎

Here she was in her daughter's house and in her granddaughter's bed, and when Julia did odd things, like hold her hand, or lie down beside her and give her a kiss, she didn't feel it was something sexual, it just felt like an aspect of love.

She had never thought of Julia as her daughter before, which was odd, but there you are. Now she looked at this woman – no longer young, a bit too thin and different from her in so many ways – and rather shyly she said, 'Hello, daughter!' trying the word out, and that made Julia smile.

'What a lovely smile you have!' she said and it was as if she was seeing a familiar face for the first time.

◎ ◎ ◉ ◎ ◎

All her life she had been so busy searching for happiness; one spiritual quest after another and sometimes it was quite exhausting. She must have started with the Gurdjieff group just after Geoffrey died. They all went off for weekends together and that made her feel less lonely and she stayed with them for years. She can't remember any of Gurdjieff's teachings now, except for the importance of doing meaningless things; once they spent a whole day sewing buttons on to a piece of cloth, and then they had to cut them off again, and that was the lesson.

Transcendental Meditation came next, with a secret word to chant silently in your head. It was nice to drift off for a while, but not half as nice as an orgasm, that's what she told them, and some of the members of the group were a bit cross with her, because they thought she was being disrespectful, but she hadn't meant it like that.

And then EST and discovering her own Inner Power. She went for a weekend conference in a hotel in Paddington and they were in a big hall, hundreds of them together and she took the microphone and, with the tears streaming down her face, she told everyone about the pain she had suffered when her daughter ran off with Geoffrey. Such a cruel, cruel daughter and everyone in the hall listened with bated breath and when she had finished talking and had put the microphone down, everyone in the hall let out a great sigh of collective grief and indignation, and they clapped their hands as a way of thanking her for sharing something so awful and intimate with them. Once she was back in Suffolk, she tried to tell Julia about what had happened and how important it was for *their* relationship, but Julia hadn't wanted to listen and that spoilt everything.

After EST there had been Osho. He of the sixteen – or was it twenty-six? – gold-plated Rolls-Royces. She went all the way to India to stay on his ashram, even agreed to have an AIDS test before leaving England, which was exciting for a seventy-eight-year-old. She was brought to stand before him and he had lovely eyes and a voice as soft as butter, and he took her hand in his and gave her a special name, which was hers to keep. And then there was learning about the One Truth and dancing with no clothes on in the big hall and chanting all together so that you felt wonderfully close to total strangers. But Osho had gone and died a few days after she arrived and it was awful. It almost felt like her fault. *I have just found my eternal guru and now he is dead,* she wrote in her diary.

Since then she had tried going to the local church, but it was really for something to do on a Sunday morning. She had never been keen on Christianity. The vicar was a dreadful bore and he said that sin was like the molehills on your lawn and you wanted to stamp it out. But she didn't want to stamp on molehills, she loved to see them bubbling up.

During the last couple of years there had been nothing much. Only a gradual slowing down of the body. She could no longer manage walks or bicycle rides on her own, although sometimes Julia would drive her to the car park, the one right at the end overlooking the cliffs and the sea, and she had just enough energy to take the few steps to the bench. She would sit there with the wind on her face and watch her daughter going down the track, and usually when she reached the path beside the sea, she would begin to run with the dog running beside her. Watching a not-so-young-any-more woman running into the distance with a sandy-coloured dog dancing at her heels: it was like watching herself in a time long before this one.

○ ○ ◉ ○ ○

And then she found she couldn't get out of the bath any more, which was awful because she loved lying in a warm bath with bubbles and a big sponge; farting and wallowing and drifting and dreaming in the water, pretending it was the sea. So Julia invited her to come and stay the night, once every week, and Julia helped her to have a bath and that was lovely too and there was nothing shameful about being so big and heavy and helpless.

And now the leukaemia and the loss of an entire immune system and no cure and nothing to be done except to die. Lying in hospital with those big dark bruises gathering like storm clouds on her arms, and then Julia arrived with that notebook with a page torn out and there were all the tears that followed. And that was it. In one moment – no, in much less than one moment – all the stuff from the past had disappeared. A little taste of remorse perhaps and they both said, 'Oh, I am sorry,' and looked into each other's eyes when they said it. But having said sorry once or twice, it really didn't seem relevant to go on with it. What mattered now was the pleasure, the concentrated pleasure of the two of them being together for a while, without trouble.

It was odd to be dying, but Rosalie knew it would be like entering the sea. She quite looked forward to it. It was just a question of stepping in, first your feet on the shingle and then up to your knees and hips and then *woosh!* and you were held in the embrace of the water. The body so light it hardly existed.

41

Here

Herman and I are here in the mountains of Liguria.

Forty years have passed since we spent our first night together in Cambria Lodge, when my mother pushed me into his room, wearing that tomato-red flannel nightdress. It was such a thick and voluminous garment reaching to the floor and it had a ruffle of white lace round the neck and the long sleeves. French lace, I think it's called, but I don't know why.

And it's already eight years since he came to see me in Suffolk. I watched him step from the train on to the station platform and everything

about him was so utterly familiar, it was as if he'd only been gone for a week. I wasn't surprised by the familiarity, I simply thought, 'Here he is. He's come home.'

I brought him home and I was suddenly aware of being surrounded by so many objects that belonged to the times we had spent together: the sparrow hawk in its glass case and the sculpture of the naked old lady with her head bowed that I carried with me from place to place; the painting of a tiger he gave me when I lived at Black Lion Yard; a red china coffee pot we bought in the Amsterdam flea market; a bedspread, books, postcards, all the letters.

I cooked fish for supper and the talk was easy and quiet and without urgency. And on the next day I invited my aged mother for lunch because I had told her Herman was coming and she said she wanted to see him again.

So there she was and there we were, sitting round the table and the years of the past were whizzing around my head, but not dangerously so.

He needed to catch a train at three o'clock that afternoon and my mother offered to drive him the short distance to the station. He told me later she was so eager to talk that she hardly bothered to steer the car and twice she almost skidded into a deep ditch on the side of the road.

◦ ◦ ◉ ◦ ◦

In May 1973 my father wrote a letter to Herman saying how sorry he was to hear that we were parting again. Herman showed me the letter just a few days before we got married in December 1999, and when I read it I remember feeling it was as if my long-since-dead father had anticipated this third chapter in our lives together and he was giving us his blessing. And now I have just read it again.

Dear Herman,
. . . as far as I know the tortuous girl, I feel that with you she met her most complete involvement . . .

Goodness knows, she had enough to deal with during her formative years and one looks back on oneself like a stranger and I am amazed at the cool callousness with which I would then follow any experience that would seem to foster a poem, at the complete expense of any personal relationship.

But that is only half the story . . . In a curious way I feel that as with myself, your life and work will eventually round themselves together and I personally very much hope that when they do, Julia will be part of the pattern.

And then a few nights ago I dreamt I told my mother that I was writing this book and she said, 'Oh, that's nice,' and there was the same easy benevolence in her voice that I remember so vividly from the last month she and I spent together.

I would like to thank my agent, Gill Coleridge,
and my two wonderful editors, Dan Franklin and Dan Frank.